BEN JONSON'S ANTIMASQUES

To Niall, Molly and Fran, without whom this book would have been finished earlier, but in less happy circumstances.

Ben Jonson's Antimasques

A History of Growth and Decline

Lesley Mickel

Ashgate
Aldershot • Brookfield USA • Singapore • Sydney

© Lesley Mickel, 1999.

All rights reserved. No part of this publication may be reproduced, stored in a retrieval system, or transmitted in any form or by any means, electronic, mechanical, photocopying, recording, or otherwise without the prior permission of the publisher.

The author has asserted her right under the Copyright, Designs and Patents Act, 1988, to be identified as the author of this work.

Published by
Ashgate Publishing Limited
Gower House
Croft Road
Aldershot
Hants GU11 3HR
England

Ashgate Publishing Company
Old Post Road
Brookfield
Vermont 05036-9704
USA

British Library Cataloguing-in-Publication data
Mickel, Lesley
  Ben Jonson's antimasques : a history of growth and decline.
  1. Jonson, Ben, 1573?-1637 - Criticism and interpretation.
  2. Masques - History and critcism.
  I. Title.
  822.3

US Library of Congress Cataloging-in-Publication data
Mickel, Lesley
  Ben Jonson's antimasques : a history of growth and decline.
  Includes bibliographical references and index.
  1. Jonson, Ben, 1573?-1637 - Dramatic works.   2. Masques - History and criticism.   3. Politics and literature - Great Britain - History - 17th century.   4. Authors and patrons - England - History - 17th century.   5. Political plays, English - History and criticism.   6. Aristocracy (Social class in literature).   7. Satire, English - History and criticism.   8. Courts and courtiers in literature.
  I. Title.
  PR2642.M37 M53 1999
  822'.3-dc21
                                                                98-50896
                                                                    CIP

ISBN 1 84014 272 3

Phototypeset by N²productions.
Printed on acid-free paper and bound in Great Britain by
MPG Books Ltd, Bodmin, Cornwall

Contents

Acknowledgements   vii

Introduction   1

    The antimasque: a history of growth and decline – Jonson and Barthes – Readers as understanders: Jonsonian masque in the twentieth century – Some speculative conclusions on the growth of the antimasque

1 'Free from servile flattery': panegyric and the formation of the antimasque   26

    Jonsonian panegyric: a textual criticism of 'To Sir Robert Wroth' – Desire and difference: *The Masque of Blackness* and *The Masque of Beauty*

2 Arthur and Augustus: masque and the historical myth   63

    History and myth – Jonson and the chivalric ideal – Reading the chivalric masques – Harsh and unendurable government: the Roman plays – Reconciling Rome and London

3 Present occasions and removed mysteries: the topicality of the antimasque   101

    Hymenaei – *Love Restored* – *Mercury Vindicated from the Alchemists at Court* – To make readers understanders – Satire and the authoritative community

4 Jonson's consuming satire and the carnivalesque antimasque   133

    Bartholomew Fair and the antimasque – The carnivalesque antimasque: *Love Freed from Ignorance and Folly* and *The Irish Masque at Court* – Some conclusions on the expansion of the antimasque

5   Heavenly love and the collapse of the court masque   171
    Love's Triumph Through Callipolis – The collapse of the
    dialogic masque – Caroline masque as the absolutist ritual

Postscript   186
    Jonson's heirs: Shirley and Milton
    The Triumph Of Peace – *Comus*

Bibliography   193

Index   205

Acknowledgements

This book is the fruition of an eight-year gestation and started life as a doctoral thesis. Since then, it has undergone many revisions as my thoughts about the Jonsonian antimasque evolved. This evolution would have been impossible without the guiding hand of Alison Thorne, whose patient reading of early drafts and tactful suggestions for refinements have been invaluable, both for the book's and my own intellectual development, and I am fortunate that an academic mentor has become a friend. While rewriting was often painful, it was always worth it. If there is anything of merit about this work, it is largely attributable to her influence; any errors or inconsistencies in argument are, of course, my own.

Michael Bath's cheery encouragement and interest has been supportive and inspiring. Ceri Sullivan, Barbara White and Julie Sanders all provided stimulating conversation and correspondance on the fantastic in Jonsonian antimasque which was most useful in the latter stages of writing. Further academic debts are almost too numerous to list and include my interpretations of the work done by Leah Marcus, Allon White and Peter Stallybrass, Roy Strong and, of course, Stephen Orgel. Practical support was provided by Strathclyde University, where a bursary enabled the thesis stage of this book, and by the University of Northumbria at Newcastle, whose award of a small research grant allowed me time to do some vital research and rewriting.

I also owe thanks to Rachel Lynch at Ashgate for having faith, and to Ashgate's reviewer, whose comments prompted some vital refinement.

Lastly, but most importantly, my family has shown unfailing encouragement and interest, particularly my husband, Niall; while he may not always have understood my enthusiasm for the Jonsonian antimasque, he has lived with it in good humour for many years and provided a therapeutic distraction.

Introduction

This book focuses on the court masques of Ben Jonson, but the sheer number of these masques (there are twenty-eight) makes a selective discussion of them necessary, although I have tried to pick out those masques that seem to be particularly significant for a study of the genre's development. My primary objective in this book is to chart the growth and demise of the antimasque in Jonson's court entertainments, and to explore the way in which they respond to both his poetic aims and their historico-political conditions of production. I will suggest that the Jonsonian court entertainment develops into a dialectical investigation of contemporary affairs and is far more complex than the simple act of homage that it has sometimes been assumed to be.[1] Two distinctive aspects of this book are its broadly chronological approach and an acute consciousness of the court entertainment as a fundamentally hybrid form. This diachronic emphasis is occasioned by my concern to explore the growth of the antimasque within the context of the masque entertainment as a whole. The generic melange that is the antimasque dictates a consideration of Jonson's handling of other literary modes, and how the hybridisation of these contributed to the evolution of the antimasque. It will soon become apparent in the main body of this book that I am primarily interested in the antimasque/masque as a discursive form and I explore the ways in which it was shaped by contemporary cultural and socio-political practices. Thus, one of the most obvious facts about the masque that we should remember is that it was created for an aristocratic elite of courtiers who were directly involved with it, both as masquers and as participants in the revels at the end of the entertainment. The court masque was a symbolic form used by the aristocracy to represent themselves to themselves, and as such, it was a vital constituent in the social and personal formation of their identity. Perhaps unsurprisingly, the identity that such masquers sought to confirm was one at the top of the hierarchical ladder, surpassed only by the King himself, whom the masque figured as God's representative on earth. Viewed in these terms, the court masque would seem to be little more than a propaganda exercise that sought to rehearse and consolidate the dominant ideology of an increasingly absolutist monarchy supported by a powerful aristocracy. However, this book is intended to demonstrate that Jonson's version of the court masque is far more interesting and complex than such a description implies. This is chiefly because he was responsible for the creation of the antimasque, which introduced elements of dramatic dialogue and plot to the emblematic tableau that was the court masque. Moreover, much of this book rests on the central belief that the antimasque itself harnessed and evolved out of the subtle contradictions and ironic anomalies manifest in the early Jonsonian masques, and developed these into significant textual structures of dissent that go against the grain of the royalist masque. This dissent is both formal and ideological; in the antimasque formal dissonance manifests itself through the combination of inverted dance steps and ludicrous, nonsensical prose, producing a disruption of the ideals of harmony, unity and order that are eulogised in the masque proper.[2] And because ideological values are asserted or challenged in and through language and gesture, this formal dissonance questions the motivating ideology of the following masque. Although the nonsensical, punning language and twisted movement of the antimasque are ultimately usurped by the orderly poetry and dance of the masque, the whiff of dissonance hangs in the air like smoke and remains as a set of implied values to counterbalance those voiced in the rest of the entertainment.[3] Even in early masques where the antimasque has not yet evolved into a separate structure, ironies and contradictions are embedded in the official discourse of panegyric and unbalance the confident assertions of monarchical rule. Furthermore, the topicality of the antimasque may be shown to reveal the historical and political contingency of the court entertainment, rather than sharing in the masque's practice of obscuring its material base and motivation. Yet we should remember that the masque also addressed matters of political and social concern to the Crown, but unlike the antimasque, it did so in order to confirm the *status quo* and mystify the state as a universal and divine order.

In my discussion of the antimasque I wish to suggest that it has a history of evolution and decay, with the fully developed version of the form emerging roughly at a mid-point in this process. The antimasque develops, as I have said, out of inconsistencies in the masque itself and becomes an important and dominant part of the court entertainment. In fact, it evolves and expands to the point where it seems to threaten the masque it was originally designed merely to prelude, and to destabilise the traditional structure of the form. The antimasque's implicit questioning of the masque's assertions sets up a dialectic within the court entertainment, or we could say that the whole structure of the court masque becomes dialogic. In manipulating the court entertainment in this way, Jonson demonstrates his desire to be a public educator on political and moral issues, and this didactic impulse is also often revealed in his poetic pronouncements. In the court entertainment the antimasque explores the extremes of chaotic 'democracy', while the masque offers a vision of all powerful absolutism. Yet it is crucially significant that the masque also shows how the agents of absolutism might deal with popular unrest. In the ideal world of masque, the monarch is shown to create peace and happiness because he treats unruly subjects with mercy and justice. In Jonson's view, effective rule is inherently moral, and the state can only achieve prosperity if a *via media* is steered between the possible extremes of imperious tyranny and anarchic democracy.

A further point that needs to be stressed at the outset is that this study primarily focuses on the textual and literary nature of the antimasque/masque, while acknowledging that other elements of the form, iconography, dance and music, are all crucial to its significance. This approach is justified by the fact that I am interested in the masques composed by Jonson, an author who sought to give these works a definitively literary spin and textual longevity that allowed them to outlast their temporal moment. Jonson achieved this by publishing his masque texts, first in quarto form and then as constituent parts of his 1616 folio of *Works*. This approach counters certain critics proposing that the court masque's significance lies solely in its visual display and music; a view which is simply not tenable when we are considering the Jonsonian masque, with its barrage of literary allusion and annotation – Jonson meant these texts to be read after their original performance. In a recent book Peter Walls has argued that the determining factor of masques is their music and that the antimasques are a minor element within the entertainment as a whole. Jerzy Limon takes a similar view, dismissing 'so-called antimasques' and differentiating between the masque in performance and the masque as literature, to the latter's detriment. However, this may be counterbalanced by attention to what Joseph Loewenstein has termed the 'semiotic plenitude' of the masque text, which bristles with allusion and textual authority, oscillating between languages and type face. Loewenstein argues that while Jonson seeks to preserve his status as author, the masque text itself preserves something of the instability of performance. While I agree that Jonson does not possess the ultimate authority over these works, he certainly attempted to dominate them, and with the addition of prefaces and notes to the masque texts he sought to create a space for his own voice to be heard. Those who wish to sideline the literary nature of the antimasque/masque seek to displace Jonson from the form, a manoeuvre which attention to the masque text cannot allow us to perform.[4]

The Masque of Queens (1609) is usually cited as the first example of the

Jonsonian antimasque, but there may be grounds to regard this as a false start. Jonson's unhappiness with his first attempt at this literary mode may be inferred from the fact that he omitted to incorporate an antimasque into his next court entertainment, *Prince Henry's Barriers* (1610). Although the antimasque of *Queens* is distinguished by the inversion of orthodox dance and song that characterises the antimasque (in the form of rhyming incantations and backward dance steps), it appears to lack any significant rhetorical or dramatic strategy to offset the dominant discourse of the masque. Consequently, the resulting antimasque is one-dimensional in its expression of formal chaos, whereas later antimasques would have a more fully developed strategy of dissent expressed through chaotic language and movement. The combination of formal and ideological dissonance is the signature of the evolved Jonsonian antimasque, and on these grounds it is arguable that *Oberon the Fairy Prince* (1611) provides the earliest proper example of the form, because its representation of unruly and often vicious satyrs and sylvans debunks the orthodox pastoral myth of bucolic innocence. However, a refrain running through this book emphasises that although the antimasque develops thereafter to a point where it threatens to consume the masque, this process is never completed, as the masque is always reinstated at the end of the court entertainment. It will soon become apparent that my primary interest is the socio-political nature of the expanded antimasque and the poetic ideals behind it, and I discuss in some detail those entertainments that feature this type of antimasque; these include, *Oberon* (1611), *Love Freed From Ignorance and Folly* (1611), *Love Restored* (1612), *The Irish Masque at Court* (1613/14) and *Mercury Vindicated from the Alchemists at Court* (1616). The trajectory of the full-blown antimasque does not end here, however, but continues for some years to come, although in the late 1620s and early 1630s it becomes enfeebled and shrinks from its former dominant position in the court entertainment. Moreover, the antimasque is stripped of its dialogue and returns to its prototype, that is, a court entertainment that merely manifests latent anomalies and anxieties that Jonson had later exploited to create the fully evolved antimasque. The silencing of the Caroline antimasque is related to the suppression of any significant structure of dissent within the masque form as a whole, and what was the dialogic Jonsonian court entertainment seems to collapse into royal monologism. The demise of the antimasque can be related both to a change in the monarchy and in the leading figures at court and in government, and to aesthetic developments. The intensified interest in neo-platonism, sponsored by Charles and Henrietta-Maria, identified the conduit to philosophical truth and virtue in the beauty of visual forms, thereby trivialising the importance of the spoken or written word, the medium in which Jonson excelled. James I had responded to Jonson's primarily verbal art as he viewed himself as a royal *litterateur*; conversely, the Caroline masques reflect Charles's overriding interest in the visual arts. This aesthetic sea-change was compounded by the fact that Jonson's antimasques often depend on topicality for much of their impact, a feature which made them seem even more outdated to a Caroline court experimenting with a more metaphysical mode of understanding and to a King who actively discouraged public discussion on matters of state.

While my priority in this book is to reach an understanding of the ephemeral antimasque, and the reasons for its evolution and decay, I hold the view that this can only be achieved by comparing these entertainments with Jonson's other works. Accordingly, Chapter 1 involves an extensive discussion of his poetry, while Chapters 2 and 4 draw on the Roman tragedies and the dramatic comedy, *Bartholomew Fair*, respectively. It would clearly be inappropriate to study Jonson's masques in isolation, and a study of the poetry enables the reader to glean some idea of Jonson's view of the relationship between satire and panegyric, a relationship of crucial relevance for any study of the antimasque/masque entertainment. Attention to the poetry is also vital as it reveals the semiotic network within which Jonson operated and the received humanist poetic ideals that he also espoused, as well as demonstrating his very personal way of combining satire and panegyric in a single didactic purpose. It seems to me that the Roman tragedies particularly complement the masques as both are stylised expressions of the state and its political mechanisms; the former offers a dark and pessimistic view of the *Realpolitik* that lies behind the complacent public image propagated by the governing powers, whereas the latter offers an ultimately optimistic and symbolic celebration of the monarchist state. Moreover, while the impulse towards chaos and anarchy that emerges in the Roman plays may be viewed as a consequence of the corrupting nature of power, the court entertainment explicitly relates anarchy to the antimasque, whereas the masque figures the monarch's absolute power and demonstrates the order and morality that are the natural consequences of Kingship. Thus, Jonson's work within different genres demonstrates two oppositional but profoundly related views of state power, where a corrupt Roman leader escalates the collapse of a great empire, and a virtuous King ensures his island's prosperity – clearly the belief that emerges in these portraits of power is that the monarch is morally responsible for the prosperity of his nation, and we can extrapolate from this Jonson's often repeated belief that only a morally upright individual can be an effective ruler or poet. Returning to the question of genre, the antimasque also shares common ground with the dramatic comedies; Jonson's treatment of both these genres includes a festive inversion of received hierarchies, and a bawdy, often scatological humour; the prose dialogue is fast paced, incorporating vivid detail in the form of incongruous lists of disparate objects. Thus Chapter 4 looks at *Bartholomew Fair* in conjunction with the antimasque and uses Bakhtin's theory of the grotesque carnival to suggest how these anarchic comic elements work to elide traditional social and cultural categories.

The antimasque: a history of growth and decline

Given that the central axis of my argument is the principle that the antimasque was an innovative performative and literary mode growing out of sixteenth-century European court entertainments, that it became fashionable for a short while in the brief history of the ephemeral masque, and died out thereafter, I am obliged to take a largely chronological approach in this book; however, in tracing the history of the antimasque I am interested in its synchronic impact, as well as its diachronic evolution, that is to say, I examine in depth certain entertainments, exploring how they generate meaning in relation to their precise historico-political moments, in addition to charting the history of a steadily evolving form. Somewhat predictably, therefore, Chapter 1 considers Jonson's first court masques, while Chapter 5 and the postscript discuss his final masques and those composed by later writers who were significantly influenced by Jonson. This structure means that each chapter springs out of the previous one, and that they are inextricably linked rather than separate units. Any consideration of the antimasque and masque, and the relation between them, requires an understanding of Jonson's use of satire and panegyric. Accordingly, Chapter 1 draws on his non-dramatic poetry to explore these questions and attempts to link the deployment of satire and panegyric in poetry and the court masque. Jonson was accused of hypocrisy in his own day, and many current students of his panegyric voice similar accusations; indeed, Jonson himself often expressed a fear that panegyric may degenerate into flattery, but he defuses this fear with the view that praise bestowed where it is undeserved actually works as covert satire. A latent irony springs up in the gap between historical reality and its poeticised image, and a dynamic operates in certain poems where overt praise becomes so hyperbolic that it collapses into irony. This kind of ironic interpretation is made available not only by Jonson's rhetorical strategies but also by reading the poem in its historical, synchronic context, where discrepancies between poetic assertion and historical actuality can be measured. The irony running through such a text does not, however, demolish its standing as panegyric; rather, it constitutes a voice of dissent that contradicts and destabilises the poem's overt meaning. In a textual criticism of the well known poem, 'To Sir Robert Wroth' I show how covert irony might work in tandem with the poem's more obvious panegyric towards a single didactic purpose of reform. This manipulation of irony and panegyric in the poetry is clearly related to their function in the mature Jonsonian masque where antimasque/masque form a dialogic structure. I extend my discussion of the dialectic impulse within the poetry to a consideration of Jonson's first court masques, *The Masque of Blackness* (1605) and *The Masque of Beauty* (1608), where it is directed at reforming the monarch and the court. *Blackness* is the earliest example of Jonson's court masques and lacks an antimasque, a separate form which has yet to develop within the genre. That is not to say, however, that this masque is an unalloyed celebration of the state, for, as I try to show, it features certain inconsistencies and anomalies that subtly permeate the masque as a whole. Rather than seeking to eradicate such 'faultlines' within the masque, Jonson proceeds in his later court entertainments to develop these anomalies into fully worked out strategies of dissent within the antimasque. These elements of dissent are not contained by the formal boundaries of the antimasque, as some critics have argued, but permeate the entertainment as a whole and interrogate the assertions of the masque, producing a dialectical exploration of the state of the contemporary monarchy. This mature phase of the Jonsonian court masque indisputably develops out of the 'fractured' nature of *Blackness* and *Beauty,* and is clearly related to the kind of dialectic at work in much of Jonson's poetry.

Chapter 2 explores the next phase of the Jonsonian court masque, those mythopoeic entertainments that appear to embody a Humanist rewriting of history, so that it becomes an edifying and didactic exemplum rather than a simple list of events lacking moral form or purpose. This chapter focuses on the chivalric masques of 1610/11, *Prince Henry's Barriers* and *Oberon, The Fairy Prince*. These masques are fascinating in the way they attempt to negotiate between competing historical traditions or myths; for example, the Stuart espousal of a chivalric tradition became associated with Prince Henry and militant Protestant values, whereas King James had his own version of the historical myth, that of the *Rex Pacificus* or Roman Emperor, a role obviously more suited to his conciliatory foreign policy. It is immediately obvious that these mythic discourses are potentially incompatible, and constructed around clashing political ideals. Yet in these masques Jonson mounts a valiant and ingenious attempt to mediate between these historical myths, and to reintegrate them as they had been under the Tudors. This project to integrate rhetorically polarised myths is visually mirrored in the set designs provided by Inigo Jones, making attention to the visual dimension of these masques imperative. The strategy of negotiation we find in the chivalric masques is a dialectic approach that Jonson developed and centred on the relationship of antimasque to masque, yet a vital *caveat* to such an assertion is the point that whereas the chivalric masques seek to integrate conflicting elements into a coherent discourse, the later antimasque/masque structure does not result in this kind of harmonised integration, it is rather moulded into an open and dynamic dialectic. Thus, the chivalric masques are important because they are an early example of the dialogic impulse that is both responsible for and emphasised by the growth of the Jonsonian antimasque, producing the dialectical court entertainments that are the main focus of this book. The last section of this chapter turns to Jonson's use of historical myth in his drama for the public stage, and just as the poetry illuminates the dynamic of satire and panegyric in the masques, so the drama, in conjunction with the masques, reveals a long term project on Jonson's part to anatomise the fundamental structure and nature of political power. Whereas the chivalric masques seek to integrate competing genealogies in order to legitimate the monarchy, the Roman plays put such claims to authority under pressure and reveal them to be a spurious public image far from the political reality of Rome. Analysis of *Poetaster* (1601), *Sejanus* (1603) and *Catiline* (1611) shows that Jonson's Rome has much in common with Jacobean London and its court, thereby representing covert criticism of the early modern British state. This project of covert criticism clearly aligns the Roman tragedies with the later antimasques, but whereas the anarchy of the antimasque is offset by the masque's confirmation of the monarchy, *Catiline*, the last of the Roman plays, ends in the dissolution of Rome. While the antimasques and the Roman plays may be said to share much common ground, one vital difference between the chaos they depict is that the antimasque places it in an essentially comic context and, although the claims of masque are destabilised, they are not completely negated or eroded. But the masque's symbolic confirmation of the state is not available in the Roman plays, which finally result in the disintegration of the body politic; this collapse is the logical outcome when the antimasque elements of dissent and anarchy are played out to the bitter end. Therefore, it is possible to read the chivalric masques and the Roman tragedies together as parts of a dialogic enquiry in to the nature of authority (the contiguous dates of these works encourage this view). Although the Roman plays and the chivalric masques embody very different historical myths as a means of analysing the modern state, it may be argued that, when juxtaposed, they represent an early version of the dialectic which characterises Jonson's later court entertainments, where the antimasque ironically comments on the state while the masque unequivocally lauds it.

Chapters 1 and 2 are largely sustained by the belief that Jonson's poetry and court entertainments are fundamentally dialectical in nature, and this view is in turn generated by an historical reading of the texts. Accordingly, Chapter 3 examines and justifies some of the principles behind this historicism before going on to demonstrate why an historical perspective is essential for an understanding of the court entertainment. I draw on particular masques (*Hymenaei* (1606), *Love Restored* (1612) and *Mercury Vindicated from the Alchemists at Court* (1616)) to reveal the historicity and contingency of the antimasque in particular, and I show how the antimasque is directly engaged with its historico-political moment of production. I then develop some of the more pressing implications of this historical approach; for example, if the antimasque was a vehicle for irony, as I argue, how is it that the contemporary audience did not object to some of its more risque suggestions? This apparently intractable problem is resolved by a theory of literary interpretation determined by genre, and made more intelligible by the fact that Jonson counted upon understanding readers and viewers of his work, whilst assuming them to be a rare commodity.

Chapter 4 maintains the historical perspective and I develop my argument by drawing comparisons between the antimasque and carnival; both as actual events and as aesthetic forms they share ambivalent relations with the structures of socio-political authority, and I am particularly interested in the way in which the now enlarged and well established ironic antimasque destabilises the masque. In a discussion of the comic drama, *Bartholomew Fair*, I suggests that it shares the anarchic qualities of the antimasque and I draw upon Bakhtin's theory of the Carnivalesque in demonstrating how this play and the antimasque symbolically invert received structures of authority. In my view, the social and cultural instability provoked by the fair is similar to the antimasque's effect on the masque, as both question the 'truths' espoused by the dominant hegemony. This discussion leads to a detailed analysis of two antimasques, *Love Freed From Ignorance and Folly* (1611) and *The Irish Masque at Court* (1613/14); these antimasques not only destabilise the masques they preface, but even threaten to consume them, although as I have noted before this consumption is never complete as the masque and its values are automatically reinstated at the end of a court entertainment, albeit such a reinstatement may seem wooden and rather unconvincing – it is a ritual that has been emptied of much of its traditional significance by the expanded and encroaching antimasque.

The closing chapter of this book considers Jonson's Caroline masques, which, like his late plays, have often been dismissed as 'dotages'. And indeed, after the full-blooded and expanded antimasque, these late masques appear to be a watery dilution of a richer dish. But the late plays are being rehabilitated by contemporary critics, which is perhaps an indication that these masques should not be dismissed too lightly. In terms of the evolution of the court entertainment these masques do represent a collapse of dialogism into monologism, and this must surely be connected with the new political climate and shift in aesthetic taste. I examine *Love's Triumph Through Callipolis* (1631), and suggest that the antimasque's edge of dissent is blunted to such a degree that it occludes any significant contradiction of monarchical values. And yet, the masque itself in this entertainment does express certain anxieties about the nature of monarchy. *Love's Triumph* also represents a departure in form as well as content because both the King and Queen perform in it, thus eliminating the need for all lines of perspective to meet in one focal point where the King is seated in the audience. Moreover, the traditional focus of the entertainment shifts from the King to the Queen and expresses certain concerns about the gender and role of the Queen and her excessive influence over royal authority. These anxieties are, however, embedded deep within the royalist discourse of the masque, rather than being part of an evolved structure of dissent of the kind that we find in the antimasque of *The Irish Masque*; it is for this reason that *Love's Triumph* appears to be rather like a pantomime embodying the monarchy's political agenda, rather than the dynamic examination of authority based on the relationship of antimasque to masque that distinguishes earlier court entertainments.

My assertion that *Love's Triumph* witnesses the marginalisation of the antimasque must be qualified by the fact that the Caroline antimasque is never completely disabled by the renewed dominance of the masque, just as the main masque in earlier court entertainments was not totally undermined by the expanded antimasque. Cultural Materialist critics would argue that the antimasque is never completely disempowered by the masque because in order to occlude dissent the court entertainment must first represent it in the antimasque and thus perversely empower it to some extent. In terms of the evolution of the form, we might say that the Caroline court entertainment thus reverses an earlier pattern of development where the expanded antimasque threatened to consume the masque. Rather than closing this book with a set of conclusions, I am more interested in stimulating debate around the topic of the court entertainment, so I offer a postscript instead. Here I try to show that the Caroline antimasque did indeed survive attempts to erase it, and this assertion is borne out by later masques such as Milton's *Comus* (1634) and Shirley's *Triumph of Peace* (1633); although these masques were written during Jonson's last declining years, they are clearly successors to his dialogic court entertainments.

Jonson and Barthes

Jonson and Barthes make anachronistic and uncomfortable bedfellows, but in the age of literary theory it is virtually impossible for a writer or academic to lay out an argument without subjecting its methodology to close analysis. Such analysis is perhaps even more important in this book as I draw on a melange of critical approaches in producing an overview of the antimasque and its evolution. For example, I combine formalist, historicist, reader-centred and author-centred theories of writing, but rather than including all of these in an overpowering and confusing mix, it is my intention to draw on selected elements of these separate theories where it best suits my argument. While I may be accused of theoretical promiscuity, I have no wish to pin Jonson down on the rack of theory, and to twist the antimasque to fit a particular methodology in all respects. The formalism of this book manifests itself in my concentration upon the way in which the antimasque is shaped by Jonson's poetic ideals and use of genre, and in the close study of particular masque and poetic texts. This formalist approach, including textual and rhetorical analysis, is accompanied by an historicist emphasis that locates individual court entertainments in their political and cultural contexts. This combination of formalist and historicist approaches reflects a view of texts as cultural productions, and literature as a system of signs embedded in a wider culture. On the one hand, attention to the formal properties of masque texts is imperative in order to avoid relegating them to the function of mere historical reflection or to the exclusive expression of ideology. But on the other hand, the meaning of the masque is largely contingent upon its historical moment. Moreover, these court entertainments have at times a strident ideological message as a result of their being commissioned by the King and the court. What may be described as a cultural approach to the masque text seeks to juggle all these perspectives, viewing the court masque as a heterogeneous production. This heterogeneity expresses itself in the generic hybridisation that is found in the masque, that is, it possesses elements that we also find in Jonson's tragic and comic drama, as well as his epideictic and satirical poetry. Furthermore, the court entertainment answers the propaganda requirements of the monarch as well as responding to Jonson's very personal sense of poetics; it simultaneously seizes hold of philosophical 'universal truths' and deliberately addresses topical issues, engaging energetically in contemporary debate. The very nature of the Jonsonian masque is also mixed or heterogeneous in that it was designed to be an ephemeral and exclusive celebration of the court, of which no trace should remain (the masque set was ritually torn down as part of the revels), yet Jonson preserved his masque texts, altering and annotating them for the market-place. Even before they were preserved in his stately volume of works (thus becoming his property rather than the monarch's), many of these elite texts were released to the public in the humble quarto edition.

The historicism in this book is based on a view of the text as directly engaged in its moment of production rather than as a passive reflector of its historical period. This approach empowers the text and can be extended to suggest that the relationship between text and history is interactive, each shaping and determining the other; this is certainly true in Jonson's case, as he self-consciously sought the role of the Horatian poet, whose work actively shaped royal policy.[5] This historical emphasis necessitates my engagement with various historically based critical theories such as New Historicism and Cultural Materialism and the broadening of focus from text to historical context not only highlights the discursive practices within which Jonson worked, but also the importance of Jonson as an individual writer among his contemporaries. The masques, poetry and plays reflect his self-appointed role as social educator and moral commentator on the times, and can only be brought into perspective when placed within this wider historical context. Furthermore, the argument for an historicist approach is strengthened by the fact that Jonson often used his work as a platform from which to address contemporary literary debate, involving him in vigorous and often vicious attack and defence.

I have already referred to the manner in which I draw on a variety of literary theories in this book, and while this approach may encourage a more sensitive engagement with the complexities of much of Jonson's work, it does mean that I need to articulate clearly my position on certain major critical issues such as the role of the author and the relationship between text and context. The very fact that in the main body of this book I often cite 'Jonson' as the originator or manipulator of texts shows that I accept (with some qualification) the notion of intentionality, the author's authority over his text, although many of the theories deployed in this thesis generally work to displace or decentre the author. It seems to me that this multivalent approach is dictated by Jonson's conscious erudition and meticulous craftsmanship; while contemporary theory can illuminate some of Jonson's more difficult texts, it should not be allowed to drown out the author's distinctive and often strident voice. His self-conscious fashioning of a poetic voice and persona demands attention to his authorial aims, and this attention is often given where I refer to his recurring proclamations of poetic intent and principle that preface many of his masques as well as his plays and collections of poetry. However, it must also be recognised that such authority is limited, a limitation that seems to have irked Jonson from time to time. My reliance on text – or reader – based theories of interpretation is demonstrated at the beginning of Chapter 1, where I quote Catherine Belsey's appeal for, 'A radical criticism... not to replace one authoritative interpretation of a text with another, but to suggest a plurality of ways in which texts might be read'.[6] Clearly, Belsey displaces the authority of the writer in favour of the self-generating significance of the text, but while my use of Belsey's critical injunction as a starting point for a textual analysis of Jonson's poem, 'To Sir Robert Wroth', may appear to contradict and undermine assumptions about intentionality I employed earlier in Chapter 2, I want to argue that such inconsistencies can be resolved by a dialogic emphasis on both the author and the text. (Such dialogism could be regarded as a typically Jonsonian strategy). The writer does author a text with clear aims in mind, but any notion of total authority is limited by the text's power to become self-divided and autonomous in its production of meaning. In writing of the death of the author, Roland Barthes famously declares:

> The removal of the Author (one could talk here with Brecht of a veritable 'distancing', the Author diminishing like a figurine at the far end of the literary stage) is not merely an historical fact or an act of writing; it utterly transforms the modern text.[7]

In my view, it is significant that what Barthes is describing here is not so much the death of the author, as is often assumed, but the distancing of the author, whereby the author is relieved of his/her privileged status and becomes another textual element. This is not to deny, however, that the author is the one responsible for the arrangement of the words on the page or the pages in the text despite the fact that he or she cannot possibly account for the proliferation of different readings of the text, produced by intentional and unintentional ambiguities within it.[8] Jonson seems to have been acutely aware of this aspect of the author's position and his extensive redrafting of work prior to publication may be seen as partly a demonstration of the author's attempt to maximise his control over words and their meaning and to minimise ambiguity within the text, although it would perhaps be more accurate to assert that Jonson wanted only specific ambiguities that he had deliberately built into his texts to manifest themselves, rather than the more arbitrary ambiguities produced by the uninformed readings of others. This paradoxical attempt to fix the ambiguity of the text stems from the fact that Jonson often relied on and exploited ambiguity for his own purposes, for example, to protect himself from the wrath of his censors when they detected what was thought to be subversive material in his work. The attempt to expel from the text random ambiguities not sanctioned by the author is, of course, impossible – a fact of which Jonson seems to have been well aware and which is signalled in the first poem in his collection of epigrams. Pointedly, the poem is addressed to the reader,

> Pray thee, take care, that tak'st my book in hand,
> To read it well: that is, to understand.

In exhorting the reader to read well, that is, to understand his poems, Jonson implicitly acknowledges that there will be many who misunderstand or read his poems badly. The poet cannot prevent such alternative readings, and can only warn against them, but such a warning is ineffective because there is no prescription laid out for a good reading, and because Jonson cannot tell how bad readings may take shape in the future after he has relinquished control over his epigrams by releasing them into the market-place. Jonson effectively articulates the author's bind (this time with an air of resignation) in a poem dedicated to Alphonso Ferrabosco on the publication of his book of music:

> When we do give, Alphonso, to the light,
> A work of ours, we part with our own right;
> For, then, all mouths will judge, and their own way:
> The learned have no more privilege, than the lay.
>
> (*Epigrams*, CXXXI)

Jonson, however, attempts to reclaim an authentic text by exhorting Ferrabosco to remain true to the text within himself in the face of misinterpretations of his book:

> Then stand unto thyself, not seek without
> For fame, with breath soon kindled, soon blown out.

In resorting to an authentic text of the self Jonson's poem resists the spiralling relativity of competing readings, however, as my emphasis on Jonson's dialectical approach suggests, he was well aware of the possibilities inherent in the polysemic qualities of language and exploited them to produce dialogic texts where a doubleness of meaning is crucial to their significance. A criticism that searches for alternative readings embedded in the overt content of a poem or a masque (see my treatment of 'To Sir Robert Wroth' in Chapter 2) is justified by Jonson's practice of exploiting a doubleness in meaning for deliberate and obvious satirical or sarcastic effect. Perhaps the best example of such a poem is the ironically acidic and amusing 'On Giles and Joan':

> Who says that Giles and Joan at discord be?
> The observing neighbours no such mood can see.
> Indeed, poor Giles repents he married ever.
> But that his Joan doth too. And Giles would never,

> By his free will be in Joan's company.
> No more would Joan he should. Giles riseth early,
> And having got him out of door is glad.
> The like is Joan. Oft-times, when Giles doth find
> Harsh sights at home, Giles wisheth he were blind.
> All this doth Joan. Or that his long-yarned life
> Were quite out-spun. The like wish hath his wife.
> The children, that he keeps, Giles swears are none
> Of his begetting. And so swears his Joan.
> In all affections she concurreth still.
> If, now, with man and wife, to will, and nill
> The self-same things, a note of concord be:
> I know no better couple better can agree!
>
> (*Epigrams*, XLII)

Playful equivocation is perhaps the most outstanding of Jonson's poetic 'voices'; he mobilises polarised extremes to produce, paradoxically, the neo-classical ideal of the rational *via media*.

If the relationship between text and author is one potential methodological problem arising out of the combination of critical theories in this book, another is thrown up by the variations in emphasis within the historicist critical approach upon which I draw widely in my study of the antimasque. New Historicists are especially interested in the court masque as a topical and occasional event, viewing it as the prevailing hegemony's symbolic confirmation of power, and as a text/occasion that merely rehearses discontent or dissent in order to contain or banish it. Stephen Orgel is one well known critic who espouses this view; he emphasises the masque's power to aestheticise and codify the monarchy as a divine principle and its ability to contain and disable any dissent expressed in the antimasque. However, there are other critics writing under the broad umbrella of New Historicism who manifest some discomfort with such a totalised view of royal power in the masque and emphasise the masque as a site of contestation, which then results in the royal containment of dissent. In shying away from this totalising concept of royal power, exponents of what might be called the 'contestation to containment' theory, such as Leah Marcus, suggest that the operations of power are not monolithic but contingent and prone to instability and flux. Such contingency is seized upon by Cultural Materialists who view the dominant ideology's attempt to reproduce dissent for its own ends, and to disable it in ritual, as often backfiring. These critics assert that a dominant ideology and its cultural vehicle are liable to appropriation, and incapable of protecting themselves against a potentially subversive adoption of their discourse. Such a view would posit that the antimasque appropriates the monarchical discourse of the masque only to subvert it radically. I broadly agree with the last supposition; for example, the antimasque is distinguished by dance and song just like the masque, but the former celebrates disintegration and chaos, whereas the latter extols harmony and national unity presided over by the divine monarch. But I would like to add an important *caveat* to the Cultural Materialist position, and suggest that the antimasque does not completely subvert the masque, but the juxtaposition of antimasque to masque enables a dialectical exploration of the nature of royal authority. In my view, the function of the court entertainment is far more complex than simple subversion or containment, and it does seem that in focusing on one or other of these options New Historicist and Cultural Materialist critics have become locked into a theoretical and confrontational binarism. Indeed, Theodore B. Leinwand has detected that both these critiques are grounded in a Foucauldian analysis of power that depends on conflict, and that they are propelled by a view of critical debate based on polarity and clear-cut opposition. In his rejection of this *zero/sum* approach Leinwand writes, 'Implicit in the subversion-containment binarism... is the conviction that sociopolitical and cultural practices have conflict as their operator.'[9] In Chapter 3, while making use of a New Historicist/Cultural Materialist frame of reference to discuss the ideological strategies of the antimasque, I have tried to avoid the reductionism of the containment/subversion debate. Moving away from this essentialist view of texts as either inherently conservative or subversive, I turn to the work of the Marxist critic, Pierre Macherey, who asserts the polyvalency of the text. Macherey emphasises the contingency and instability of the text as opposed to Foucault's stress on entrenched power relations that predetermine the production of the text; such instabilities are, he argues, generated not only by the text but also by its interaction with its socio-political context. Macherey's theory can be used to liberate the court masque from the essentialist subversion/containment options and enables it to be considered a site for the articulation of contingent power relations and negotiation. With these points in mind we can view the court masque as reproducing an absolutist discourse while destabilising it at the same time. Moreover, according to this theory of textual production, it is impossible for such instability to be fully recuperated or resolved by the absolutist masque. In this book I have borrowed the key term 'negotiation' from Leinwand, who justifies his rejection of the reductive binarism of recent historicist theory thus:

> Perhaps we can reconceive the binarisms of social process as other than conflict leading to one-sided victory. Compromise, negotiation, exchange, accommodation, give and take – these bases for social relations are as recognizable as those mentioned thus far... I am not interested in throwing

out insights and interpretations generated by the binarism of conflict; rather, I believe that a model based on negotiation and exchange may prove useful where now familiar paradigms seem unsatisfactory. In particular I want to attribute change to something other than subversion. While it may be argued that forces of containment perceive all change, in the last instance, as subversive, change has, I think, been effected through the efforts of ostensibly antagonistic parties negotiating toward settlement, adjustment, even alteration. It is a thorough falsification of historical processes to argue that subversion offers the only alternative to the status quo. And it is a comparative falsification to argue that anything short of authentic subversion is but another instance of discipline.[10]

This view of power relations and their cultural expressions as contingent and shifting is, I suggest, a more useful historicist methodology for discussing the growth of the antimasque. Leinwand points a way out of the stalemate inherent in the containment/subversion debate that has dogged New Historicists and Cultural Materialists, and his emphasis on the social processes of negotiation and accommodation is consistent with the dialogism within Jonson's work as a whole for which I argue throughout this book. The antimasque's appropriation and inversion of the traditional terms of masque, followed by the official reassertion of these values in the masque proper sets up the dialectic that is, in essence, a process of negotiation and this form of Jonsonian dialectic seeks neither to undermine the state nor to laud it without qualification, but to produce a conditional endorsement of the monarchy. Such an endorsement is dependent upon the monarch following the model of rule laid out in the masque, where the King is seen to administer mercy and justice and to eschew tyranny as a means of quelling the disruptive elements of the 'democratic' antimasque; Jonson's ideal of monarchical government embodies a golden mean between extremes of tyranny and anarchic democracy. Significantly, the court entertainment is not monolithic in either its subversion or containment of the ideal of monarchy, but rather a dynamic text/event that initiates and depends on change, movement, and alternative formulations of power. The very dynamism of the Jonsonian masque lies in the fact that the balance for or against the Crown is never predetermined, but a contingent process that can appear to favour one set of ideologies and then another in different masques; and we should remember that such contingency is inherent in the structure and history of the antimasque as well as in its ideological processes. For example, while the Jacobean antimasque expanded and threatened the masque, it later became marginalised by the Caroline masque and virtually disappeared. There is no better example of the ebb and flow, the shifting nature of power relations than the history of the antimasque; it experienced an expansion, followed by decay and a tentative renewal. The history of this most courtly of texts is not only determined by the poetics and political leanings of its author but, undeniably, also by its conditions of production.

Readers as understanders: Jonsonian masque in the twentieth century

Jonson's reputation as a whole has been rehabilitated in recent years, resulting in no less than three major conferences devoted to him in the UK alone in 1995/6 and an academic journal solely devoted to Jonson recently established. But this process was started many years ago and has been gradual to say the least. For example, if Jonson the poet and dramatist enjoyed a new climate of admiration, Jonson the masque maker was treated with some suspicion until recently, and his court entertainments are still seen as problematic in many ways, particularly in relation to questions of authorial intention and integrity, audience reception, and the interactive balance between the masque as a visual as well as a written event. Moreover, Feminist critics are beginning to struggle with the masque, and to ponder issues such as the meaning involved in female costume design, where the female masquers appear to be bare breasted in certain entertainments when the plot neither requires such a device nor alludes to it, and when the performers are aristocrats who presumably placed a value on decorum and status. Unfortunately, these questions lie outwith the scope of this book, but I include them to indicate the ways in which masque criticism is likely to develop in the future before outlining a history of twentieth-century masque criticism to date.

No work on the Jonsonian masque can omit to mention Enid Welsford, whose seminal book, *The Court Masque* (1927), was the first serious work to examine the origins of the court entertainment, and its structure and function under the Stuart monarchs. Welsford takes great pains to trace the embryonic development of the masque in the folk customs and literary traditions of medieval Europe, themselves indebted to Roman saturnalia. Perhaps her most important contribution to the study of Jonson's masques is her emphasis on them as part of a major European tradition, and she indicates where Jonson may have taken his inspiration from contemporary Italian or French examples of the form, thereby counteracting the influence of those critics who stress the Stuart masque as an introspective and claustrophobic event. Whereas Welsford painted a grand perspective of the masque, another British critic, D. J. Gordon, attended to the intricate details of various entertainments. Gordon's importance rests in the fact that he was the first to decode the iconology of Jonsonian masque in a comprehensive and comprehensible manner, and his analyses of *The Masque of Blackness*, *The Masque of Beauty*, and *Hymenaei* remain text book examples of a fine tradition of criticism that rests on close reading and painstaking analysis. Perhaps the most monumental contribution to the twentieth-century study of Jonson was the publication of his complete works in eleven volumes (1925-52), edited by Charles Herford and Percy and Evelyn Simpson. The major significance of these volumes lies in the fact that they made available for the first time the whole body of Jonson's work, rather than the few plays and volumes of poetry that he was mostly known for. This meant that academics and students could actually read the masques for the first time in many years, and even attempt to stage them.[11] Herford and Simpson's volumes are still vital reference points, perhaps not so much for their editorial comment, but for their comprehensive coverage of accounts of the masques' original reception, and documents relating to their performance. A new edition of Jonson's complete works is currently being prepared by the British scolars Ian Donaldson and Martin Butler, a welcome development which will doubtless enhance masque criticism.

It may be argued that the efforts of Welsford, Gordon, Herford and Simpson made the achievement of the American critic, Stephen Orgel, possible and that, while these earlier British critics laid the foundations of current masque criticism, it was really Orgel who first brought the Jonsonian masque to the serious attention of students of Renaissance literature. His work, *The Jonsonian Masque* (1965) made an impact partly because it completely disregarded certain aspects of the court entertainment that plainly made the British critics uncomfortable and shuffle around their subject from time to time, that is, the masque's status as unqualified flattery of the King and the philosopher-poet's function as royal servant. Such a view sees the authorial integrity of the masque maker as unavoidably compromised, and Jonson's apparent political and poetic compromise dictated that the masque would always be considered a degenerate and lesser art form by certain critics. Orgel, however, proclaimed the folly of burdening the public and epideictic literature of the Renaissance with the literary values of the Romantics, and placed the masque within the context of royal panegyric where issues of flattery or integrity are completely irrelevant. His triumph in terms of Jonsonian masque was that he demonstrated how it had to be viewed in its literary and historical contexts to be understood properly. Contemporary with Orgel's efforts on behalf of Jonson is John C. Meagher's book, *Method and Meaning in Jonson's Masques* (1966); he also re-evaluated the masque and examined its structure and function, although his perspective seems to lack Orgel's clarity. Orgel also explored the visual aspects of the court masque, and in conjunction with Roy Strong produced, *Inigo Jones. The Theatre of the Stuart Court* (1973). Strong has produced and continues to produce independently significant work relating to masques, but this book is the most important record of the visual impact of the masque in terms of set design and costume, replicating many of Inigo Jones's original sketches. The text of this book largely reworks the hypothesis of Orgel's earlier book, but in addition to the emphasis on the masque as panegyric, it stresses the importance of platonic philosophy in shaping the masque's content and form. There is no doubt that between them Orgel and Strong have made a great contribution to the study of Jonson's masques, but my major reservation relating to their work is that the emphasis on panegyric and philosophy fails to take into account adequately the evolution and role of the antimasque. More recently, critics such as Leah Marcus, Martin Butler, David Lindley and Graham Parry have expressed discomfort with such a totalised view of masque, but while they may pay attention to elements within the masque that do not fit with the panegyrical model they generally subsume them in the masque's greater goal of monarchical praise. However, just as masque criticism seemed to change gear in 1965, so it seems to be shifting again today thanks to the impact of critical theory on the masque. Anne Lake Prescott reflects a growing interest in the related cultural paradigms of the classical and the grotesque in her examination of Jonson's antimasques and their debt to Rabelais. Furthermore, Anthony Barthelemy, Suzanne Gosset, Kim Hall and Hardin Aasand have charted the discourses of race and gender at work in the court masque, and shown how the masque harnesses certain assumptions in these areas to legitimate and celebrate a nascent British imperialism. These American critics represent a new wave in masque criticism and are united in an interest in unravelling the masque and highlighting those elements that resist the masque's wider project of totalising panegyric. Similarly, I believe that the impact of the antimasque has been too easily dismissed and in this book I draw upon many of the insights generated by recent critical theory in an attempt to understand it and its relationship with the court entertainment as a whole. Critics are now listening to what is spoken beyond or behind the panegyric of masque, to the murmuring voice of dissent within the chorus of praise and examining the ideologies masque negotiates in relation to issues of class, politics, sexuality, gender and race. In this way the Jonsonian masque becomes the truly dynamic text/event that I suspect its author intended it to be.[12]

Some speculative conclusions on the growth of the antimasque

I realise that an introduction is an odd place in a book to offer conclusions, but as I have been concerned thus far to outline some of the problems involved in examining the rise of the antimasque, and some of the theoretical issues involved, it may be useful to sum up here the direction of my argument as far as it has developed. I have already asserted that the antimasque developed out of anomalies and discrepancies within the more orthodox court masque, and in Chapter 1 I discuss *The Masque of Blackness* (1605) at some length as an example of an early masque permeated with inconsistencies that give rise to certain subtextual ironies which go against the grain of a royalist reading. The way in which the antimasque developed is in keeping with a dialogic impulse found in much of Jonson's other work and as an early example of Jonson's impulse towards dialogism I discuss the chivalric masques, *Prince Henry's Barriers* (1610) and *Oberon* (1611), in Chapter 2. The antimasque proceeded to evolve into the full-blown strategies of dissent typified by *The Irish Masque at Court* (1613) and *Mercury Vindicated From the Alchemists at Court* (1616), which I discuss in Chapter 3. If the subtle ironies in the earlier masques pointed out flaws within royalist ideology, these developed antimasques overtly articulate values which contradict and invert those of the following royalist masque.

This emphatic expansion of the dissenting antimasque resulted in a destabilising of the masque and its values. The question that needs to be asked here is what was the point of such a radical restructuring of the court entertainment. The answer to this lies, I suggest, in both Jonson's very personal brand of poetics and the masque's socio-political context. Both Jonson and King James immersed themselves in Roman culture, and used classical precedent as a model for their own roles within the state. James promoted himself as the Augustan king who presided over a political and artistic golden age, the *Rex Pacificus*. In his plays Jonson also recognised the value of this version of the classical ruler and portrayed the ideal state structure in *Poetaster* (1601) where Caesar is the just and merciful ruler, advised by the philosopher poet Virgil. In the same play the poet Horace is vindicated as commentator on and arbiter of social values. Jonson sought to take on the roles of both these poets and become a Virgil to James's Caesar. He readily recognised James's claims to a classical heritage and presented the monarch with a reflection of them in the accession day entertainments that he helped to create. In according James imperial status, Jonson simultaneously empowered himself, and upgraded himself from lowly playwright to royal advisor and keeper of public morals. Jonson's desire to monitor and comment on private and political morality is partly responsible for his distinctive manipulation of the court masque into a dialectic structure, that addresses both the private behaviour of courtiers and the impact of royal policy on the nation as a whole. The role of moral arbiter entailed dissent from time to time, as the poet thought it appropriate to criticise public fashion or even royal policy. Such an apparently daring and risky strategy was implicit in his chosen function because a philosopher poet in the Virgilian/Horatian mode was expected to maintain a critical independence and a distinctive poetic voice that responded to individual conscience rather than merely echoing imperial policy. This emphasis on poetic integrity dictates that dissent is an essential function of the poet.

Importantly, the ironies of the masques and antimasques embody this dissent without overturning the absolutist discourse that is present; so that these entertainments are neither simply subversive nor conservative but enact both these discursive strategies as a means of exploring exactly what constitutes secure and just government. Moreover, this dialogic aspect of the court entertainment was a means of defence against the many accusations Jonson incurred through his position as the unofficial *poet laureate*. As a philosopher poet Jonson could take the King's shilling and maintain his poetic integrity, because he was not involved in unalloyed flattery in his creation of the antimasque/masque. Furthermore, his dialogism often involves an equivocality that can slip into deliberate ambiguity, again protecting Jonson from those detractors who wished to pin on him accusations of subversion or royal flattery. The dialogic tendency of the court entertainments is not, however, chiefly a self-protective measure, but, more significantly, the embodiment of Jonson's political and poetic values. It seems to me that the fundamental motivation behind the Jonsonian antimasque/masque is the desire to produce a conditional and didactic endorsement of the monarchical ideal, and to represent a negotiation of extremes through a counterbalancing of oppositional formulations of royal authority, arriving at a classical *via media*.

The development and growth of the antimasque not only promotes the poet as both critic and eulogist of the monarchy but can also be viewed as a response to the socio-political climate. As I will show in the following chapters, historical documentation seems to demonstrate that there was a definite increase in public scandals throughout the reign of James I, or, at the very least, a heightened public consciousness of such matters. Predictably, such scandals involved members of the aristocracy, whose fall from grace, then as now, attracted the prurient interest of their less elevated contemporaries. However, the very genuine horror expressed by Stuart society at matters such as the Howard-Essex divorce stems from the fact that the dominant ideology of the period attributed to the aristocracy an unassailable authority within the divinely appointed social hierarchy surmounted by the monarch.[13] In behaving badly, the aristocracy violated this assumption, destabilising those 'norms' of power and status so central to the ideology of early modern Britain. Furthermore, if the aristocracy's position was undermined in this way, what was to prevent this instability radiating up the hierarchical ladder and putting the monarch's position at risk? Because the security of the monarch and the security of the state were seen to be indissoluble, the questioning of status occasioned by scandals at court has wider implications than is first apparent. Many of Jonson's antimasques tackle this crisis at court and ridicule such behaviour in an attempt to reform it. This is the kind of human folly that the antimasques, plays and poetry feed on. It appears that, as the court increasingly seemed to lack the virtues it was expected to have, Jonson expanded the antimasque in order to comment on this situation. Additionally, constitutional issues were the subject of intellectual enquiry during this period.[14] Many of Jonson's antimasques address the effects of real and potential social instability, and yet despite these crises, the political *status quo* was relatively secure. On the whole, those who criticised court society or sought to curtail the monarch's prerogative did not express a wish for the abolition of the state and its rulers but for reform. These reformists included Jonson as well as more marginal pampleteers and playwrights such Gascoigne and Deloney.[15] Thus, the relative security of the state meant that the dialogism of the court masque was not felt to be a danger by the monarch. It is most important to remember that the antimasque developed in response to a monarchy which was sufficiently secure to tolerate oblique criticism. It is in what we might term these fertile conditions that the antimasque thrived, its dissent protected by a veil of antic humour. However, a change of monarch and leading personnel at court in 1625 led to the antimasque experiencing a reversal in fortune. There is no doubt that the demise of the antimasque is attributable in part to the fact that Charles I introduced to the court a new, inward-focusing aesthetic. As royal productions, Jonson's masques were called upon to reflect the fashionable cult of neo-platonism, and, in doing so, they focused on the royal couple more than on any note of dissent in the antimasque. In fulfilling the new royal agenda the poet marginalised himself from the entertainment. Rather than the advising poet-philosopher, who exploited the antimasque to contradict royal policy where appropriate, Jonson became the royal servant whose only task was to provide a suitable vehicle to display royal splendour. Nevertheless, we should not dismiss the Caroline masques too readily, or overlook the fact that they express anomalies similar to those that feature in the early Jacobean masques, flaws that resist the total recuperation of the masque as a monolithic confirmation of the state.

Notes

1. It may be appropriate to clarify my use of the terms 'antimasque' and 'masque'. 'Masque' refers to the Court entertainment as a whole, but it is also used to describe a constituent part. Critics also refer to the 'masque' when alluding to the courtly component of the court entertainment, which was often prefaced by an 'antimasque'. I have tried to make my use of the term 'masque' clear from the context of the sentence in which it appears. Exponents of the view that the court masque is a simple act of homage to the Crown include Jonson's contemporaries as well as recent critics. The masque maker Samuel Daniel declared his view that the most significant aspect of masque entertainment was 'pomp and splendour', and covertly attacked Jonson's more intellectually ambitious entertainments: 'And whosoever strives to show most wit about these punctilios of dreams and shows are sure sick of a disease they cannot hide and would fain have the world to think them very deeply learned in all mysteries whatsoever. And peradventure they think themselves so, which if they do, they are in a far worse case than they imagine'. Philip Edwards is a recent critic who dismisses masques in terms similar to Daniel, but also brands them as distasteful displays of egregious flattery on the part of the poet and as an outstanding example of royal vanity. See Daniel, *The Vision of the Twelve Goddesses*, in Spencer and Wells (eds) (1967), 30; and Edwards (1979).
2. There is a clearly defined tradition of this type of nonsensical, punning language, which is outlined by Rhodes (1980). Also see Weimann and Shwartz (1978).
3. My interest in the literary nature of the antimasque and its conditions of production unfortunately precludes a consideration in any depth of other formal characteristics of the court masque, such as music, set design and the use of perspective. Informative works considering these aspects of masque include Chan (1980); Walls (1996); Orgel and Strong (1973); Peacock (1995).
4. Walls (1996); Limon (1991), 212; Loewenstein (1991), 180.
5. For an excellent rehearsal of the New Historicist view of the interactive relationship between text and history see Howard (1987).
6. Belsey (1985a), 167.
7. Barthes (1977), 145.
8. In an excellent essay, however, Stephen Orgel shows how this notion of the author is made even more complex by the conditions of textual production in the Renaissance period, and that the book seller, the printer, and the theatrical company all exerted a measure of authority over the text in addition to its writer. See Orgel (1991), 'What is a text?', in Kastan and Stallybrass (1991).
9. Leinwand (1990), 478.
10. Leinwand (1990), 479.
11. While there may have been more recent amateur efforts to stage a Jonsonian masque, the last courtly production was in 1911 as part of the coronation festivities for George V. For details see Herford & Simpson (1925-52), vol. X, 570.
12. See Welsford (1927); Gordon, D.J., in Orgel (1975b); Herford and Simpson (1925-52); Orgel (1965); Orgel (1969); Orgel (1975a and b); Orgel and Strong (1973); Meagher (1966); Marcus (1986); Butler and Lindley (1994); Prescott (1984); Gossett (1988); Barthelemy (1987); Hall (1991); Aasand (1992).
13. Lindley (1994).

14. This shift in power away from the monarch and towards the Commons is demonstrated in Wooton (1988). This book is an anthology of political writing in Stuart England, with an excellent introduction describing the political wrangling and competition between the House of Commons and the monarchy.
15. Gascoigne's prose fiction *The Adventures of Master F. J.* satirises the aristocratic pose of courtly love and reveals it to be the pastime of bored and licentious nobles. Gascoigne does not, however, suggest that the social hierarchy should be abolished, but satirically hints that aristocratic behaviour may benefit from some reformation. In *Jack of Newbury*, Thomas Deloney also examines and puts pressure on the concepts of gentility and courtly behaviour. Jack makes his fortune through his trade as a merchant, and becomes a prince. Deloney apparently suggests that princeliness may depend on industrial service rather than aristocratic birth and values. For both these pamphlets see Salzman (1987).

1
'Free from servile flattery': panegyric and the formation of the antimasque

An understanding of Jonson's deployment of panegyric in both poetry and masque is an essential prerequisite for any analysis of the antimasque and its growth. The question that needs to be addressed here is why did Jonson obviously believe that the panegyric of masque needed to be offset by the irony of the antimasque? I believe that we will find the germ of an answer by scrutinising the poetry and paying attention to the ways in which the most hyperbolic of Jonson's panegyric can, at times, subtly incorporate a note of mockery. I hope to demonstrate that rather than being a weakness in his poetic eulogies this rhetorical instability is, in fact, a great strength, ensuring the poet's integrity and simultaneously fulfilling the terms of patronage. So it is to Jonson's poetry I turn initially in an attempt to account for the antimasque's evolution from ironic suggestion to overtly ambiguous satire; this entails taking into account both the historical context of certain poems as well as the implications of such an instability for Jonson's personal philosophy and poetics. These are continuing concerns threading through the book, but my primary aim in this chapter is to demonstrate that the characteristic features of the antimasque are present from the first in an embryonic form in the earliest masque and poetry.

In laying the groundwork for an examination of Jonson's early attempts to combine panegyric and irony in the masque, the first section of this chapter will explore the nature and purpose of Jonsonian praise, using his non-dramatic poems to present a rounded interpretation of a form that has so often been misunderstood and underrated.[1] Such misapprehension extends from Jonson's contemporaries to present day readers, and in tackling some of the assumptions on which it rests I hope to offer a rationale for the poet's accommodation of irony and satire within the masque. Focusing specifically on the early masques of *Blackness* (1605) and *Beauty* (1608) I will suggest that fracturing tensions arise in the masque, partly due to discrepancies between the historical and the ideal, and partly due to clashing philosophies of poetry, where, rather than sharing a 'consociation of offices', poet and monarch harbour different notions about the function and authority of each other. These tensions appear to be in danger of undercutting the previously established artistic unity of masque where music, drama, and dance are harmonised to 'present the figure of those blessings' bestowed by a divinely inspired monarch on his people.[2] Significantly, the kinds of contradictions that distinguish *Blackness* and *Beauty* are turned to advantage by Jonson and developed into the antimasque, creating a masque form capable of flexible interpretation, accommodating both the poet's and the monarch's sense of poetics. It is this very flexibility in masque that results in a particularly Jonsonian dynamic interchange between satire and panegyric that will be the subject of following chapters. At this stage in my discussion, however, I want to emphasise that satire and panegyric are complementary aspects of a Humanist tradition of didactic literature – an interrelation that the current critical preoccupation with 'subversion' can encourage us to gloss over.

Jonsonian panegyric: a textual criticism of 'To Sir Robert Wroth'

For many years Wesley Trimpi's pronouncements on Jonson's 'plain style' dominated criticism of the author, but in the recent past this simplifying view of Jonson's poetry has been opposed by critics such as Richard Peterson, who are more alert to the subtle complexities of much of Jonson's verse. In his indispensable book, *Imitation and Praise in the Poems of Ben Jonson*, Peterson reveals the plasticity of Jonson's verse, its capacity to house the three-dimensional shapes that are the monuments of praise.[3] Moreover, Peterson demonstrates that Jonson's classical learning is far from academic pedantry and rather a gathering in of all that is excellent in ancient literature to reshape it into poetry that meets the needs of his own age. Jonson and his contemporaries recognised this practice as *imitatio* and it involved studying and learning from the works of the best authors; selectivity was viewed as a crucial aspect of *imitatio* and rather than a parasitical dependence on an earlier literature it was an exercise in discretion: 'to draw forth out of the best ... with the bee, and turn all into honey' (*Discoveries*, ll.3069–71). Peterson suggests that the poems of praise are transmitters of demanding ideals and concepts, and reveal an intricate structure with multiple layers of meaning. We may extrapolate from this argument a view of Jonson's poetry as inherently dynamic, a poetry of rhetorical movement and debate that rejects the orthodox monologism of poetic praise for something more demanding.

Peterson's critical approach offers an alternative to the common criticism of Jonsonian epideictics as the superficial tribute of a hireling poet to his patron, a poetry which lacks the personal integrity that we have come to associate with the more subjective poetry of the Romantics. Although Jonson himself, as well as his contemporaries, expressed varying degrees of reservation about his use of panegyric, much of our modern bias against the poet stems from a contextual misapprehension of Jonsonian praise, and the imposition of anachronistic ideals upon the public poetry of the Renaissance.[4] As if in anticipation of such criticism, the poet himself justifies panegyric (ironically, whilst conceding that there are some grounds for the charge of flattery) in 'An Epistle To Master John Selden':

> I have too oft preferred
> Men past their terms, and praised some names too much,
> But 'twas with purpose to have made them such.
>
> (*Underwoods*, XIV)

These lines pointedly allude to the didactic drive of Jonson's poetry and should remind us of the fact that the poet seeks to praise what is admirable in his subject in order to encourage him/her to maintain and pursue excellence; typically, Jonson also extends the same kind of exhortation to readers of the poem as well as to himself. In Jonson's verse there is often a classically based searching self-criticism, which in this poem is prompted by the poet's praise of Selden's authorial integrity. Bearing these ideals in mind, we should not be troubled by reading in Jonson's *Conversations* criticism of a man whom the poet also saw fit to praise in his public verse (See 'To Sir Robert Wroth' and Jonson's private remarks made upon the historical Wroth to Drummond in *Conversations*, ll.359-60). Similarly, in the masques of *Blackness* and *Beauty* Jonson praises James in the form of an alchemical sun-king; this is not empty eulogy, but praise of James in his symbolic capacity as a divinely inspired monarch ruling over his nation. In these masques Jonson poeticises the prevailing political order and makes it morally comprehensible, and the same kind of exhortation to virtue that Jonson extends to Sir Robert Wroth also applies to the King.[5] It seems clear then, that in these instances masque and poetry are governed by similar didactic principles and operate on both a symbolic and an historical level: the real is idealised in an attempt to encourage Wroth/King James to emulate his better image, thus creating the possibility of transforming an ideal image into reality. However, despite Jonson's practice of reading history symbolically, some tensions still remain, rising out of the gap between the symbol and the historical fact that lies behind it. In later court entertainments, rather than glossing over such a potentially embarrassing discrepancy, Jonson exploits it through the antimasque. This part of the court entertainment articulates a satirical discourse which emphasises the less elevated aspects of life under the early Stuarts, offsetting the masque's philosophical eulogy of the state and its monarch. The dynamic interaction between antimasque and masque will be discussed in later chapters, but for the moment I want to examine these initially problematic discrepancies, firstly referring to his poem on Wroth, and secondly to the masques of *Blackness* and *Beauty*.

The fundamental ideals behind Jonson's poetry of praise have been discussed by Jongsook Lee with particular reference to the two poems on Cecilia Bulstrode:

> In the poems, Jonson is concerned with something more universal and less particular than the things that have happened to Cecilia Bulstrode, and he addresses far more general audiences than Cecilia Bulstrode and those associated with her.[6]

Lee focuses on the symbolic and broader public nature of Jonson's eulogistic poetry rather than viewing it as specific commentary on historical persons. This critical perspective seeks to negotiate the tensions generated by Jonson's alternate criticism and praise of the same historical figures, by arguing that the gap between so-called historic fact and idealising poetic fiction is not relevant for a study of Jonsonian verse. As a qualification of this premise, I would suggest that the historical aspect of Jonson's panegyric is as important as the ideal; in disregarding the importance of fact and history, Lee misses the plasticity of Jonson's verse, poetry which can operate simultaneously as both irony and praise. According to Lee, all historical persons are turned into allegorical figures; in my view this attempt to homogenise Jonson's epideictics into one-dimensional symbolic meaning glosses over the dialectic set up within a poetry that can encompass both historical and idealistic aspects, fact and fiction, blame and praise.

In recognising the dialectic set up between the universal (ideal or symbol) and the specific (history or fact) in Jonson's work, Anne Barton has brought to light the significance of names in the poet's dramatic art.[7] Similarly, names and naming are of the utmost importance in Jonson's treatment of the subjects of non-dramatic satire or eulogy; for example, the 'Court Pucelle', Cecilia Bulstrode is stripped of her own name and given a more telling title that reveals her moral identity, (*Underwoods*, XLIX). This also has the effect of dehumanising the subject of the poem; she is no longer Cecilia Bulstrode but more akin to the traditional 'vice' figure of a mediaeval morality play. It is mere chance that we know the true identity of the subject of this poem; but for the pertinent note in *Conversations* (ll.646-8), the historical figure behind this vitriolic piece of satire would be just as mysterious as that of Lord Ignorant, Court-Worm, and Sir Cod the Perfumed (*Epigrams*, X, XV, XIX). The recipients of panegyric, however, experience the reverse of this symbolic renaming. Their historical names are the axis upon which the poem hangs, but their names also come to signify virtues beyond those of the specific individual referred to by that name. The focus upon name in eulogy has the same distancing and universalising effect as the renaming process of satire; the moral qualities synonymous with the name are of more importance than the individual behind the name. At the same time, however, the subjects of praise, unlike the generic figures of satire, do retain their real names and this invites cross-referencing with specific historical figures. Thus in his epitaph to Cecilia Bulstrode Jonson declares:

> She was 'Sell Bulstrode. In which name, I call
> Up so much truth, as could I it pursue
> Might make the *Fable of Good Women* true.
>
> (*Misc.* XXIV)

By invoking Chaucer's *Legend of Good Women* in the last line, Jonson acknowledges the fabulous nature of his portrayal of Cecilia Bulstrode, yet in naming his subject he also pointedly refers to an historical person. Around the historical subject of this poem Jonson weaves abstract values, much as a moralistic fable juxtaposes caricatured personifications of vice and virtue against a background of historical specificity. This approach is an integral part of a satiric tradition, which can be traced back to texts such as Chaucer's *Miller's Tale*. While fabliaux is a genre often described as an anarchic celebration of animal appetite, this does not preclude a moral direction to the satirical content of the tale. This is demonstrated by a text such as the *Miller's Tale* where most of the characters meet their just deserts (albeit certain characters are exempted from this general rule by virtue of their youth and wit). John the carpenter is the foolish old man who marries a younger wife; cuckoldry is his moral nemesis. By contrast, Nicholas is the wily scholar who triumphs through his wit, whereas his rival, Absolon, is a ridiculous lover whose humiliation is directly related to his egregious personal vanity. Alison is the prize they all compete for, the physically desirable and bored wife who is no better than she should be. Clearly, such characters are generic types created for an entertaining tale of comic satire, but despite the universality of such characters they are specifically based in a particular geography and time. Chaucer tells us that the carpenter lives in Oxford and travels to Oseneye on business; he also takes pains to make his tale visually immediate, thus it is set among tubs and kneading troughs. We learn that Nicholas plays the psaltery in his room which also contains his astrolabe and augrym stones, and is scented with sweet herbs, and so on; Chaucer heaps up circumstantial details to create a vivid and lively backdrop for his universal character types. This combination of the universal and the specific is a continuing literary tradition, and has been translated to the medium of television and film entertainment, a logical development when we remember the status of fabliaux as the popular culture of its day. Both *The Miller's Tale* and many contemporary screen thrillers use moral stereotypes to illustrate the universal conflict between vice and virtue, and at the same time place these within a recognisable historical setting, creating an accessible morality tale.

A similar dialectic between a universalising impulse and the temporally relevant is at work in the famous ode, 'To the Immortal Memory and Friendship of that Noble Pair, Sir Lucius Cary and Sir H. Morison'. These renowned friends became an undying symbol of altruistic friendship, and their specific names synonymous with this quality:

> You lived to be the great surnames,
> And titles, by which all made claims
> Unto the virtue. Nothing perfect done,
> But as a Cary, or a Morison.

(Underwoods, LXX)

That this dialectic could be perceived as hypocritical, a cloaking of fact in flattery for unscrupulous ends, is a problem of which Jonson was acutely aware. In the dedication of his epigrams to the Earl of Pembroke Jonson shows his desire to resolve any unease his readers may feel towards his concept of panegyric,

> If I have praised, unfortunately, anyone, that doth not deserve; or, if all answer not, in all my numbers, the pictures I have made of them: I hope it will be forgiven me, that they are no ill pieces, though they be not like the persons.

We are asked not to judge the poems on their historical accuracy as portraits, but to see them as works of art that operate within their own terms. At the same time, however, such a statement acknowledges an uncomfortable discrepancy between ideal portrait and historical fact. In the 'Epistle To Master John Selden', from which I have already quoted, Jonson asserts that his aim in panegyric was to encourage great men to emulate their poetic image. In emphasising the moral utility of poetic fiction Jonson was engaging in a debate that exercised some of the foremost intellectuals of the Renaissance; that of poetic fiction versus historical fact. In his *Defence of Poetry* (published 1595), Sidney famously maintains the superiority of poetry over history in the belief that poetry can create a golden world of virtue that man is encouraged to emulate by the poem's rhetorical power to please and move the listener/reader. Conversely, history is tied to 'the truth of a foolish world', which 'is many times a terror from well-doing and an encouragement to unbridled wickedness'. Sidney also draws an important distinction between lying as deception and lying as an assertion of figurative truth, and to illuminate this distinction he refers to the poet Aesop who, 'though he recounts things not true, yet because he telleth them for true, he lieth not ... so think I none would say Aesop lied in the tales of his beasts; for who thinks that Aesop writ it for actually true were well worthy to have his name chronicled among the beasts he writeth of'.[8] In a similar vein, Erasmus justified eulogies of princes with the belief that they functioned as didactic exemplars of virtue,

> When the prince listens to the usual panegyrics, let him not straightway believe them or be well disposed toward praises of himself, but if he is not yet such an one as his praises proclaim him, let him take that as advice and give his attention to making his acts correspond to his praises. If he already fulfils them, then he should strive to be better.[9]

Jonson's didactic panegyric was grounded in a dialectical relationship between the universal and the specific, and this allowed him to praise his subjects in their ideal capacities, and to demonstrate the value of a good king or aristocratic landowner, while also employing an ironic implication (incorporated through rhetorical strategies and a topical emphasis) that marked the distance between this King or that aristocrat and their ideal incarnations. In this way, Jonson defends the principle of an hierarchical society, but reveals that it is in need of improvement. This fundamentally didactic project involves a restoration from within and improvement of traditional structures of authority, rather than an anarchic criticism that aims to destroy the *status quo* because of unsatisfactory elements within it. What we may call Jonson's restorative criticism functions as a dialectic dependent on the interaction between irony and panegyric; these apparently polarised critical perspectives co-exist and produce an examination of the state as it is, however unsatisfactory, and its ideal potential. This exemplary ideal is intended to move its audience to mirror it, while the ironic implication works to motivate it further by implicitly outlining how far the audience or readers of Jonson's panegyric fail to meet this exemplary ideal. We could say that Jonson's panegyric attempts to exploit simultaneously the human qualities of noble aspiration and sense of mortal failure.

Although Jonson's panegyric clearly does not involve unqualified flattery, and although he could claim the ideological support of important Renaissance thinkers on the value of panegyric as a poetic form, it does appear that, at times, Jonson himself felt uneasy with poetic panegyric. His 'To My Muse' (*Epigrams*, LXV) is a scathing piece of self-castigation deriding the poet as a servile flatterer:

> Away, and leave me, thou thing most abhorred
> That hath betrayed me to a worthless lord;
> Made me commit most fierce idolatry
> To a great image through thy luxury ...
> But I repent me: stay. Whoe'er is raised,
> For worth he has not, he is taxed, not praised.

The anguish caused the poet by what one critic has called a 'crisis in reference' is resolved by Jonson's theory of undeserved praise working as covert satire.[10] As the poet praises his patrons for what they should be, rather than for what they are, the gap between fact and fiction reflects upon the patron, not upon the poet, and thus operates as covert satire. The suggestion that eulogy and satire should form a dialectic in poetry that is traditionally seen as undiluted panegyric is an important clue to understanding why and how the poet shifts from creating eulogistic masques with ironically suggestive discrepancies to an accommodation of fully developed satire within the form. With this hybrid form of poetry Jonson will now truly be able to mean what he speaks, presenting an apparently symbolic fiction, yet one that also alludes to specific historical contexts, resulting in flexible and multivalent texts that manage to house traces of dissent within the monument of praise. The importance Jonson attaches to his poetic integrity is voiced in the 'Epistle to Master John Selden':

> Since, being deceived, I turne a sharper eye
> Upon my selfe, and aske to whom? and why?
> And what I write? And vexe it many dayes
> Before men get a verse: much less a Praise;
> So that my reader is assur'd, I now
> Meane what I speake: and still will keepe that Vow.

Yet speaking true is never an easy task, and in his poem, 'Epistle to Katherine, Lady Aubigny', Jonson underscores the constant difficulties involved in honest speech in an age where traditional values are continually degenerating and 'both the prais'd and praisers suffer' (*The Forest*, XIII). In discussing the significance for Jonson of the virtuous individual (often symbolised by the centred circle) besieged by a society in a state of degenerative flux, Thomas M. Greene writes:

> He travels well who in a sense never travels (or travails) at all, who circumscribes hell with his courage and whose mind knows no exile, keeping one foot still upon his centre, compass-like, and lives through tempest, here in his bosom and at home.[11]

Given this acute social instability, of which Jonson was keenly aware, any monolithic, static analysis of an historical person must be untrue at times, and yet, paradoxically, it is precisely a virtuous and even monolithic stability that Jonson attributes to Lady Aubigny; she remains her centred self in a world of change, a measure of her extraordinary virtue. More usually, however, historical change appears merely to compound the 'crisis in reference', the gap between the ideal and the real. In such a context, praise of the few centred souls like Lady Aubigny becomes crucial as a means of resisting the contaminating spread of moral degeneracy. Greene illuminates the terms of this Jonsonian praise:

> Jonson seems to see his centred figures moving perpetually through this purgatory of the Protean, still at rest when active, just as the vicious are unstable even when torpid.[12]

Jonson responds to this social and moral instability by creating poetry of extreme plasticity and multivalency, with the potential to be interpreted as either satire or eulogy or both. An outstanding example of poetry which possesses this fluidity of meaning, or shifting reference points, is 'To Sir Robert Wroth'; a detailed analysis of the poem's subtextual irony and referential ambivalence is illuminating at this point in my argument and will prepare the ground for my reading of the masques of *Blackness* and *Beauty*. At first glance this poem is most obviously a genre piece belonging the classical tradition of pastoral, and it is often paired with 'To Penshurst' as the earliest example of the seventeenth century country house poem. Successors in this tradition include Carew's 'To Saxham' and Marvell's 'Upon Appleton House'. A certain irony in poetic stance seems to be inherent in all these poems and could be seen to be characteristic of this sub-genre.[13] I have already noted Jonson's private criticism of Wroth and an historically based criticism of the poem dedicated to him alerts us to an alternative perspective on Wroth available to Jonson, one which forms a dialectic with the more apparent allegorical panegyric that the aristocrat benefits from. Careful attention to rhetorical structures within the poem and its historical context has led Gary Waller to counter the standard view of this poem as a hymn to aristocratic hospitality rooted in the heart of the country with the suggestion that Jonson deploys a sly irony at the expense of Robert Wroth, attempting to please multiple audiences rather than Wroth alone; in particular, he suggests that the poem may be informed by a partisanship towards Pembroke and his cousin Mary Wroth, Sir Robert's wife. Attention to this alternative perspective may encourage us to develop certain traces of ambivalence in the poem into an ironic, historicist reading which co-exists with the more obvious panegyric of the piece.[14] According to this interpretative approach, each level of meaning modifies and qualifies the other, arriving perhaps at some kind of truth through compromise. The influential critic Catherine Belsey has justified this kind of critical project in the following terms:

> A conservative criticism reads in quest of familiar, obvious, common-sense meanings, and thus reaffirms what we already know. A radical criticism, however, is concerned to produce readings which challenge that knowledge by revealing alternative meanings, disrupting the system of differences which legitimates the perpetuation of things as they are. The project of such a criticism is not to replace one authoritative interpretation of a text with another, but to suggest a plurality of ways in which texts might be read in the interests of extending the reach of what is thinkable, imaginable or possible.[15]

The first lines of the poem eulogise Wroth's capacity for self-containment away from the court:

> How blessed art thou, canst love the country, Wroth,
>   Whether by choice, or fate, or both;
> And, though so near the city, and the court,
>   Art ta'en with neither's vice, nor sport.
>
> (*The Forest*, III)

Through his interest in the historical contexts of renaissance poetry David Norbrook has uncovered a view of Wroth quite at odds with that expressed in Jonson's poem:

> The young Sir Robert was subject to social pressures that worked against respect for traditional rural standards of fair behaviour. Someone living so close to Theobalds was bound to feel the need to keep up with the massive scale of conspicuous consumption indulged in by Cecil and by the King... Sir Robert felt the need to keep up appearances in order to gain the King's favour; he overspent so drastically that according to one contemporary, he died in debt to the tune of £23,000. His court contacts gave him valuable grants of land, and he was described on his death as, 'a great commaunder or rather by the Kings favor an intruder in Waltham forrest'. In the light of this accusation Jonson's portrait of Sir Robert seems somewhat over-idealised. Perhaps he intended the poem as a tactful hint, a reminder to Sir Robert that he could draw more real satisfaction from a traditional rural existence than from frenzied gambling on court favour.[16]

In noting the tension between the ideal and the real, Norbrook suggests reading the poem as an oblique exhortation to better conduct, in the same sense that Erasmus defended panegyric. Extrapolating from Norbrook's argument we could say that the poem functions in a symbolic way, with the possibility of irony latent in the gap between fact and fiction. Irony is a term often loosely employed so it may be useful here to define exactly what I mean when I use the term; the dictionary definition is, 'an expression of one's meaning by language of opposite or different tendency, especially simulated adoption of another's point of view or laudatory tone for the purpose of ridicule...' (*Oxford English Dictionary*, 1911, 1984). Part of Jonson's purpose in the first lines of 'To Sir Robert Wroth' may be a simulated adoption of a point of view far removed from biographical truth, but the crucial point to remember here is that, for Jonson, satiric humour is corrective much as the exhortation of panegyric should be corrective; the poem involves two different but interacting approaches to the same end.

Such irony is not confined to the figure of Sir Robert; in a blunt dismissal of masque Jonson implicitly condemns both himself and Lady Mary Wroth, himself as masque maker, and Lady Wroth as an enthusiastic participant:

> Nor throngs't (when masquing is) to have sight
> Of the short bravery of the night;
> To view the jewels, stuffs, the pains, the wit
> There wasted, some not paid for yet!

These lines adumbrate the poet's moral reservations about masque as an occasion of meretricious consumption rather than a Jonsonian ritual shadowing forth universal truths. They seem to reveal a profound questioning of the function of praise in epideictic verse and masque, and intimate that capacity for a probing and often painful self-criticism that Jonson exhibits from time to time. For Jonson, praise was intended to be instructive, but, it was possible for the recipients of praise to grasp the occasion for unthinking self-congratulation; the implications of this kind of misapprehension are grave for a poet who valued his reputation for integrity and critical detachment. Perhaps it is for these reasons that Jonson seems even to have enjoyed being condemned for the severity of his satire. In *Epigrams* II, 'To My Book', he writes:

> It will be looked for, book, when some but see
> Thy title, Epigrams, and named of me,
> Thou should'st be bold, licentious, full of gall,
> Wormwood, and sulphur, sharp and toothed withal;
> Become a petulant thing, hurl ink, and wit,
> As madmen stones: not caring whom they hit.

Though Jonson appears to admit an apparently anarchic compulsion behind his satire, he may have thought it better to strike vice directly than to correct it obliquely through praise with the danger that the splendour of praise may mask the need for improved and continued excellence. It is arguable that the poet's reservations about the efficacy of epideictics, however, qualified, to improve and teach contributed to his development of the ironic implication of court masque into the full-blown satire of the antimasque.

Typically, the artificiality of pastoral is acknowledged by the genre itself, and Jonson satisfies this expectation by writing that Wroth lives,

> Free from proud porches, or their gilded roofs,
>   'Mongst lowing herds, and solid hoofs:
> Alongst the curled woods, and painted meads.

The reference to painted meads in this poem suggests that they owe more to artifice than to the natural world, although we should remember that the image of nature as artificer is a common Renaissance trope that does not always have negative connotations. However, the suggested artificiality of such a landscape casts doubt over the wider vision of rural contentment that this poem offers to the reader, and perhaps foregrounds the fact that the vision of Jonson's poem is an ideal construct rather than a faithful imitation of 'nature'. It may be that in offering an ironic counterbalance to the mainstream genre of pastoral Jonson is developing a marginalised impulse that he found specifically in Horace; 'To Sir Robert Wroth' owes much (in the sense of *imitatio*) to Horace's second epode which Jonson himself translated as 'The Praises Of A Country Life'. The paradisal vision conjured up by this poem is sharply undercut in the last four lines when the poet's coolly ironic tone informs the reader that such a vision is merely the fleeting fantasy of a hard-nosed man of business:

> These thoughts when usurer Alphius, now about
>   To turn mere farmer, had spoke out,
> 'Gainst the ides, his monies he gets in with pain,
>   At the calends, puts all out again.
>
> (*Underwoods*, LXXXV)

Horace's version of pastoral questions the very framework on which it rests, and it is arguable that this impulse is taken up in 'To Sir Robert Wroth', with its exploration of the received ideology surrounding the land-based aristocracy.[17]

Throughout the whole vision of 'To Sir Robert Wroth', 'A serpent river leads', an image suggestive of the sly subtlety of Jonson's wit, especially when we remember that Renaissance iconography employed the snake to symbolise cunning deceit as well as wisdom. Strictly speaking, in the prelapsarian world of Wroth's estate the snake does not yet symbolise evil; but, as a meticulous poet, Jonson must have been aware of the ambivalent implications of this imagery, and may have deliberately exploited such doubleness to comment upon the duality of meaning and technique permeating the poem as a whole, enabling an accommodation of both irony and panegyric. With these points in mind, therefore, the boon of royal patronage can be read as bringing contamination by the court and it does seem that in this poem Jonson questions the *mores* of the landed aristocracy by offering a critical reading of the court that offsets the more obvious panegyric of the piece – the poem has already indicted the court as a place of vice and yet Wroth allows the court into his home.[18] In particular, the central section of the poem hints at the court's corrupting effect on the paradise of Wroth's estate; we read that in the course of the noble hunt, which is 'More for exercise, than fare,' the courtiers commit inessential slaughter, and quarry that is legitimate as sustenance is redundant in a society that is nourished enough not to need the extra food. To designate the thrush as 'greedy' in this context can be seen as deliberately ironic. It is this social economy of consumption that Raymond Williams notes in 'To Penshurst', which involves a tyranny over the land rather than any notion of a natural cycle of reciprocity between man and earth;[19] this is the slash and burn social economy suggested in such lines as:

> The hogs returned home fat from mast;
> The trees cut out in log; and those boughs made
> A fire now, that lent a shade!

The suggestion of egregious consumption is broadened in this poem to adumbrate a view of the courtier's life as empty of profitable employment. As the historian Lawrence Stone has shown, in the seventeenth century, an aristocratic position excluded any notion of wage-earning work, so the onus on the courtiers is to find occupations that will 'With some delight the day outwear'.[20]

The day's hunting is followed by an evening of apparently democratic feasting when, 'The rout of rural folk come thronging in'. Jonson leaves unsaid that this occasion is exceptional and only staged at certain times of the year, like the 'Feasts that either shearers keep'. Comus, the deity presiding over the feast, symbolises mirth and cheer; Charles Wheeler has suggested that Jonson was inspired by Euripides in his creation of Comus.[21] In the *Bacchanals* Comus is referred to as the Clamour-King and this suggestion of raucousness is born out by the Comus of Jonson's masque *Pleasure Reconciled To Virtue* (1618), who is represented as the god of the bouncing belly. Such classically based associations with Comus as the herald of uncontrolled revelry undercut the atmosphere of quiet, centred moderation that Jonson has carefully woven around Sir Robert Wroth; the evening feast may be more influenced by the *mores* of the court than by those of the rural folk. Milton pushes the latter version of Comus even further in his eponymous masque, where the classical god is the son of the witch Circe and the god Bacchus, and is figured as the seducer of virtue. In Milton's masque Comus entices men with magical liquor and turns their faces into those of beasts, reflecting their moral degeneracy. While this aspect of Comus is not overtly emphasised by Jonson in 'To Sir Robert Wroth', it is a latent implication that contributes to an alternative reading of the poem. This manipulation of mythological symbols into ambivalence is continued by the poet's comparison of the feasting with the classical golden age when the world had not yet degenerated into vice:

> The jolly wassail walks the often round,
>   And in their cups, their cares are drowned:
> They think not, then, which side the cause shall leese,
>   Nor how to get the lawyers fees.
> Such and no other, was that age, of old,
>   Which boasts to have had the head of gold.

This vision of men soothed to oblivion by alcohol so that they forget the wheelings and dealings of the competitive business world in which they are involved must surely be a comic parody of the golden age. Praising these men by means of negatives is part of Jonson's covert satiric strategy; the latent implications of the lines being that although the guests are too drunk to care about their business concerns, they would normally be occupied with such matters; these are men more likely to be found around the Strand or Fleet Street than in a pastoral arcadia. It is perhaps unsurprising that Jonson, he of the 'mountain belly', ostensibly approves of the revellers:

> Let others watch in guilty arms, and stand
>   The fury of rash command,
> Go enter breaches, meet the cannons' rage,
>   That they may sleep with scars in age.

These lines could be read as from a poet who appreciated fraternal revelry and who had himself experienced the frustrations of war in the Netherlands. Yet Jonson wrote other poems offering a very different perspective on the value of going to war. In his eulogy, 'To Sir Henry Cary', the poet boldly asserts,

> That neither fame, nor love might wanting be
> To greatness, Cary, I sing that, and thee.
> Whose house, if it no other honour had,
> In only thee, might be both great, and glad.
> Who, to upbraid the sloth of this our time,
> Durst valour make, almost, but not a crime.
>
> (*Epigrams*, LXVI, ll.1-6)

Moreover, Jonson considered the subject of valorous combat worthy of a long poem, 'An Epistle to a Friend, to Persuade Him to the Wars':

> Wake, friend, from forth thy lethargy: the drum
> Beats brave, and loud in Europe, and bids come
> All that dare rouse: or are not loth to quit
> Their vicious ease, and be o'erwhelmed with it.
>
> (*Underwoods*, XV, ll.1-4)

Perhaps Wroth's feasters are also overwhelmed with vicious ease, perhaps the avaricious lawyer and miser that Wroth is favourably compared against, are extreme satirical images of qualities that panegyric would praise as prudence and thrift.[22] With historical hindsight, it seems that the opposing policy of excessive consumption caused Wroth to die with debts worth £23,000. In praising Wroth's scorn for the business of gathering wealth and property Jonson screens the real source of his wealth, inviting speculation about how this was acquired; this speculation is soon answered when we remember Norbrook's comment that Wroth was known by his contemporaries as a great encloser of land at the expense of the 'rout of rural folk'.[23]

The last lines of the poem take on a new *gravitas*:

> Thy morning's, and thy evening's vow
> Be thanks to him, and earnest prayer to find
> A body sound, with sounder mind:
> To do thy country's service, thyself right;
> That neither want do thee affright,
> Nor death; but when thy latest sand is spent,
> Thou mayst think life, a thing but lent.

These lines certainly lend support to Norbrook's view of the poem as an exhortation to Wroth to lead a better and more self-sustained life, while the ironic subtext of the poem implies that Wroth's retirement is not from the world but from the ideals of self-knowledge and self-discipline. The gravity of Jonson's tone here echoes that in his other poetic meditations on death such as *Epigrams*, XXII, 'On My First Daughter', and LXXX, 'Of Life And Death'. The contrast such seriousness makes with the jovial tone of the preceding lines (albeit they involve a doubleness in meaning) lends these last lines an air of profound admonitory significance.

Jonson's anxiety that his epideictic poetry would be misunderstood has been well founded from his own day up to the present time.[24] Jongsook Lee's concentration upon the symbolic aspects of Jonson leads to the view that the hyperbolic nature of 'To Penshurst' is purely an aspect of the symbolic, and yet in championing the symbolic Lee seems to undercut this argument by reminding us that Jonson insists on the factual reality of his idealised picture. Lee is one of many critics who have difficulty in reconciling Jonson the satirist with Jonson the eulogist, and indeed, my account thus far has suggested that Jonson himself experienced similar difficulties which prompted him to experiment with more flexible forms of epideictic verse; however, despite this developing aspect of his poetics, it seems that many of his peers remained sceptical about his motives.

The same kind of misapprehension of Jonson's poetic ideals is apparent in contemporary responses to the masque, highlighting certain tensions that seem to be inherent in panegyric and the masque in particular; tensions which can be briefly summarised as the thorny problem of royal or aristocratic representation. How does the masque suggest the monarch's divinity and yet presume to comment critically on the King's policies? The first seems to involve unalloyed flattery and the second seems incompatible with the project of panegyric. The development of the court entertainment is inextricably linked with Jonson's desire to preserve his poetic integrity and critical voice, while meeting the eulogistic requirements of masque. To this end, he developed dramatic elements within the antimasque as a way of disputing the emblematic certainties of masque. With the movement from antimasque to masque, the monarch is shown to resolve conflict among his people with justice and mercy; this movement from conflict to divine resolution involves a simple plot line and dramatic dialogue. However, the masque was largely viewed as generically superior to drama and Jonson's dramatic innovations to the form often resulted in charges of indecorum. The poet's response in his early masques to these problems is to negotiate a delicate middle way between the emblematic and the dramatic. The dramatic antimasque is his most important introduction to the masque form, and is exploited both to shore up the monarchy through an emphatic demonstration of the monarch's power to quell dissent, and to expose it to a pragmatic criticism incorporated through covert irony. In this way, the court entertainment becomes a dialectic exploration of what constitutes good government, and implicitly measures current authority against this ideal. Much of what has been said so far in this chapter about the nature of Jonson's epideictics will be relevant to my following discussions of his masques; in attempting to elucidate the problems inherent in Jonsonian panegyric and discussing their implications for the masque I will focus on the masques of *Blackness* and *Beauty*. In doing so, I hope to show that an ironic subtext was present in the Jonsonian masque from the first, and was later developed into the overtly satirical antimasque. Furthermore, my analysis of these masques will demonstrate that the ironic implication of even the earliest court entertainments is firmly rooted in its historico-political context; this feature is retained and enlarged by the developing antimasque. In the instances of *Blackness* and *Beauty*, the texts attempt to address issues of race, colour, gender, and authority, thereby refracting a nascent British imperial project.

Desire and difference: *The Masque of Blackness* and *The Masque of Beauty*

In its primary function masque is a vehicle of praise and therefore has much in common with Jonson's epideictic poetry, and indeed, it was this function of masque that was most readily recognised by Elizabethan and Jacobean contemporaries, often eliciting well articulated if varying responses. Francis Bacon's aloof disapproval of such 'toys' is well known, while Samuel Daniel focuses on the prescribed and specific nature of masque, delimited and defined by its strict adherence to the principle of royal panegyric:

> Only to present the figure of those blessings with the wish of their continuance, which this most mighty kingdom now enjoys by the benefit of his most gracious Majesty, by whom we have this glory of peace, with the accession of so great state and power.[25]

For Daniel then, masque is a ritual of totemic significance ensuring the continuation of an already established tradition, it is empty of the political content and rhetorical agitation out of which Jonson composed his court entertainments. Rather unsurprisingly, the two masque poets publicly clashed on this issue, with Daniel implicitly criticising Jonson for exploiting masque as an occasion to parade his erudition, a vain display that Daniel believed to be superfluous in a context of royal praise. Daniel adds that Jonson appears to be more interested in eulogising himself as a poet than praising the King; although he does not actually name Jonson in this piece of literary polemic, there seems no doubt that Jonson believed the attack to be directed at himself and he responded in kind in his preface to *Hymenaei*.[26] The bitterest of insults smart because they contain a salty grain of truth, and, while Jonson refused to suffer silently Daniel's attack, twentieth-century critics have found his analysis of Jonson a useful starting point for an examination of how Jonson manipulates, departs from or builds on the convention of panegyric to create a form that is strikingly dynamic, intellectual and critical. It is this very intellectualising of masque that distances Jonson so far from Daniel; Jonson creates and works through poetic tropes to adumbrate the platonic mysteries of the universe and render them morally comprehensible to an audience and in doing so reveals some of the dominant cultural and political concerns of his day. Thus, while *Blackness* and *Beauty* draw on platonic symbolism and link it with the current political order they also disclose concerns of racial and national difference, a difference that seems to be ultimately gendered. Jonsonian masque typically operates on several levels as D. J. Gordon has incontrovertibly shown, the poet's skill is demonstrated in the way that he manages to address simultaneously platonic mysteries and political realities. The masque's critical edge emerges as the poet manipulates the form to create a space for his own voice to be heard in tandem with the chorus of royal praise. So it seems that there are valid grounds for inverting Daniel's attack and making it work in Jonson's favour – compared with Jonson, Daniel's interpretation of the form seems little more than a choreographed genuflection to the King.[27]

Jonson took great pains to emphasise the depth of learning and universality of meaning his work contained, which may suggest he was conscious that the genre could be accused of empty flattery or even that uncomplicated praise was generally assumed to be all that masque should aspire to. The famously tart preface to *Hymenaei* (1606) articulates the terms of this controversy:

> Though their voyce be taught to sound to present occasions, their sense, or doth, or should always lay hold on more removed mysteries. And howsoever some may sqeamishly cry out that all endeavour of learning and sharpness in these transitory devices, especially where it steps beyond their little or (let me not wrong 'em) no brain at all, is superfluous, I am contented these fastidious stomachs should leave my full tables and enjoy at home their clean, empty trenchers, fittest for such airy tastes, where perhaps a few Italian herbs picked up and made into a salad may find sweeter acceptance than all the most nourishing meats of the world.

Clearly, Jonson intends to present the Banqueting House with more food for thought than Daniel's 'Italian salad' would provide, and at the very inception of his career as a masque maker he publicly rejects those entertainments based on Italian *intermezzi* where stylish dance and song were foregrounded at the expense of philosophical content.

Yet masque has to negotiate the same dilemmas as epideictic poetry, and while we may be fascinated by the latent ironies running through an individual entertainment or the way in which its official discourse is fractured, it has to be remembered that the most important function of the form is praise, and praise of the King in particular. Earlier in this chapter I examined the discrepancy between fact and idealising fiction in Jonsonian panegyric, and the way in which irony may spring up in the gap between the two. In a process similar to that traced in 'To Sir Robert Wroth' Jonson has the delicate task in his masques of mediating between the fact of a potentially degenerate court and the fiction inherent in an idealisation of that court. If we attempt an historical recuperation of the immediate context of Jonson's poetry and masques the problematic nature of such a gap becomes clearer (I perform this historical recuperation in later chapters); just as in 'To Sir Robert Wroth', the poet must find a way of incorporating his own poetic aims and voice into a form ostensibly created as a symbolic, eulogistic expression of the King and state. Overt criticism of the court would be rejected by the body that sponsored these festivals, while unqualified flattery would be morally repugnant to a poet who spent much of his life and work defining the qualities of independence, truth and didacticism that mark worthy poetry. Jonson's commonplace book, *Discoveries*, is packed with illustrative examples of his fierce adherence to these ideals, and he writes there:

> I do not desire to be equal to those that went before; but to have my reason examined with theirs, and so much faith to be given them, or me, as those shall evict [evince?]. I am neither author, or fautor [faulter?] of any sect. I will have no man addict himself to me; but if I have anything right, defend it as truth's, not mine (save as it conduceth to a common good). It profits not me to have any man fence, or fight for me, to flourish, or take a side. Stand for truth, and 'tis enough.
>
> (ll.187-96)

It is my contention that Jonson attempts to manipulate masque as he does epideictic poetry; that is, to equip it with the required rhetoric of praise and yet use semiotic structures of such ambivalence that the poet's own ideals can find an expression in a dynamic relationship between satire and panegyric. In Chapter 3 I will try to address the issue of the audience's reception or reading of the ironic element in masque, and indeed their response to its more overt meanings. For the moment, however, I want to detect the ways in which Jonson widened the scope of masque in order to allow himself a critical voice within it. In the early masques it seems indubitable that an implicit comparison of the King with the masque's ideal entails oblique criticism and, while this criticism may seem significantly more muted than that in 'To Sir Robert Wroth', this more tentative approach can be explained by the fact that Jonson was experimenting in *Blackness* and *Beauty* with an ironic content that would develop later in to the contradictory antimasque. In focusing on the exalted nature of Kingship, Jonson exhorts James to emulate his poeticised image, to close the gap between the ideal and the real, and expel the threat of reductive irony. In analysing these two masques it is my purpose to demonstrate the shiftings, accommodations, coherence or lack of it, between the monarch's requirements and the poet's requirements of masque – not forgetting Queen Anne's key but often marginalised role in the conception of these entertainments. This analysis will reveal an early stage in the poet's development of the masque, a development towards the definitively topical antimasque which compliments or counterbalances the universalising nature of masque. As I have already stated, *Blackness* and *Beauty* represent in embryonic form the satire that becomes prominent in Jonson's later antimasques. Moreover, these masques are of particular interest as they demonstrate a relationship between irony and panegyric that is based on didacticism. In offering an historically informed reading of these entertainments I hope to demonstrate exactly how Jonson uses the language of emblems to praise the monarch, while at the same time, offering subtle criticisms of royal policy and probing the potential weaknesses of James's monarchical discourse. In addressing itself to both the King and the courtiers, the masque simultaneously praises and challenges the ruling elite, encouraging its subjects to mirror their idealised image, while intimating how far these individuals fall short of their ideal.

Richard A. Burt is one of many critics now employing more sophisticated political analyses of texts and their place in the social formation. He argues persuasively against the temptation to view Jonson as either exclusively subversive or eulogistically authoritarian, and urges a more complex reconciliation of the two views.[28] Burt approaches this difficult topic through a study of the ambivalent issue of 'license' in Jonson's plays and masques, and concludes:

> The fact that Jonson's view of license is neither in clear alignment with the court nor with the Puritan opposition makes apparent the difficulty with construing the politics of the theater in terms of a radical antithesis between authority and subversion.
>
> (p.553)

Jonson cannot be indicted as anti-royalist, because he spent years in literary service to the court and his king, yet, the presence of the masque's ironic content, and later, the full-blown satirical antimasque indicates that Jonson did not unconditionally subscribe to the practices of the early Stuart government. Jonson's position is located somewhere between the polarised axes of containment and subversion, and the ironic or satiric content of his masques may best be understood as an exhortation to the monarchy and court to reform themselves from within, and become an ideal pattern of virtue. Jonson was a royalist in the sense that he believed in the *potential* of the monarchy, that is, he believed that the principle of monarchy was a sound one, but that it might be temporarily marred by misguided policy – this is a traditional position for would-be advisors to the Crown to occupy, their criticism rendered palatable by the fact that they never presumed to attack the monarch directly but through his advisors.[29] Jonsonian masque proffers the King an image of his potential as a didactic exemplar, thereby gaining an unassailable validity as the vehicle for such improving didacticism and distancing Jonson from the Puritan anti-theatrical lobby where some critics have sought to place him.[30] Leah Marcus is one influential American critic who views Jonson's masques as exhortations of varying degrees; in her study of *Pleasure Reconciled To Virtue* Marcus not only argues that this masque is a defence of the King's recently issued *Book of Sports*, but she also suggests that Jonson's intention was, 'to indict carnival excess at court even as he praised royal mediation in the countryside'. Yet while proclaiming the masque's critical and didactic edge Marcus blunts it by echoing Orgel's assumption that the ideal vision of the entertainment automatically encompasses the court:

> As the masque is being performed, the royal *via media* acts upon the court itself, which, illuminated by the shining light of hesperus, becomes a Hesperidean garden, a place for virtuous pleasures. The main masque's 'distant landscape' of pastoral felicity is brought home to Whitehall and made a living reality.[31]

However, if masque is to function as an exhortation to improved virtue it must retain a sense of difference and distance from its audience. Panegyric offers an idealised image of the court, while irony and satire point to the gap between the reality of the court and its idealised poetic image; if masque automatically extends its ideal status as a 'hesperidean garden' to the court, the court is no longer exhorted to live up to is idealised image and the didactic edge of the masque is dissolved. Thus, while *Blackness* offers an image of potential harmony to be achieved, the miracle of transformation is not performed in this masque, but we are presented with its results in the later *Beauty*. However, we never witness this transformation, and while it is ascribed to the King we are forced to accept this assertion of his powers in good faith. This is a strange withholding of the miraculous effects of royal power in a form that was chiefly noted for their spectacular representation. The problematic transition from black to white in these masques suggests a lack of closure and deferred attainment of perfection. *Blackness* provides a vision of the miracle of transformation and encourages the King and the court to strive for it; the fact that neither it nor *Beauty* presents us with a view of the King's transformative powers in action suggests how far he falls short from his divine representation. It seems to me that a fatal flaw in the Orgel/Marcus conception of masque is that in celebrating the virtuous, pastoral wonders of the Stuart court they fail to take into account the full effect of Jonson's dissenting voice or the ironic/satirical antimasque. I have already argued in some detail for the view that satire and panegyric operate simultaneously in masque, modifying and qualifying each other to arrive at a *via media* that is fundamentally didactic. To ignore the effect of covert satire on the more obvious panegyric of masque results in a one-sided, partial view of a multifaceted form that is defined by its propensity for a dialectic conducted between layers of meaning.

Blackness and *Beauty* are of particular interest here as they predate Jonson's later strategy of displacing the eruptions of irony that accompany his idealisation of the King; in later masques the poet exploits these ironic implications but sites them within the arena of the antimasque, and follows them with the masque proper which *appears* to dissolve the anarchic and satirical impetus of the antimasque. Conversely, a subliminal and muted voice of dissent echoes all the way through these early masques. In his analysis of the emergence of the antimasque Orgel has designated the topos of 'blackness' as an element of misrule that would usually be confined to the antimasque along with witches and other deviants from the norm of Stuart culture.[32] Yet more recent critics such as Kim Hall, Yumna Siddiqui and Hardin Aasand have objected to the way in which Orgel glosses over the significance of issues of colour and race in this masque with his remarks that black disguise was certainly not an innovation in court entertainment. Any historically based analysis of this masque and its ironic undertones must take into account the way in which it addresses these issues in relation to a nascent imperialism, while exhorting James to become an ideal ruler, signifying in this context, the ideal ruler of an emerging British empire.

Turning to the text of the first of these masques we notice immediately that *Blackness* eulogises the King for bringing unity and mercy to 'Britain', yet images of disharmony, disunity, strife and excess form a counterpoint to such panegyric. While Sol obviously represents James in his role as omnipotent Sun-King, the other striking image of paternal kingship is provided by the figure of Niger, a ruler who is bemused and puzzled by the events in the masque and consistently errs in his interpretation of them; clearly, these two rulers embody complementary although contradictory views of kingship. Additionally, anxieties about bodily and geographical excess are figured in the plot detail of this entertainment and linked with the representation of royal power. In an earlier part of this chapter I analysed in some detail the value Jonson places on moral stability which he often represents in physical terms, while spiritual and moral degeneration is suggested by a nervous energy and undirected movement. In accordance with this typically Jonsonian equation between mental and physical properties Oceanus, the godly ruler of the seas surrounding Britain, is constructed out of images of fixed circularity, he resides in his empire's heart, while

Niger has abandoned his usual course in his search for the land to which he has been directed by Aethiopia; it is entirely in keeping with this paradigm that Niger's efforts are increasingly fruitless and desperate until he is rescued by the goddess Aethiopia herself. At the very outset of the masque we discover Oceanus's amazement that Niger has broken his banks, as it were, and wandered so far from his native lands into the west:

> And, Niger, say, how comes it lovely son,
> That thou, the Ethiop's river, so far east,
> Art seen to fall into th'extremest west
> Of me, the king of floods, Oceanus,
> And in mine empire's heart salute me thus?
> My ceaseless current now amazed stands
> To see thy labor through so many lands
> Mix thy fresh billow with my brackish stream ...
>
> (ll.89-96)

Oceanus's weighty moral position is partly expressed by his authoritative rhetoric which conflates Asia and Africa into one powerful image of exotic foreigness, an image that literally streams into the West, and while this flood may not be an inundation, it certainly mixes with the native element. Yumna Siddiqui has pointed to the fear of miscegenation that lurks within these lines, caused partly by an early modern fascination with and desire for the exotic.[33] Admittedly, the terms Jonson employs seem to elevate Niger's 'fresh billow' above Oceanus's 'brackish stream', but it may be that this language indicates early seventeenth-century preconceptions about the New World, free from the taint of civilisation and urban development, and rich in natural resources, thereby meriting the attention of navigators and entrepreneurs. I think it must also be significant that Oceanus greets Niger with language that acknowledges the pristine and implicitly fertile exoticism of the African river, while emphatically asserting the military pre-eminence of Britain. Niger is obliged to 'salute' Oceanus who sits in the heart of his empire, a verbal gesture towards the fact that military occupation and domination usually accompanied economic exploitation of the New World by adventurers hailing from the old world. Thus, this masque is not only important for the way in which it exhorts James and ironically hints at some of the pitfalls of kingship, but also for the way it reveals early modern worries about the impact and consequences of exploration and trade. Siddiqui informs us that not only were Africans a visible presence in Britain in this period (a consequence of Britain's involvement with the slave trade) but also that anxiety about the proliferation of black people caused Queen Elizabeth to issue a proclamation in 1596 (nine years before the performance of this masque) commanding that 'those kinde of people should be sent forth of the land'.³⁴ Yet Jonson's masque shows us that far from being freed of this anxiety early British society continued to be gripped by the fearful fantasy of an 'orient flood'.

If we look to another aspect of the historical context of this masque it becomes clear that the notional neglect of a geographical or bodily centre and intellectual confusion applies to the monarch, particularly with reference to religious matters; in 1604 James had presided over the Hampton Court conference, where he vigorously opposed the aims of the moderate Puritan lobby, and yet, in 1605, the Gunpowder Plot revealed that the King was also perceived by some as an inveterate enemy to Roman Catholicism. To the Puritan lobby James was unacceptably sympathetic to a Roman style of worship and church hierarchy (Queen Anne, for example, was known as a practising Catholic), and to the Catholics he was an iconoclastic Puritan. It seems that even early on in his reign, James's religious policies seemed unsatisfactory to many of his subjects, and perhaps his intermittent leaning towards one faction and then another promoted a view of the King and his policies as wavering, unstable and self-contradictory. Niger is certainly self-contradictory and supernatural powers in the shape of Aethiopia are required to correct him, thereby consolidating the masque's implication that James needs to develop a more consistent and centred set of policies befitting a royal ruler.

D. J. Gordon's seminal work established that the Sol in *Blackness* is a representation of King James whose divinely inspired powers are enough, 'To blanch an Ethiop, and revive a corse'; this image of omnipotent kingship overwhelms that of the bumbling Niger, yet does not erase it entirely.³⁵ The line quoted indicates an extension of the trope of royal paternity to potentially lucrative African lands; in bleaching the Ethiop so that he or she resembles British subjects the King establishes his 'natural' authority over an alien race of people, and in tying this transformation with the ability to 'revive a corse', Sol/James is attributed the regenerative power of Christian tradition. If we accept that Niger remains as an implied vision of kingship to offset the dominant Sol, it may be argued that by focusing on the exotic and extreme foreignness of Niger and his daughters, the masque gestures towards James's own foreign status as a Scottish ruler based in London – a foreignness that had been the butt of xenophobic jokes and resentment.³⁶ Nevertheless, with the glorification of Sol, this masque illustrates the way in which imperial power and ambition typically figures itself as morally benign, and paternal in nature. It may be tempting to declare that Jonson colludes in the forging of imperial manacles, but although such an accusation may be crude, it does seem that while he pointed up the potential weaknesses of the current monarch he was also a key figure in the evolution of an imperial discourse that held sway well into the twentieth century, whereby British imperial occupation was seen to entail educational and cultural improvement for the new world, whose subjects were moulded according to a British pattern, thereby becoming 'white' in outlook although not in skin colour.[37] Yet, as I have suggested, Niger's mistakes, although well intentioned, counterbalance Sol's power. He asserts his role as father to his daughters, who are subject to him, as the citizens of Britain are subject to James, and declares his wish:

> To do a kind and careful father's part,
> In satisfying every pensive heart.

In this he closely resembles James who often described his role as that of a father to his children (alarming some of his subjects who feared an authoritarian rule). In the widely circulated and read *Basilikon Doron* James asserted:

> A good king... employeth all his studie and paines, to procure and mainteine... the well-fare and peace of his people, and (as their naturall father and kindly maister) thinketh his greatest contentment standeth in their prosperity.[38]

The equation between fathership and kingship has been remarked on by many commentators on the Renaissance, but perhaps nowhere else is it more authoritatively expressed than in James's own writings.[39] Whereas Niger represents the King as patriarch, Oceanus stands for the body politic, guarded by an immortal line of hereditary kings, and as such he symbolises Britain. The fact that he refers to Britain as Albion, using its ancient title, serves to emphasise the longevity of this body politic that continues to function on a principle of 'divine right', and its innate cultural and racial 'whiteness' ('albus' is Latin for white, with the connotation of fortunate or propitious). Thus, Oceanus claims complete political authority, not only within his own realm, but also beyond it. Appropriately, the language of Oceanus is full of allusions to circularity, signifying closed perfection. The Banqueting House at Whitehall is his 'Empire's heart', this 'squared circle of celestial bodies'. As ocean, Oceanus encloses the island of Britain, protecting and sealing its whiteness from the less exalted lands of 'Black Mauretania, swarth Lusitania and rich Aquitania'. Yet if it is a truism that revulsion bears the impress of desire, it is surely significant that Oceanus welcomes his renewal in the form of a new king, the African Niger, who is hailed as his son. Again, Jonson mirrors early modern revulsion and fascination for Africa and the East, and expresses an intuition that British power and authority will be reborn and enlarged through the inclusion of foreign bodies.

The goddess Aethiopia addresses James as the unifier of Britain, as she declares, 'Britannia, which the triple world admires, / This isle hath now recovered for her name' (ll.211-12), and the song opening the masque welcomes a great prince arriving in the West:

> Sound, sound aloud
> The welcome of the orient flood
> Into the West.

This recalls the songs of the welcoming entertainments staged for James as he travelled down from Scotland to take up his throne in London. The resemblance between this masque and the civic entertainment grows when it is recalled that the conceit of Britain as a separate and favoured island in the west was popular; Jonson refers to it again in this masque and also in *Love Freed From Ignorance And Folly* and *The Masque of Queens*.[40] James appears to fulfil this myth of the western isles as he was reputed to be the first monarch since King Arthur to unite the different countries of the island into one Britain. Britain may be united, but Jonson's celebration of Sol cannot be totally separated from the presentation of the flawed paternal ruler, Niger. The mythologising of the King, together with the expression of certain reservations about him that Jonson performs here may be seen as typical. For example, in her study of *Pleasure Reconciled To Virtue* Leah Marcus suggests that the representation of King James as Hercules is significant, because the masque recognises the classical hero's great strength, but a contemporary audience would have also been aware of his reputation as a drunkard; Hercules, however, is shown responding to his nobler impulses.[41] This is also the kind of satirical implication that accompanies Jonson's use of Comus in 'To Sir Robert Wroth'; *Blackness* similarly urges the King to maintain his status as Sol and to avoid Niger's mistakes, perhaps the greatest of which is his obssession with the outer, black, appearance of his daughters rather than their inner qualities;

> Fair Niger, son to great Oceanus,
> Now honoured thus,
> With all his beauteous race,
> Who, though but black in face,
> Yet they are bright,
> And full of life and light,
> To prove that beauty best
> Which not the colour but the feature
> Assures unto the creature.
>
> (ll.79-87)

These lines are puzzling until we read them bearing in mind the masque's simultaneous discourses of platonic metaphysics and race (Jonson's masques demand of the interpreter this kind of 'multi-tasking'; attention to merely one strand of meaning running through the entertainment risks a partial and distorted reading). In their notes Herford and Simpson assert that 'feature' means 'goodly shape', and while this gloss may not be inaccurate it is certainly limited and fails to take into account Jonson's habit of using physical shapes to symbolise moral or philosophical virtues, a habit amply demonstrated by the poet's use of the circle or circular imagery both in this masque and elsewhere in his work.[42] Kim Hall remarks that this passage is a pointed reminder directed at the audience and reader that the lady masquers were not black; although they had stained their skins a dark colour, they retained their distinctive European features ('but black in face') as opposed to the stereotypically rounded African face and features. Hall's point is clarified when we remember Dudley Carleton's famous objection to the masquers as 'a troop of ugly lean cheek'd Moors', an attack that highlights the cultural disturbance provoked by the masquers' mingling of African and European physical attributes. Anthony Barthelemy has shown how centuries of western Christian and cultural discourse elides the categories of blackness, ugliness and, ultimately, evil. Jonson extends traditional Western assumptions abour fair beauty and black ugliness to the daughters of Niger, who are the blackest of all, but he employs the conventional paradigm of beauty only to reject it. Jonson's language here points to the popular wisdom that the appearance of beauty is only skin-deep, whereas true and lasting beauty is of a moral kind, thus 'that beauty [is] best / Which not the colour but the feature / Assures unto the creature'. So the thesis of this masque is that it is of no importance that the daughters of Niger are black, and thus by definition, ugly, because they have a more lasting beauty within. The fact that the daughters themselves reject this weighty, moralising rhetoric and persist in their wish to be bleached brands them as inconstant and wilful, and is a representation of female gender that spills into *The Masque of Beauty*. Perhaps the emphasis placing inner virtue above physical form is particularly pertinent with regard to a King who was well known for elevating good looking favourites to high government office.[43]

In fact, the masque as a whole is intimately related to the balance of power at court; Hardin Aasand has shown how Queen Anne played a fundamental role in commissioning and shaping *Blackness*, and argues that she chose this rather startling disguise, transgressing traditional aesthetics and notions of beauty, in order to signal her marginalisation at court where 'fair' young men had greater access to her husband than she did. In the homoerotic and Protestant atmosphere of the Jacobean court, she was a female Catholic and thus largely excluded from it despite her position of Queen. Aasand sums up this situation: '*The Masque of Blackness*, on several

The formation of the antimasque   53

levels, is a document of marginalization, and it records analogically, historically, and ethically, the intersection of socially excluded forces'.[44] It may be that in attempting to down play the importance of skin-colour in his analysis of beauty Jonson was trying to smooth over some of the latent cultural disturbances provoked by Anne's choice of disguise, which presents a view of female sexuality to offset the homosocial and homoerotic atmosphere of the court. One of the common assumptions held about Africans is that they were lascivious, and this assumption can be traced in the remarks of observors of the masque. One writes, 'At night there was a sumptuous shew represented by the Queen and some dozen Ladies all paynted like Blackamores face and neck bare and for the rest strangely attired in Barbaresque mantell to the halfe legge'; Dudley Carleton's famous comments include the charge that, 'Their apparel was rich, but too light and Curtizen-like for such great ones' and he anxiously remarked that, '[The Spanish ambassador danced with the Queen], and forgot not to kiss her Hand, though there was danger it would have left a mark on his Lips'.[45] The emphasis on revealed flesh, and the kiss that entails the risk of taint or symbolic infection, points towards common male fantasies and fears about women and sex and is enabled primarily by Anne's black disguise. She presents the court with an alternative female sexuality, which could not normally be articulated within the traditional, often male authored discourse of aristocratic, female, and ultimately fair beauty.

In adopting the disguise of a black woman, albeit an aristocratic one, Anne creates a disturbance by confusing the cultural categories of black and white and their attendant associations: vice and virtue, sin and redemption, lasciviousness and chastity. Moreover, the impact of this cultural confusion must be partly attributable to its suggestion of miscegenation, as Dudley Carleton's horrified comments quoted above testify.[46] There is a discrepancy between Orgel's assertion that black characters had performed or been represented in court theatricals long before this particular masque, and his normalising of this puzzling disguise, and the efforts of Hall and Aasand to recuperate some of the shock they argue the court must have experienced on viewing Queen Anne as a blackamore. Both of these views are reconciled when we remember the fact that while blacks had appeared or been represented in court entertainments previously, it is most likely that professional performers took on these roles, and certainly not any member of the court. Thus, the shock of Queen Anne's disguise becomes comprehensible as an extreme breach of decorum, particularly as blacks had often been presented in servile roles. Anne must have present at at least two earlier masques featuring blacks which had been performed at the Scottish court, a fact strongly suggesting that she consciously anticipated the impact her disguise would make on the Stuart court in London.[47] This point reinforces Aasand's comments regarding Anne's deliberate choice of this disguise to signal her marginal and suppressed position at court and proves a compelling instance where the categories of race and gender seem to overlap temporarily.[48] My remarks here show that both Queen Anne and Jonson were undeniably co-authors of this masque, and that her choice of disguise largely determined its content. Jonson's later battles with the masque designer Inigo Jones, and his attempts to wrest authority within the form have been well documented, and perhaps even in this early masque Jonson is involved in a subtler kind of competitive synthesis with the Queen; she commissioned this entertainment to express her personal concerns, and Jonson also inserted into it his views on kingship and the role of the poet.

At the outset of the masque, Niger employs typically Jonsonian terms to praise the virtue and constancy of his daughters:

> How near divinity they be
> That stand from passion and decay so free.

However, he goes on to declare that his daughters are disturbed by 'The fabulous voices of some few / Poor brainsick men, styled poets here with you' (ll.130-1). Such distress has grave implications, as it involves the daughters' alienation from Sol, and their charging 'his burning throne / With volleys of revilings'; the daughters also express frustration with their father, Niger, whom they expect to bring about their colour transformation. Niger alleges that poets are responsible for stirring up this distress, which may be analogous to political dissent when we remember James's frequent description of his relationship with his subjects as that between a father and his children. But Niger, as we have seen, has weak judgement and the denouement of the masque justifies the daughters' demands to be white and the poets' celebration of fair beauty and the virtue it physically reflects. Aethiopia, the luminous moon goddess appears promising transformation to the daughters and she possesses an indisputible divine authority; she is the female exotic other complementing Sol and these elemental deities are the ultimate authorities in the masque. Given that Jonson is responsible for the plot and dialogue, it is hardly surprising that these joint rulers implicitly defend the wisdom and position of poets.

Niger has already tried and failed to exert his royal and paternal authority and 'To frustrate' the 'strange error' that perplexes his daughters. In this context, it is intriguing to note that although Niger's views are expressed in the weighty terms of Jonson's moral rhetoric, they are blatantly dismissed as 'errors' by the goddess Aethiopia. Initially, he does not recognise the goddess when she first appears to urge him on his quest for a kinder climate, and he fails to interpret her cryptic clue indicating that 'Britannia' is the land for which he should be looking. Eventually, Niger's incompetence calls for direct intervention from Aethiopia, and she explains to him the meaning of her original message:

> Niger, be glad; resume thy native cheer.
> Thy daughters' labors have their period here,
> And so thy errors. I was that bright face
> Reflected by the lake, in which thy race
> Read mystic lines...
> This blessed isle doth with that *-tania* end,
> Which there they saw inscribed, and shall extend
> Wished satisfaction to their best desires.
>
> (ll.202-10)

Niger is clearly shown to be in error and implicitly criticised for his failures here, but there is also a sense of an apologetic exoneration of him at work in this masque; Aethiopia does not condemn Niger, but rather steers him on the right course with a heartening wish for him to 'be glad'. Yet the goddess does not bring the quest for true beauty to a resolution and the masque closes with the miracle of colour transformation withheld but tantalisingly promised; the daughters are told by Aethiopia:

> So that, this night, the year gone round,
> You do again salute this ground,
> And in the beams of yond' bright sun
> Your faces dry, and all is done.
>
> (ll.322-5)

It may be that this twist of the plot, guaranteeing a sequel masque, was partly motivated by a wily and aspiring poet who wished to ensure his employment in the following year. Jonson was retained, not for his planned sequel, but to compose the 1606 *Hymenaei* celebrating the wedding of the Earl of Essex and Lady Frances Howard. Thus, the promised transformation of the daughters of Niger was further postponed until *The Masque of Beauty* in 1608 (another wedding masque had occupied the festivities of 1607). The fact that Aethiopia's promise was frustrated for two years aptly demonstrates the contingency of the court masque, shaped and informed by fashions and occurrences at court despite Jonson's attempts to dominate it. There is some awkward tweaking of the plot in order to explain the gap between *Blackness* and *Beauty* and the inclusion of four more lady masquers. Jonson's own notes at the beginning of the masque record that, 'it was her highness' pleasure... that I should think on some fit presentment... still keeping the same persons... but their beauties varied according to promise, and their time of absence excused, with four more added to their number'. It is entertaining to speculate on Jonson's immediate reaction to this exacting request, but he meets it with much ingenuity. Boreas, the North wind, tells us that on their way to the court, as directed by Aethiopia, the daughters of Niger have been captured by Night, who, envious that their glorious whiteness will cast her into shame, has 'tossed / The nymphs at sea, as they were almost lost, / Till on an island they by chance arrived, / That floated in the main; where yet she gyved them' (ll.70-3). Trapped on their floating island, the daughters of Niger repeat their earlier pattern of directionless wandering that in *Blackness* led them to exceed their natural boundaries and arrive in Britannia. The daughters are victim to the whims of elemental nature, Night holds them in her grip, and while Boreas reports their imprisonment, Vulturnus, the East wind, tells of their release by Aethiopia, goddess of the moon Thus, the daughters are wrapped up in a series of tropes that feminist scholars have previously noted in relation to depictions of the female body, tropes of wandering, incorporating physical and geographical excess, emotional outpouring, intuition and impulse as opposed to intellect, and a cyclical nature attuned to the cycle of the moon. There is no doubt that within the discourse of the masque this unstable female nature is shown to be in need of policing; indeed, *Blackness* intimates that James's weaknesses are rooted in his connection with whimsical female nature and his rejection of constancy: Aethiopia instructs him that the ideal king should cultivate a 'light sciential', 'past mere nature'. The daughters of Niger are extreme examples of this wandering female nature, because even the island they land on is unfixed and floating. They are only stabilised when the island is fixed to the British land mass and placed under the authority of the Thames:

> Rise, aged Thames, and by thy hand
> Receive these nymphs within the land;
> And in those curious squares and rounds
> Wherewith thou flow'st betwixt the grounds
> Of fruitful Kent and Essex fair,
> That lend thee garlands for thy hair,
> Instruct their silver feet to tread,
> Whilst we again to sea are fled.
>
> (*Beauty*, 251-8)

In *Blackness* we witnessed Niger's failure as *paterfamilias* (failure that reflects on King James), and in *Beauty* his role as father is usurped by Thames, who will discipline the whitened nymphs and fix their movements; no longer will they be led far from home on a wandering and directionless journey by Niger, but schooled in the merits of order and obedience as they follow the geometrical 'rounds and squares' through which Thames orders the countryside. African excess, both geographical and physical, is erased in favour of an English pastoral order, thereby rendering once alien and uncontrollable foreigners into acquiescent British subjects. It is surely significant that these masques depict the African subject as essentially feminine and thus insert embryonic imperial aspirations within a traditional ideology of gender, naturalising a relatively new discourse with the language of an accepted one. The fixing of the daughters is given the full weight of Jonsonian rhetoric as by the end of the masque they are commanded to return to their throne which the notes tell us 'turns'. The daughters, however, remain seated and personify a fixity in motion that distinguishes many Jonsonian representations of virtue:

> Still turn, and imitate the heaven
>   In motion swift and even,
>   And as his planets go,
>   Your brighter lights do so.
> May youth and pleasure ever flow;
>   But let your state, the while,
>   Be fixed as the isle.

(ll.336-42)

Yet attention to the historical context of these entertainments demonstrates that many of the female masquers refused to be contained in the way that *Beauty* represents. As I have noted, Hardin Aasand focuses on the cultural disruption provoked by Anne's choice of disguise and describes her as a 'Lady of Misrule' embodying those grotesque elements that would later be assumed by the antimasque. Moreover, Kim Hall has shown us that many of the aristocratic women who danced in the masques were notoriously unruly, concluding that, 'From the first entrance of James into England, the ladies at court are associated with lawless, transgressive behavior'.[49] It may be that while the poet provided the court with a spectacular fantasy operating as wish fulfilment on many levels, Jonson also attempts to wrest domination of the masque from Anne and her ladies. The Queen may have commissioned the masque, but she is fixed in a moral landscape by the poet, and through rhetorical means (principally metaphor and metonymy) rendered subject to his metaphysical universe.[50]

By the end of the masque the daughters of Niger have achieved a platonic essence that elevates their beauty and virtue onto a metaphysical sphere, where issues such as skin colour are irrelevant. Thus, although *Beauty* may be seen to consolidate Britain's foreign ambitions, it also has a strong domestic resonance. Anne and her ladies are shown to surpass mere physical beauty, and the masque implies that King James must learn to appreciate these qualities in his wife and Queen. In this way these entertainments articulate both Anne's concerns as an alienated royal consort, and the philosopher poet's concerns that James's personal preferences interfere with the government of the nation. But it is vital that we do not gloss over the fact that the *Blackness* and *Beauty* also acknowledge James as the omnipotent monarch while hinting at his weaknesses. It is this juggling of multiple perspectives, and dialectical negotiation between alternative analyses of monarchical government that distinguishes the Jonsonian masque, and prepares the ground for the coming antimasque, where dialectic becomes an integral part of the court entertainment.

Notes

1. Jonson's contemporaries as well as later critics suspected the motives behind his panegyric. A squib written by Jonson's 'friend', John Eliot, clearly accuses him of prostituting his talent:

   > Your verses are commended and tis true
   > That they were very good, I mean to you;
   > For they return'd you Ben as I was tould,
   > A certain sum of forty pound in gold:
   > The verses then being rightly understood
   > His Lordship not Ben Jonson made them good.
   >
   > (HS, XI, p.406)

   In 1680, the character writer, Izaac Walton, also suggested that Jonson financially exploited his talent for satirical invective, because he received, '100li a yeare from the king, also a pention from the cittie, and the like from many of the nobilitie, and som of the gentrie. W^{ch} was well pay'd for love or fere of his rayling verse, or prose, or boeth' (HS, I, p.181, ll.13-17). However, it appears that it is Jonson's panegyric that leaves current critics feeling most uncomfortable, and it is often suggested that it constitutes an immoral and egregious flattery. David Lindley has written of 'Embarrassing Ben' when reflecting that the masque, *Hymenaei*, eulogises newly wedded courtiers who were later convicted of crimes including murder, and that the companion entertainment, *The Irish Masque at Court*, unashamedly subscribes to the Crown's brutal foreign policy on Ireland. Philip Edwards goes further and asserts that he has to dissociate the masques from their historical contexts in order to enjoy them as literature, but he goes on to assert that the masques are tainted by their lack of integrity or truth in reflection of the monarch. Edwards declares, 'When we look at most of the praise which is given in poems and masques to James and his family it is straightforward panegyric, and it seems to me that the educational potential for the recipients is totally outweighed by the real damage flattery does.' See Lindley (1987), 248-64; Edwards (1979), 168.
2. Spencer and Wells (1967), 259.

3. Peterson (1981).
4. Jonson expressed some anxiety that his panegyric could be misrepresented or misunderstood as idolatry. This seems to be related to the poet's serious self-doubt that, in fact, his panegyric may have been little more than empty flattery (see 'To My Muse', *Epigrams*, LXV). Such crises in confidence are offset by his many poems asserting poetic integrity (see 'To Robert, Earl of Salisbury', *Epigrams*, XLIII). This concern with the validity of his panegyric must have been partly provoked by the carping of some of his contemporaries and friends who publicly voiced the view that Jonson betrayed his status as a poet by selling his skill to the highest bidder (see John Eliot's squib, HS, (1925-52), vol.XI, 406, quoted in note 1).
5. In proclaiming 'His light scientiall is, and, past mere nature' (*Blackness*, 1.226) Jonson exhorts the King to rule according to the precepts of philosophy rather than according to human whim (nature). This exhortation grows in significance when we remember that in the early part of his reign the King off-loaded many burdens of state on to the shoulders of his secretary, Robert Cecil, Earl of Salisbury, enabling the King to devote his hours to his favourite sport of hunting. In the later 'To Sir Robert Wroth', we see a similar didactic exhortation mediated through panegyric. The praises of an idealised country life, and Wroth's function as its focus, suggest that he should eschew the court influences that David Norbrook has shown Wroth to have been swayed by; Norbrook (1984a).
6. Lee (1989), 79.
7. Anne Barton (1984), ch.8.
8. Dutton (1987), 130.
9. Erasmus (1515/16?: 1936), 199.
10. Lee (1989), 36.
11. Greene (1970), 331-48.
12. Greene (1970), 332.
13. Carew's 'To Saxham' and Marvell's 'Upon Appleton House' are usually mentioned with 'To Penshurst' and 'To Sir Robert Wroth' as important examples of the minor genre of the country house poem. Both these poems adopt a hyperbolic rhetorical approach in the description of the abundance of these great houses. As with Jonson's poems, the hyperbole often goes to such extremes that it collapses into a 'tongue in cheek' type of irony. Carew's poem suggests that in the winter season, animals offer themselves gladly as sustenance for Saxham in the lean time:

> The willing ox of himself came
> Home to the slaughter, with the lamb,
> And every beast did thither bring
> Himself, to be an offering.
> The scaly herd more pleasure took,
> Bath'd in thy dish, than in thy brook;

The image of fish leaping happily from stream to platter is so ridiculous as to become ironic; I would suggest that this is a deliberate rhetorical strategy on Carew's part, and probably adopted from Jonson's country house poems.
14. Waller (1993), 117. At this point in my argument there is a shift from an author-centred criticism to a reader-centred criticism. This is because I consider both approaches vital for the understanding of Jonson's panegyric. The acceptance of

'Jonson' as a writer with a specific agenda and literary strategy is necessitated by his conscious erudition and forging of a poetic voice. However, despite Jonson's many statements of authorial intention. I recognise that any literary authority must be limited, as texts are always open to misreading by the reader, who may also exploit the ambiguity within the text and allow it to produce an autonomous meaning. In this book I place a dialogic emphasis on both author and text; such dialogism may be seen as a typically Jonsonian strategy.

15. Belsey (1985a), 167.
16. Norbrook (1984a).
17. The tendency of pastoral poetry to undercut ironically its own orthodox assumptions that we find in Horace and then Jonson, fits in with what Bakhtin has described as the novelistic tendency of literature to question the very framework on which it rests. Bakhtin (1981).
18. The comparison of court and country is, of course, traditional in pastoral, but Jonson uses this binary opposition in a more complex way. Although the court is indicted initially and the country held up as a virtuous exemplum, the poem goes on to suggest that the landed aristocracy also subscribe to the courtly values of lavish abundance and ostentation. In fact, these country aristocrats act out a pastoral fantasy that has little to do with the values of moderation and good husbandry that are readily associated with the country. Jonson's poem exhorts Wroth to eschew the pastoral fantasy, to become self-contained in his country estate, and to refrain from modelling his life style on that of the court.
19. Williams (1985), 26–34.
20. 'Active personal occupation in a trade or profession was generally thought to be humiliating. The man of business was inferior to the gentleman of leisure who lived off his rents. Retail trade was always degrading, and overseas trade only a respectable occupation for a son and heir if pursued as a hobby rather than as a profession.' Stone (1967), 24.
21. Wheeler (1938), 68.
22. Renaissance rhetorical strategies often evince an ability and a readiness to interpret absolutes in terms of their polar opposites according to the current moral imperative. Thus, the avaricious lawyer and miser that Wroth is favourably compared with, could easily be reascribed as prudence and thrift, with Wroth's generosity becoming profligacy. This rhetorical strategy was known as *paradiastole*. For more detail on this trope see Whigham (1984), 40-2.
23. Norbrook (1984a), 192.
24. See note 1.
25. Bacon (1597: 1986), 115; Daniel (1604: 1967), 25.
26. Daniel (1604: 1967), 30, 194-212.
27. Jonson's innovations in the masque entertainment include the dramatisation of the form, he also intellectualised it and published heavily annotated versions of his masques explaining their dense classical allusions. Moreover, he stressed his masques' autonomy as literary texts rather than using the masque text merely as a journalistic record of a particular spectacle.
28. Burt (1987), 359-559.
29. In *Discoveries* (ll.1493-9) Jonson articulates his view of the monarch's divinity, but at the same time suggests that much depends on the individual character of the monarch:

   Let no man therefore murmur at the actions of the prince, which is placed so far above him. If he offend, he hath his discoverer. God hath a height beyond him. But where the prince is good, Euripides saith: God is a guest in a human body.

30. For historical examinations of Jonson's anti-theatricalism see Barish (1981). Barish writes, 'Somewhere in Jonson there lurks a puritanical uneasiness about pleasure itself, and also a distrust of movement, which connects with what we shall presently see to be an ideal of stasis in the moral and ontological realm. But whatever exists in time, and unfolds in time, and utilizes human actors, must also involve motion as one of its mainsprings. To banish motion, to attempt to arrest or disguise it by ruling out the devices of stagecraft that exploit it, is in a sense to deny the intrinsically kinetic nature of the theatrical medium' (p.135). Later, Barish goes on to say, 'The masque proves vulnerable on two related counts – showiness and ephemerality' (p.152). Although these reflections on Jonson's view of the theatre are valid in a sense, they are distorted into an 'anti-theatrical prejudice' as Barish neglects the didactic content of Jonson's work, which may be described as its *raison d'etre*. For more on Jonson's 'anti-theatricality' see Sweeney (1985). On the publication of Jonson's *Works* as a specific instance of anti-theatricalism, see Murray (1983), 641-63; Loewenstein (1988), 265-77.
31. Marcus (1986), 117.
32. Orgel (1965), 118-23.
33. Siddiqui (1992), 139-63, 144.
34. Siddiqui (1992), 142.
35. Gordon (1975), 134-56.
36. Jonson himself fell into serious trouble when he was charged by Sir James Murray 'for writing something against the Scots in a play *Eastward Ho*', (*Conversations*, l.271). Popular attitudes in London to the Scottish 'invasion' are aptly demonstrated by a piece of doggerel circulating at the time:

> Hark! hark! the dogs do bark,
> The beggars have come to town.
> Some in rags, and some in tags
> And some in velvet gowns.
>
> (Akrigg (1962), 48).

37. For an eloquent description of how the 'native' middle classes are westernised see Fanon (1994), 36-9.
38. James I (1599: 1969), 29.
39. See, for example, Greenblatt (1992a), 256-75.
40. For a review of this topos of Britain as a favoured isle in the West see Edwards (1979).
41. Marcus (1986), 113-14. Jonathan Goldberg suggests that Jonson recognised James I's multifaceted identity in an early poem that celebrates him both as poet and King:

> How, best of Kings, do'st thou a sceptre beare!
> How, best of Poets, do'st thou laurell weare!
>
> (*Epigrams*, IV)

See Goldberg (1983), 17.
42. HS, (1925-52), vol.X, 452.
43. Hall (1991), 8; Barthelemy (1987), 18-41. For a fuller account of James's favourites see Bingham (1981).

62   Ben Jonson's Antimasques

44. Aasand (1992), 273.
45. HS, (1925-52), vol.X, 448-9.
46. On the cultural associations surrounding the categories of white and black in the Renaissance, and their derivation from a more ancient Judeo-Christian discourse see Barthelemy (1987), 1-41.
47. 'There were at least two masques with Moors at the Scottish court, George Buchanan's *Pompae Deorum* and the anonymous masque performed on August 30, 1594, to celebrate the baptism of Prince Henry of Scotland. It is doubtful whether the Turma Aethiopium in *Pompae Deorum* were played by courtiers. In the baptism masque a Moor pulls a triumphant chariot, he was certainly not a courtier. See Anna Jean Mill, *Medieval Plays In Scotland* (New York, 1924, 50)'; Barthelemy (1987), n.2, 19.
48. Critics have become increasingly interested in the representation of gender and race in Renaissance literature, and how these categories often cross-fertilise; see, Hendricks and Parker (1994).
49. Aasand (1992), 272; Hall writes, 'In actuality female unruliness was not so easily contained: the performance itself featured many women who resisted patriarchal standards of female decorum. Along with Philip Sidney's "dark lady", Penelope Rich, who was the mistress of Edward Blount and the mother of four illegitimate children, the play cast Lady Arabella Stuart, who would later be sent to the Tower (again) for her secret marriage to Lord Seymour; Frances Howard, who later became notorious for poisoning her husband in the Overbury affair; Lady Mary Wroth, who had two illegitimate children by her first cousin and was sent down from court after the publication of her prose romance (the first by a woman), *The Countess of Montgomerie's Urania* (1621).' (Hall (1991), 12.
50. It may be that Jonson was seeking to guide the Queen as he hoped to guide the King, or that the closing scene of the masque suggests that he sought to subject what he considered a weaker female intellect to his superior masculine mind. Jonson is often termed a misogynist yet his attitude to women is complicated. While representations of women in his work often fall into the stereotypical categories of either virgin or whore, women can play a more significant role than first appears. For example, it is Dol Common in *The Alchemist* who mediates between the competing Face and Subtle, and without her none of the action of the play would be possible. Jonson's ambiguous attitude to women is amply demonstrated by his short poem, 'Song. That Women Are But Men's Shadows, *The Forest* VII):

>Follow a shadow, it still flies you;
>Seem to fly it, it will pursue:
>So court a mistress, she denies you;
>Let her alone, she will court you.
>Say, are not women truly, then,
>Styled but the shadows of us men?
>At morn, and even, shades are longest;
>At noon, they are or short, or none:
>So men at weakest, they are strongest,
>But grant us perfect, they're not known.
>Say, are not women truly, then,
>Styled but the shadows of us men.

2
Arthur and Augustus: masque and the historical myth

History and myth

In the last chapter I examined *Blackness* and *Beauty*, Jonson's first court masques, in order to show that even in these early entertainments fractures in the dominant ideology of masque manifest themselves, fractures which, I argue, would later be developed and exploited with the emergence of the antimasque. Jonson's chivalric masques, *Prince Henry's Barriers* (1610) and *Oberon, The Fairy Prince* (1611) share much common ground with these early masques, as they too, express tensions between competing ideologies, tensions which Jonson attempts to reconcile. The chivalric masques are of particular interest here as they witness the emergence of the antimasque, and we see Jonson working out a strategy whereby the court entertainment can express openly values contradicting those of the monarchy. My argument hinges on the view that *Oberon* offers us the first example of the Jonsonian antimasque, that is, a prelude to the main masque that interrogates its dominant assumptions. Most critics, however, follow Orgel in detecting the presence of the first antimasque in *The Masque of Queens* (1609). While this is true to a certain extent, I view this antimasque as a kind of false start as the antimasque of witches in *Queens* is one-dimensional in presenting us with stereotypical hags who chant and dance in a bizarre fashion, thus parodying the choreographed harmony of the following masque, yet the witches fail to articulate any views counterbalancing the content of the latter. That Jonson was unsatisfied with this first attempt at an antimasque may be deduced from the fact that the entertainment for the following year, the *Barriers*, omits an antimasque, although Jonson makes a more successful attempt with the form in *Oberon*. These are, however, the embryonic stages of the antimasque, and the chivalric entertainments on the whole attempt to reconcile all the competing ideologies that find expression in the masque, whereas Jonson would capitalise on this problematic aspect of the masque in later entertainments and produce the fully developed, dramatic antimasque; an innovation ensuring a critical space for the poet's political and poetic values and for challenging, topical reflection on current issues as opposed to the masque's universalising and idealising expression of monarchical government.

The competing ideologies of the chivalric masques are rooted in classical and Arthurian historical myths and in order to unravel the political motivation behind Jonson's mythopoeism here it is necessary to review these myths as well as Jonson's personal attitude to history, myth and literature and the relationship between them. This leads me to a brief analysis of Jonson's Roman plays, which are roughly contemporaneous with the chivalric masques, and together constitute the complementary parts of a rigorous analysis of autocratic government; at one extreme Jonson offers us in masque the ideal harmony conferred by monarchical government, and in the Roman plays we have a view of autocracy turned sour, infecting Rome with its values of greed and tyranny. In this sense, the chivalric masques and Roman plays demonstrate Jonson's dialectical impulse that would later be centred on the masque and antimasque; and in this respect it is surely significant that Jonson's last Roman play, *Catiline* (1611), and his first proper antimasque, *Oberon* (1611), coincide chronologically.

Like many of his contemporary dramatists, Jonson set much of his work in an historical context, yet he was not a slave to historical fact but rather selected and recast his material into forms more suitable for his dramatic purpose.[1] In reshaping history this way Jonson conforms to the humanist view of history famously espoused by Sidney, that the idealised golden world of didactic poesy is a more effective instructor of moral virtue than history which is often obliged to rehearse acts of immorality; however, while Jonson's portrayal of Rome is certainly intended to be didactic, it is hardly golden.[2] Sidney's ethos legitimates the dramatist's manipulation of history, although the distinction between history and poetry, in any event, was less clear for Jonson and his contemporaries than it is now and suggests an instructive insight into the way history is written. At the beginning of the seventeenth century, the perspective from which scholars and poets approached history became a subject for hot debate; in fact, the distinction between history and poetry was a recent innovation that contrasted with the practice of earlier Tudor thinkers such as Sir Thomas Elyot who readily included historical material in his discussions of poetry and *vice versa*.[3] Although, as Sidney's *Defence* demonstrates, poetry became aligned with fiction, and history with fact, these distinctions, in turn, became blurred, as historiography could be perceived as flawed, incomplete or distorted through bias. Francis Bacon's method of categorising the different forms of historiography as perfect, unfinished or defaced, perceptively points to the danger of accepting historical record as a monolithic representation of truth, and he condemns the fact that the line between history and creative writing is blurred in those texts where the author interprets the historical material presented.[4] In the chivalric masques Jonson demonstrates this more flexible or relativist approach to history, as he places known fact within an obviously fictionalised or poeticised context, and in the Roman plays, he manipulates history to make it fit his dramatic purpose. Just as Bacon suggests, Jonson erases the line between history and fiction, to create a hybrid form of literature functioning as mythopoeism. Moreover, Jonson's manipulation of historical myth within the masques is distinguished by his attempts to mediate between polarised historical traditions, to reshape established myths. My assertion that the chivalric masques and Roman plays are the constituent parts of an analysis of autocratic power is not a specious attempt to link differing literary forms for the purpose of criticism, but rather a recognition that Jonson's work as a whole manifests a continuing concern with the nature of government and authority, and that the representation of these institutions is largely dictated by genre. Therefore, literary context is often responsible for either the satire or praise allotted to the poet's subject matter; what is often termed as Jonson's hypocrisy is simply this ability to see both sides of the coin, an ability recognised by renaissance rhetorical theory, and known as *paradiastole*. In his illuminating study of courtly rhetoric and literary tropes Frank Whigham describes *paradiastole* as, 'the ongoing adjustment of public information by redescribing an utterance or action in such a way as to reverse the polarity of its meaning'. So, absolute power governing the state can be described as either paternal or tyrannical depending on the context of the utterance; furthermore, the two terms are interchangeable as a means of describing the same set of circumstances. Whigham emphasises that the trope of *paradiastole* is incapable of conveying literal or fixed truth because it depends on the interchangeable and relative nature of known reference points; so that, for example, 'the kaleidoscopic relations between praise and blame, flattery and slander, finally shift uncontrollably at every turn'.[5] This means that the absolutist state may always be construed as both paternal and tyrannical; Jonson's chivalric masques and Roman plays are not rooted in a factual account of history, and this enables them to grasp the dual nature of absolutism, and perhaps more importantly for this study, they embody a dialectical impulse that would later be centred on the interaction between the masque and antimasque.

The chivalric masques are of particular interest as they represent a synthesis of myths peculiar to the early Stuart period; although these mythic discourses had previously flourished in the Elizabethan court, they were adapted and integrated in a completely new way under Stuart patronage. Roy Strong has recognised that the Stuart chivalric masques were intended by their creators as a deliberate continuation of Elizabethan tradition (or pseudo-tradition), and he describes the *Barriers* as, 'The last deliberate effort to revive the faltering fantasy image of late-Tudor chivalry'.[6] Moreover, the figure of Oberon in the eponymous 1611 masque suggestively harks back to the fairy prince and queen that Elizabeth had met in a stage-managed forest glade in Woodstock in 1575.[7] The format of the *Barriers* is obviously a simulacrum of the tilts staged to celebrate Queen Elizabeth's accession day, and yet, even for the Tudors, such tilts were exercises in nostalgia that exploited outdated symbols of baronial power to celebrate the newly centralised monarchy. The post-medieval tilt is fundamentally oxymoronic, in that feudal barons are nominally ascribed independence and power in order to make a publicly symbolic act of ceding this power to the Crown; the poet Peele foregrounds the contradictory nature of these stage-managed events imaging a transference of power that had long since taken place:

> What troupe of Loyall English knights in armes
> righte richely mounted and appointed all
> in shininge armes aucutred for the war,
> small number of a number numberles
> held Justes in honor of hir hollyday.[8]

Although at the period when these Elizabethan tilts took place the feudal structure had been largely eroded by the Tudors, the monarchy recognised the ideological value of exploiting an outdated socio-political structure in order to consolidate the new political *status quo*; it is clear that the discursive practice inherent in the Tudor tilt posited a powerful feudalism appreciating the benefits of the newly centralised state and graciously ceding to it – a far cry from the many petty rebellions which the Elizabethan Crown had to contend with. Strong suggestively describes the Elizabethan tilt as a grand public relations exercise: 'This saga of Elizabeth I and her knights was therefore, a vast and over-publicized romance lived out in the public arena' (p.102). This publicity is a key distinction between the Elizabethan and Stuart interpretations of the chivalric Arthurian myth; as opposed to the open and public celebrations of the Queen's accession day, the Stuart chivalric masque was performed privately in the Banqueting House at Whitehall, with the audience confined to the elite members of the Stuart court. The Stuart royal entertainment reversed the emphases of the Elizabethan model; whereas Elizabeth's royal celebrations had been geographically open they were also intellectually limited, and clearly indebted to native traditions of 'mumming' and pageantry. The Stuart court masque, however, was geographically insular and retreated within the walls of Whitehall, yet it also manifested an openness to European developments in the arts and in philosophy. The Stuart masques demonstrate Jonson's familiarity with European literature and thought and his readiness to mine these intellectual resources in the interest of the English court entertainment. Moreover, John Peacock has extensively shown that Inigo Jones's designs for the masque sets are definitively European in their inspiration, and far in advance of Tudor style, which was still pervasive in architecture and painting.[9] While the Stuart masques clearly had a political function, primarily to consolidate the monarchy, they ignored the importance, and, at times, even the existence, of the public masses. Elizabeth's tilts and progresses also performed an important political function – they allowed the Queen to meet her public and the public to meet their Queen. As a political strategy and public relations exercise these public events seem to have been highly effective in promoting a strong sense of national unity and mutual interest. Under James's influence, however, these celebrations of the monarchy were brought indoors. The implications of this shift are given a sharper focus by comparing the accession day festivities of both monarchs. It is well reported that Elizabeth's entry into London at her coronation was a celebrated success, partly because of her eager participation in the day's pageantry; she studied the emblematic motifs minutely and keenly responded to them as well as seizing the opportunity to make a number of spontaneous speeches *en route*. In stark contrast, James's reaction to the London crowds cheering him on his entry to their city was one of barely concealed revulsion and impatience; however, historians may have been somewhat unfair to James over the years and his behaviour here is certainly more understandable when we remember that he must have been acutely conscious of the risk of plague in London at this time, and that he had also been the victim of numerous plots and attempts on his life: no doubt these experiences imbued him with a horror for jostling crowds.[10] Yet whatever the explanation behind James's behaviour on his accession day, he continued to shun close encounters with his public and a newly enclosed and rarefied court atmosphere prevailed. Whereas James remained at court where he viewed masquers representing shepherds in the highly stylised pastoral manner, Elizabeth journeyed outside of London (to the financial burden of her hosts) and met real shepherds as well as their pastoral imitations. The intensified introspection of the Stuart court was undeniably a contributory factor in its increasing detachment from the outside world, although, as I have noted, it should be remembered that this political withdrawal was accompanied by a growing interest in European artistic developments. Both these trends reached their ultimate exaggeration under Charles I, an educated collector and patron of European art, who expressed his autocratic will in the increasingly contained nature of the court masque.

Strong has also emphasised that the prime mover in the Stuart resuscitation of popular Elizabethan themes of chivalry was Prince Henry, rather than his father, King James; James encouraged quite a different myth to be woven around his court. As the cultural historian R. Malcolm Smuts describes, an alternative discourse was needed to exemplify the alternative policies of the new King: 'Particular strains of Latin thought and culture, deriving from the late republican and early imperial periods, began to play an unprecedented role in shaping English court culture'.[11] Classical and chivalric myths, however, were not mutually exclusive; the myth of Troynovant had reconciled the two discourses for the Tudors who represented themselves as descended from Brutus, the founder of Britain. Significantly, King Arthur was reputedly part of this genealogical inheritance and the last king under whom the British Isles had been united. It would seem obvious for the Stuart family to continue this combined tradition, but competition between James and his son, Prince Henry, seems to have resulted in them appropriating different parts of the Tudor myth that suited their personal ideology and using one to challenge the other. In this way, the synthesised myth of Troynovant became polarised, and the component parts mutually negating as the crusading prince challenged the Augustan *rex pacificus*.[12] In the chivalric masques Jonson sought to reintegrate the Augustan and Arthurian myths but in a manner that made the two discourses question and modify each other dialectically; this is not the same as the Tudor myth of Troynovant which uncritically claimed dual status as a classical and an Arthurian inheritance, and operated as part of a propaganda ploy to legitimate the shaky Tudor claim to the monarchy. In the *Barriers* and *Oberon* Jonson explores the ideological implications involved in the appropriation of aspects of these myths, and suggests that a combination of their values would result in effective government; this is the poet's version of the political 'middle way' which James had previously asserted he always pursued (*Basilikon Doron*, p.29). The masques shy away from the militant religiosity often associated with Prince Henry, and graft the energy and enthusiasm of chivalric discourse onto the values of the classical myth. This negotiation of polarised extremes is a typically Jonsonian strategy; in poeticising political reality Jonson sought a *via media* which promoted a moral and peaceful government rather than serving the personal aspirations of any individual ruler. Moreover, the chivalric masques are a critical manipulation of the myth of Troynovant in an attempt to explore the possibilities of contemporary domestic and foreign policy; the chronological distance between us and these strange court entertainments may lead us to forget or gloss over how bold a move it was on Jonson's part to explore royal policy in these terms – both Kings, James and Charles, attacked poets and other formers of opinion who did likewise, yet Jonson's licence within the court masque must be partly born out of his intellectual affinity with King James.[13] These early examples of Jonson's dialogic practice in masque move towards integration and closure as he attempts to combine the most positive aspects of the chivalric and classical myths and to minimise any discrepancies between them. In later court masques, this dialectic is centred upon the relationship between the antimasque and masque, but any sense of closure or integration of the two is resisted. As the masque developed, Jonson seems to have been more interested in keeping its discursive practices as dynamic and open as possible; the discrepancies and ideological contradictions set up between the antimasque and masque are not smoothed over but rather produce a dialogic investigation into the nature of monarchical government.

It is probably useful at this stage to review briefly the historical myths inherited by the Stuarts from the Tudors; in understanding the provenance of these important discourses we will be able to appreciate more fully exactly how Jonson shapes and intervenes in them. As I have already suggested, while the Elizabethan revival of the cult of chivalry may seem shallow in retrospect, a triumph of style over content, it did, in fact, perform an important political function. As the Tudors sought to shift the balance of power away from the feudal structure that characterised Britain before their reign and to centralise power in the monarchy, they evolved sophisticated ideological strategies to encourage the nobles to collude in this process – their collusion was all the more important given that the monarch did not command a standing army at this time. A number of literary and cultural discourses declared the centrality of the Queen, and she became the focus of courtly love culture and the apostrophied lady of sonnets. The political importance Elizabeth attached to this role is aptly demonstrated by her angry reaction when any one of her closest male courtiers became engaged or married without her permission.[14] Just as Elizabeth placed herself at the centre of secular court culture, she also became the focal point of religious life, both as the head of the national church and as virgin Queen, occupying the iconographic space left by the removal of the Virgin Mary from Anglican worship.[15] Moreover, the consecration of the monarchy and demonisation of nations loyal to Rome justified a revivalist chivalric cult with the Queen at its centre. The rhetorical framework of the medieval cult of crusading chivalry rested on the notion that offensive foreign policy was, in fact, valiant and religiously zealous defence against pagan assaults; in keeping with this discursive practice, Elizabethan knights at arms were eager to defend Protestantism against Spanish Catholicism, both at home and in the Netherlands, and gathered themselves around the figure who simultaneously represented the church and the state, defining their virtue in their willingness to defend her from the pagan Other. While the cult of Elizabeth was thus a romantic construct in many respects, it also performed a pragmatic function in consolidating the position of the monarchy after the new religious settlement; the Crown sought to occupy a central position in national and religious life and to prevent religious or factional disruptions of the body politic. This neo-chivalric discourse often lurks behind Tudor military and diplomatic encounters with Spain and the New World, justifying acts of aggression and snatched loot from the Spanish treasure ships. The cultural historian, Smuts, carefully notes the connection between Tudor foreign policy and the revival of chivalric myths:

> Conveniently, English chivalry had long helped to justify the Crown's wars. Heroic kings – the legendary Arthur, Edward III, and Henry V – were national symbols of courtesy and prowess, and the Order of the Garter, was an exclusive society of knighthood under the monarch's leadership. Whenever England went to war in the late fifteenth and sixteenth centuries, accounts of the exploits of legendary royal conquerors circulated with official encouragement. Shakespeare's *Henry V* and Spenser's *Faerie Queene* continued a tradition of propaganda already more than a century old.
>
> (p.21)

The Faerie Queene overtly manifests the Tudor association of chivalry with militant Protestantism, a connection that is repeated poetically and visually in the *Barriers*. In this masque chivalry is located in a temple, a place, we are told, that once outshone the temple of Ephesus and the Lady of the Lake describes it in terms evoking a great medieval cathedral:

> There porticoes were built, and seats for knights
> That watched for all adventures, days and nights;
> The niches filled with statues to invite
> Young valours forth by their old forms to fight.
>
> (ll.56-9)

Pointedly, this temple of chivalry is named St George's Portico, thus trumpeting its status as a blatant symbol of crusading Protestantism. It is highly significant that in the time of his inauguration as Prince of Wales, Henry chose to present himself to the court in this setting, deliberately declaring his ambitions as a crusading Arthurian knight.

The cult of chivalry, however, was distasteful to King James, and his influence is partly responsible for Jonson's stripping the myth of its militaristic and crusading connotations as much as possible.[16] In this respect it is significant that James had refused to accept a sword presented to him as part of the festivities celebrating the King of Denmark's visit to London in

1606; presumably, this action was a symbolic rejection of the sword's military implications. It is also probable that the King's feelings in this matter prevented Henry from receiving the customary sword of triumph in reward for his victorious combat in the *Barriers*. However, in *Tethys' Festival* (a 1610 masque by Daniel and performed on the day of the Prince's investiture) Henry was presented with a sword, but the masque emphasised it as the sword of justice, bequeathed by Astrea, the goddess of justice (and a common representation of Queen Elizabeth), rather than as a symbol of crusading Protestantism.[17] Again, this rejection of the militancy inherent in the chivalric myth is probably attributable to James. Jonson seems to have been particularly aware of the monarch's requirements of state iconography and by contrast to the chivalry of the *Barriers*, created the pastoral *Oberon* for the following year; although the militancy of the chivalric cult is clearly questioned in the *Barriers*, in *Oberon* Jonson develops more fully the classical discourse that accompanied the King's pacific politics.[18] On this occasion, Henry is presented as a pastoral knight imposing peace and order on an unruly universe, quite a different persona to that of Meoliades (anagram of *Miles A Deo*), the 'soldier of God' role assumed by Henry in the earlier masque. Clearly, *Oberon* draws most obviously on the classical discourse favoured by the King, whereas the *Barriers* responds to Henry's political aspirations; both classical and chivalric discourses are present in each masque, but the relative emphasis given to them varies with their occasions. The *Barriers* is unique among Jacobean court entertainments as the masquing Prince forms a second focal point challenging the King's central position; this anomaly is accounted for by the fact that the masque was composed as part of the celebrations of Henry's investiture as Prince of Wales – as heir to the throne he partakes of the King's divinity and implicitly challenges his father's pre-eminence. While the influence exerted by Henry on this occasion is obvious in the chivalric setting and theme, Jonson foregrounds the cult of chivalry in order to question it with a classically informed discourse. Although the following masque *Oberon* is subtitled, 'A masque of Prince Henry's', its occasion was a celebration of New Year's Day, a standard celebration for the court, rather than the exceptional occasion of Henry's investiture; thus, in the second of the chivalric masques, the King's influence predominates once again and a pastoral entertainment is therefore created, but this more pacific masque is tempered with selected aspects of the cult of chivalry to produce an ideal of strength in peace.

King James was a very different monarch from England's 'Faerie Queene', he was the 'Rex Pacificus' who sought peace with Spain and France. It seems that his violent experiences as ruler of Scotland had imbued him with an almost mystical regard for peace, which explains his lifelong attempts to mediate between Catholic and Protestant Europe. The Elizabethan chivalric myth was thus patently unsuitable for a king harbouring such ideals. James described his brand of pacific classicism as 'the style of kings' and he defined this as this as the monarch's espousal of the ideals of moderation and discipline.[19] It is worth remembering that many poets, including Jonson, represented the King in these terms, even though other commentators record less glowing aspects of the monarch, suggesting that James's attempts to cultivate an Augustan image were largely successful.[20] The monarch himself describes 'the style of kings' in some detail at the outset of the second book of *Basilikon Doron*:

> A good king (thinking his highest honour to consist in the due discharge of his calling) employeth all his studie and paines, to procure and mainteine (by the making and execution of good lawes) the well-fare and peace of his people, and (as their naturall father and kindly maister) thinketh his greatest contentment standeth in their prosperitie, and his greatest suretie in having their hearts, subjecting his owne private affections and appetites to the weill and standing of his subjects, ever thinking the common interesse his chiefest particular.
>
> (p.29)

Obviously, these particular classical ideals are the result of a highly selective interpretation of the classical tradition and ignore the less edifying examples of Roman rule that Jonson explored in his dramatic tragedies. The kingly model that James encouraged poets to pursue was that of peaceful and cultured Augustus rather than tyrannical Tiberius, Nero or Caligula; and, unsurprisingly, busts of the twelve Emperors rather than the heroes of the Roman republic decorated palaces throughout Europe. By way of summary then, Prince Henry's promotion of chivalry and the King's classicism are clearly conflicting discourses, yet the *Barriers* and *Oberon* demonstrate an attempt on Jonson's part to reconcile the two, involving the interweaving and adaptation of traditional themes which had exercised Jonson's imagination prior to these masques. Significantly, even his early poetry and accession day entertainments were based on classical models, and while his later work continues to be rooted in classicism it also questions the value of chivalric ideals and myths; it is perhaps this scepticism, shared by King James and Jonson, regarding Prince Henry's attempts to galvanise a neo-chivalric cult, that shapes these masques most distinctly.

Jonson and the chivalric ideal

As I have already described, the chivalric myth was revived around Prince Henry at the same time as King James encouraged a revivalist neo-classical mythopoeism; although these discourses had been reconciled in the past under earlier monarchs, they became increasingly polarised for the Stuarts. Many who were dissatisfied with the King's pacific policies turned to the Prince, and Roy Strong has demonstrated that James was acutely conscious of the implicit challenge to his authority offered by Henry's household at St James's, which was deliberately moulded into the polar opposite of the court at Whitehall.[21] In his patronage of Elizabethan heroes such as Sir Walter Raleigh, Henry obliquely criticised his father's pacific foreign policy and domestic practice of casting off the old aristocratic Elizabethan order, to make way for 'parvenu' favourites like Robert Carr. Although he was no great scholar himself, Henry attracted the foremost artists, poets and men of letters to his circle, and the young Prince was reputed to be a future national and Protestant champion. The excitement and glamour surrounding Henry is reflected in the work of a poet under his patronage, Michael Drayton, who prophesies a military victory recalling Henry V's triumph at Agincourt:

> O, when shall English men,
> With such acts fill a pen,
> Or England breed again
> Such a King Harry?[22]

Jonson's *Barriers* also draws this glowing comparison:

> Harry the fifth, to whom in face you Henry are
> So like, as fate would have you so in worth
> Illustrious Prince! The virtue ne'er came forth
> But Fame flew greater for him than she did
> For other mortals; Fate herself did bid
> To save his life ...
> War knew not how to give 'im enough to do.
>
> (11.278-83)

The masque places Prince Henry in a genealogical line that includes the most illustrious monarchs of England; Richard the Lionheart, Edward I, Edward III, Henry V, Henry VII, Henry VIII and Elizabeth I. Yet this roll-call of illustrious monarchs is not merely flag waving on Jonson's part, but also an effective means of highlighting the implacable forces of history and time, and the way in which they ultimately erode human achievement. This emphasis is rendered particularly acute by Jonson's placing of Henry V in context among his predecessors and successors, thereby drawing attention to the ebb and flow of history under the various monarchs, because one of the more notable aspects of Henry's reign was that, although he won great military victories and tracts of land, all this was soon lost, and his kingdom embroiled in the violence of the Wars of the Roses. Shakespeare's *Henry V*, performed approximately ten years before the *Barriers* strikingly points to the ephemeral nature of Henry's triumph:

> Henry the Sixth, in infant bands crowned King,
>   Of France and England, did this King succeed,
> Whose state so many had the managing
>   That they lost France, and made his England bleed.
>
> (Epilogue, ll.9-12)

It is quite possible that this view of Henry V's achievement was in Jonson's mind as he praised the young Prince Henry through comparison with the earlier King, and that his presentation of Henry V as a role model incorporates a subtext pointing to the ultimate futility of military exploits; this is part of the *Barriers'* strategy of openly espousing chivalric sentiments, only subtly to qualify and question their validity. Furthermore, while celebrating the military exploits of these monarchs, Jonson takes pains to underline that this success has only been possible on the back of the nation's material wealth fostered by more prudent monarchs such as Edward I and Henry VII. This celebration of peace and the trade it fosters may be an indication of the moral reservations shared by many humanist thinkers about the didactic values of the Arthurian legend, where adultery and murder are legitimated by the chivalric ideal.[23]

Many critics of Jonson's masques have shown how they comment directly on contemporary affairs, and the *Barriers* is no different. Allusions to the Low Countries and Spain involve a covert reference to the recent treaty of Antwerp (1609) ending hostilities between these countries and terminating Britain's part in that conflict. Jonson tactfully rewrites the diplomatic treaty in terms of a glorious military victory, flattering Henry's dream of a victorious and militant neo-chivalry. Moreover, the Tudor victory in Wales and then England is shown to prefigure symbolically contemporary success in foreign policy:

> So here in Wales, Low Countries, France and Spain
> You may behold both on land and main
> The conquests got, the spoils and trophies reared
> By British kings, such as noblest heard
> Of all the nation, which may make t'invite
> Your valor upon need, but not t'incite
> Your neighbour princes; give them all their due

> And be prepared if they will trouble you.
> He doth but scourge himself his sword that draws
> Without a purse, a counsel and a cause.
>
> (ll.317-26)[24]

Despite the patriotic nature of the masque, it is important to note that its endorsement of militarism is at least equivocal, as it celebrates a nation strong in defence which shuns needless offence:

> Nay, stay your valor; 'tis a wisdom high
> In princes to use fortune reverently.
> He that in deeds of arms obeys his blood
> Doth often tempt his destiny beyond good.
>
> (ll.393-5)

Thus, Jonson's masque engages in the exacting task of representing and reconciling the polarised policies of King James and Prince Henry, militaristic hopes and the espousal of peace in Europe. In a dialectical exploration of the ideals and policies that befit royal authority, the masque clearly emphasises the arts of peace and valorous defence rather than offence; the chivalric ideal is invoked, but significantly modified to embrace caution and rationality. Within the ideological framework of this masque, open hostility to rival countries is treated as acceptable only when diplomatic relations have broken down and the royal coffers can bear the expense of a military campaign. Pointedly, the lines beginning, 'Nay, stay your valour ...' act as a caution against excessive pride, implying that there is a higher moral law to which even the greatest ruler must submit. This cautionary moral recalls the chilling fate of Jonson's Sejanus in the eponymous play performed in 1603, where Sejanus's overweening pride leads to his downfall and dismemberment at the hand of the mob; it is surely no accident that Jonson was pondering issues of government and tyranny in the year of James I's accession and it may be possible to speculate that even in his early drama for the public stage, predating his court masques, Jonson was attempting to instruct the new monarch about the dangers of tyranny. Returning to the *Barriers*, however, its moralising content underlines Jonson's conception of praise as an education in impersonal moral standards rather than as mere flattery of an individual monarch and in this masque Jonson manipulates opposing discourses so that they qualify and comment upon one another in seeking a *via media* for royal policy. The dialectic we find here produces a chivalry tempered with the arts of peace, and the language traditionally employed in praise of the knightly ideal, is translated into a celebration of the domestic virtues of trade and farming. In this masque, the dialectic set up between the competing historical myths moves towards integration, producing a view of

British history that draws on combined medieval and classical traditions; yet, the interpretation of these traditions is deliberately selective, to produce a celebration of the arts of peace as well as the arts of war, and to provide a blueprint for future national policy.[25]

Part of this mediation between potentially opposed historical myths involves the appropriation of chivalric symbols for James's domestic and foreign policies; this rhetorical strategy seems to be symptomatic of a wider ideological project operating during this period, and Smuts notices in the work of Jonson and his contemporaries a significant alteration in the symbolic function of Arthur, whereby, 'King Arthur was converted from a symbol of chivalric prowess into one of British unity' (p.24). This process can be detected in the *Barriers* when Arthur presents himself to the masquers as a star above (Arcturus) and reassures the Lady of the Lake:

> Nor let it trouble thy design, fair dame,
> That I am present to it with my flame
> And influence, since the times are now devolved
> That Merlin's mystic prophesies are absolved
> In Britain's name, the union of this isle
> And claim of both my sceptre and my style.
>
> (ll.72–7)

The masque is clearly informed by James's continual efforts to bring about a union between England and Scotland and assume the title of King of Great Britain; the *Barriers* engages in this task of integration by representing union as something essentially 'British' and Arthurian, as Arthur was reputedly the last king to unite the separate nations in the British Isles.[26] Significantly, the masque glosses over the available militant associations with King Arthur, transferring the energy and enthusiasm of militant neo-chivalry to the project of uniting the British Isles and representing the new state as dignified and strong in peace; a state that legitimates itself from within its own history rather than defining itself against a religious and national 'Other' as a militant discourse required.

The dialectical investigation of the classical and chivalric traditions that Jonson performed in the *Barriers* (1610) gives way in *Oberon* (1611) to a pastoral representation of the arts of peace that were adumbrated in the earlier masque. Although chivalry and folklore were often interlocked in popular legend, the Oberon of this masque is not the crusading prince evoked in the *Barriers*, such as the Black Prince, Henry V and Meliadus, but a figure moulded from classical literature.[27] Jonson justified his Hellenic 'fairy prince' with an end note to the masque text:

> And Galen observes out of Hippocrat. Comment. 3. in 6. Epidemicor: that

both the Athenians and Ionians, call'd the Satyres pheras, or phereas; which name the Centaures have with Homer: from whence, it were no unlikely conjecture, to thinke our word Faeries to come. Let the critics consider it.

Unfortunately, critics have considered it and found Jonson's etymology to be rather fanciful, and it seems that Jonson's aim of mediating and reconciling the classical and ancient British traditions for the Stuart court led him to this rather wild speculation.[28] In *Oberon* unruly satyrs and sylvans replace the chivalric kings of the *Barriers*; they are tamed by Oberon, but significantly, he does not conquer them through combat, but by example. This elaboration of the classical/pacific themes manifested in the earlier masque is a response to the dominant royal policy of the time, aptly demonstrated by the recent peace treaties with France and Spain, and *Oberon* continues the probing of hostile and militant behaviour initiated in the *Barriers*; for example, the aggressive, albeit playful, satyrs of *Oberon* are shown to be self-serving and self-defeating. So far I have been explaining the poet's distancing of this masque from a chivalric discourse in terms of King James's political preferences, yet this rhetorical and textual strategy must also be explained in terms of Jonson's personal taste. As a poet, Jonson was not attracted to romantic medieval myths and legends, and it is often remarked that his corpus of work reveals a lifelong cultivation of classical models; his vitriolic poem 'An Execration upon Vulcan', written in the 1620s, amply displays his scorn for tales,

> Of errant Knighthood, with the Dames and Dwarfs,
> The charmed boats, the enchanted wharfs,
> The Tristrams, Lancelots, Turpins and Peers,
> All the mad Rolands and sweet Oliveers.
>
> (*Underwoods*, XLIII)

And in the *Barriers* Merlin declares that 'deeds / Of antique knights' are no longer suitable examples for a young prince to follow, because the present age has different tasks that need to be met and to which a chivalric code is largely irrelevant.[29] Furthermore, in the induction to *Bartholomew Fair* Jonson scorns the use of fabulous and mythical material in drama, as part of a covert attack on Shakespeare's *The Tempest*. Given the classical models of Horace, Martial and Lucian that Jonson pursued in his verse and drama, it is reasonable to assume that the demands of a classical discourse promoted by the King would more readily provoke a positive imaginative response than those of the myth of chivalry. Richard Helgerson has even gone so far as to suggest that the evocation of chivalry in the *Barriers* is anti-chivalric, anti-militaristic and anti-aristocratic; this may be overstating the case, however, and I would suggest that Jonson's opinion of the value of the chivalric myth is rather more complex.[30] For example, Drummond records Jonson's assertion that, 'For a heroic poem ... there was no such ground as King Arthur's fiction'.[31] It seems here that Jonson recognised that chivalric material may be suitable for epic or heroic poetry and, certainly, the chivalric masques are heroic in nature as they are concerned with princely strength and virtues. Rather than being 'anti-chivalric' then, Jonson saw the value of a reconstructed myth of chivalry as he presented it in the *Barriers*; this masque clearly rejects the nationalistic jingoism that often accompanied the celebration of Prince Henry by other poets, but in both the *Barriers* and *Oberon* the chivalric virtues of fortitude, loyalty and faith are recognised and reascribed to a domestic context where industry, trade and prudence are valued.

The yoking of classical and chivalric myths can also be seen in the sets for both the *Barriers* and *Oberon*. Henry's revival of chivalry in the first masque is equated with his revival of ancient British architecture and it is King Arthur in the *Barriers* who first suggests the connection:

> that by the might
> And magic of his arm he may restore
> Those ruined seats of virtue and build more.
>
> (ll.83-5)

Yet Arthur is not heralding a simple return to medieval or gothic architecture that we might expect to accompany a renaissance revival of medieval themes. Henry's project is a restoration of both classical and gothic building styles, and the set of this masque is distinguished by classical porticoes and triumphal arches. The importance of this 'new' architecture to the Prince is adduced by the fact that he does not appear to the court in the conventional grove or bower, but in St George's Portico and framed by a significant style of architecture combining both classical and gothic traditions. This is a departure for masque, and may well have been the result of Henry's own directions; in this respect Roy Strong comments: 'We are looking at one of the major statements which the Prince was never able to bring to fulfilment because of his death: the introduction of classical renaissance architecture to England'.[32] As I have already suggested, this new style of architecture, however, is not purely classical. Jonson's collaborator in the court masque, the designer Inigo Jones, created visual images of a form of ancient British architecture reflecting the combined traditions of the chivalric masques' discourse. The first scene of the *Barriers* presents a mixed view of Roman ruins, some derived from engravings, some from sketches Jones made when he visited actual monuments. Among the identifiable ancient buildings are the Pyramid of Cestius, the Temple of Antoninus and Faustina, and the Arch of

Titus; a decayed Great Britain is presented in terms of a *Nova Roma*. Gothic architectural features are superimposed on this classical cityscape indicating the intervening centuries between ancient Rome and renaissance London; alongside Trajan's Column there is a castle, with a crenellated tower and Romanesque features. St George's Portico lies at the heart of this architectural synthesis, and in choosing to be seated within it for the opening of the masque Henry proclaims his aspirations to be the legitimate successor of the two traditions and divinely sanctioned heir to both eras of the island's history. A similar combination of architectural and historical traditions can be seen in *Oberon*, although this time they are even more directly associated with the person of Prince Henry, in terms of his costume as well as the masque set design. Jones's extant designs for Henry's costume feature classical buskins and a tunic in the same style, embellished with baroque frills and lacework; the juxtaposition is repeated with Henry's classical helmet adorned by a luxuriantly baroque plume of feathers. Jones's design for Oberon's palace also illustrates this unique combination of styles that marked so many of the cultural displays of the early Stuart period. Oberon's palace is set among rough rocks and includes gothic turrets recalling fortified medieval towers. Out of the top of the palace, however, rises a Palladian dome decorated with obscure figures and a very similar palace is featured in the masque following *Oberon, Love Freed From Ignorance and Folly* (1611). Designs for the gardens surrounding Richmond palace echo this combination of the classical and the gothic, where classically proportioned walks and parterres are interrupted by a craggy grotto.[33] J. Alfred Gotch's early work on renaissance architecture and Mark Girouard's study of the country house also demonstrate that new buildings of this period were distinguished by plans that uneasily combined traditional medieval features with a developing classical fashion in architecture, and that there were attempts to update older houses by embellishing them with classical features. There is no doubt that these attempts at synthesis were not always aesthetically successful, but it does suggest that the early Stuart period was very much on the cusp between late-medieval England and renaissance Britain.[34] Having examined the provenance of the myths appearing in the chivalric masques, and the ideological motivation behind Jonson's distinctive moulding of them, I intend next to support my conclusions thus far with a close textual analysis of the *Barriers* and to track the signs of Jonson's analysis of monarchical government, with its attendant glories and dangers.

Reading the chivalric masques

The *Barriers'* mission of integrating and adapting potentially oppositional state mythologies is perceptible from the outset with the appearance of the Lady of the Lake, who is both classical nymph and Arthurian dame; in case we miss the double significance of her iconography she spells it out for us:

> What nymph I am, behold the ample lake
> Of which I am styled, and near it Merlin's tomb,
> Grave of his cunning, as of mine the womb.
>
> (ll.7-9)

Although she declares that King James's realm far outshines Arthur's Britain, she also regretfully draws attention to the fact that the house of chivalry is in decay:

> her buildings laid
> Flat with earth that were the pride of time,
> And did those barbarous Memphian heaps outclimb;
> Those obelisks and columns broke and down
> That struck the stars, and raised the British crown
> To be a constellation; shields and swords
> Cobwebbed and rusty; not a helm affords
> A spark of lustre ...
>
> (ll.35-42)

These lines are given a double meaning by the ingenious poet who, simultaneously, manages to feed the potentially conflicting aspirations of Henry and James, for while they may be interpreted as an elegy for the decay of militant chivalry, they also ironically comment on the eventual outcome of all military victories. Moreover, it is possible to extrapolate from this reading a consistent view of militancy permeating this masque, and Jonson's *oeuvre* as a whole; in the *Barriers* Jonson questions the belief of military heroes, such as his own Sejanus and Marlowe's Tamburlaine, in the unassailable strength of their own position, culminating in a claim to usurp even the gods themselves. At the zenith of his career Sejanus expresses his bloated ego with the line, 'At each step I feel my advanced head / Knock out a star in heaven!' (V.viii). (Although they belong to different dramatic genres, Sejanus shares with *Volpone*'s Mosca an unbridled delight in his apparently more than human capacities.) While Jonson makes the folly of such claims apparent, both in this masque and in his earlier Roman play, by overstretching hyperbolic rhetoric beyond its limits, there is also a chilling quality attached to a self-regard that consumes all other considerations. Although Sejanus and Tamburlaine share a certain charisma that we admire, and that other characters in the plays find hard to resist, these overreachers are ultimately destroyed by the wheel of fate, and as they are crushed they finally experience their moral nemesis. Hindsight invests the boasts of Sejanus and Tamburlaine with dramatic irony; we know that although they may be powerful and wealthy beyond belief, they will eventually die, and their ephemeral achievements be forgotten and decay. In my view, a similar dramatic irony can be detected in the speech by the Lady of the Lake, and the hyperbolic description of 'arcs triumphal ... outstriding the colossus of the sun' is ironically undermined by the images of decay that Jonson has already used to describe the house of chivalry.

The Lady of the Lake's speech, ending in an almost hysterical hyperbole to lost valour, is counterpointed by Arthur's calm announcement of himself. He has been translated into the star Arcturus, 'Such the rewards of all good princes are'. Pointedly, Arthur's eternal status is linked not with his prowess as a warrior, but with his record as a good king. Furthermore, Arthur's eternal divinity explicitly contrasts with the images of decay and death that have been previously associated with military heroes and combat; the juxtaposition of these images powerfully suggests that, while military spoils are to be honoured, they crumble with the passage of time, whereas a more peaceful approach to kingship concentrating on domestic policy brings a lasting reward. Arthur reminds the court that James has united the British Isles, just as he himself had in an earlier time: 'Merlin's mystic prophesies are absolved / In Britain's name, the union of this isle, / And claim of both my sceptre and my style' (ll.75-7); the mythical Arthur is definitively linked with a conservative domestic policy rather than with a financially extravagant foreign policy, contributing to an image of a nation strong in peace, that could be lauded, rather than dismissed as cowardly and weak. Thus, Jonson deliberately sets up Arthur as a royal precedent legitimating King James's controversial policies.

Arthur then summons 'thy knight / Preserved for his times, that by the might / And magic of his arm he may restore / These ruined seats of virtue, and build more' (ll.82-5). This knight is, of course, Prince Henry/Meliadus who has yet to appear in the masque, and it is significant that instead of exhorting the knight to military virtue, Arthur describes the heroic task of creating a new kind of architecture, a labour requiring a princely strength and associated with national prosperity and peace. Jonson reascribes chivalric attributes and virtues to the domestic forum, implying that there are worthy and challenging occupations for a prince at home, which are of greater value and importance than the ephemeral glory of foreign battle. In attempting this task of restoration, Henry's/Meliadus's name will rank with those of the Arthurian knights of the Round Table, 'Tristram, Tor /

Launc'lot' and he will also attain an eternal status, 'His name / Strike upon heaven, and there stick his fame!'. Jonson attempts to integrate knightly prowess and fame with domestic achievement, to produce an image of a nation that can take pride in its own strength and prosperity, without resorting to the often futile glamour of foreign combat.

In order to aid Meliadus in his heroic task, Arthur calls on Merlin:

> awake
> The learned Merlin; when thou shut'st him there,
> Thou buried'st valor too, for letters rear
> The deeds of honor high and make them live ...
> For arms and arts sustain each other's right.
>
> (ll.101-7)

Clearly, Merlin fulfils the poet/philosopher role that Jonson tried to carve for himself and bestowed on his dramatic characters, Virgil and Horace, and these lines represent an example of the many instances in his work as a whole where Jonson trumpets his aspirations and his right to act as a moral advisor to those in power. Jonson's model philosopher/poet not only advises his ruler, but also records his deeds for posterity, thereby performing an important political function that serves both poet and monarch. In proclaiming Merlin's importance here, Jonson effectively demonstrates the fruitful 'consociation of offices' between poet and king that he famously described in *Discoveries* (ll.81-91). Moreover, Merlin asserts that not everyone can be a king, and by implication, not everyone can be an advising philosopher/poet:

> Call forth the fair Meliadus, thy knight;
> They are his fates that make the elements fight,
> And these but usual throes when time sends forth
> A wonder or a spectacle of worth.
> At common births the world feels nothing new;
> At these she shakes: mankind lives in few.
>
> (ll.120-5)

Again, these lines mirror a sentiment recorded in *Discoveries* (l.3017) that was, in fact, one of Jonson's favourite tags, '*Solus rex, aut poeta, non quotannis nascitur*', which may be loosely translated as 'kings and poets are not born every year'. Clearly, the elitist implication here is that the multitude should allow themselves to be guided by their wiser leaders, and, in fact, Merlin/Jonson goes on to guide precisely the masque audience and readers as to how they should interpret the masque's confusing messages about the value of the chivalric ideal, 'What place is this so bright that doth remain / Yet undemolished? or but late built O, / I read it now: Saint George's

Portico!' (ll.130-2). The typically Jonsonian imperative to read the masque well is stressed, and Saint George's Portico is presented as a symbol of the rewritten chivalric ideal. This portico is both associated with the mythological feats of England's patron saint, and, as an edifice 'late built', represents the task of peaceful achievements laid out for Prince Henry. Effectively, the symbol of the portico seeks to integrate what appeared to be the conflicting cults of Arthurian chivalry and Augustan classicism, through its titular connection with the chivalric St George and its deliberate aping of the columned portico found in classical architecture.

So far I have been suggesting the ways in which the *Barriers* enacts a tactful *rapprochement* of the potentially conflicting myths cultivated by King James and Prince Henry respectively, yet one of Jonson's main contributions to the masque form is the creation of a space within it for the articulation of the poet's concerns, and in the *Barriers* it is clear that he is not merely attempting to reconcile conflicting royal ideologies, but also to present his own view of the values that are essential for good government. As I have already suggested, Jonson's vision of the ideal body politic entails a strong ruler advised by wiser men, who concentrates on building up the domestic economy. This is borne out by the list of kings presented to Meliadus as instructive models of good kingship, because Jonson demonstrates that the military achievements of individual monarchs always depends on a strong home economy built up by their predecessors. Edward III is such a king, 'This was he erected first / The trade of clothing, by which art were nursed / Whole millions to his service, and relieved / So many poor...' (ll.185-8). These lines foreground the wider social aspects of promoting the domestic economy and suggest a model of responsible rule that strikingly contrasts with Merlin's indictment of the chivalric myth (of which he, nevertheless, is a part) as a frivolous, antiquated and irresponsible code on which to base an ideal of kingship. Pre-empting Jonson's later scornful appraisal of chivalry in 'An Execration upon Vulcan', Merlin dismisses,

> deeds
> Of antique knights, to catch their fellows' steeds,
> Or ladies' palfries rescue from the force
> Of a fell giant, or some score to unhorse.
> These were bold stories of Arthur's age;
> But here are other acts; another stage
> And scene appears; it is not since as then:
> No giants, dwarfs, or monsters here, but men.
> His arts must be to govern and give laws
> To peace no less than arms.

(ll.159-68)

Moreover, those past kings who appear to have been motivated by the gothic chivalric ideal are described in the vaunting language that I have already mentioned; for example, Edward I lets forth 'rivers of blood / Of infidels', burgeoning to a field of blood, 'And marches through it with Saint George's cross' (ll.231-3). Similarly, the Black Prince, 'flowed out like a sea' upon the French troops, 'Or like a fire carried with high winds, / Broad and spreading...' engulfed the enemy (ll.261-4). We know exactly what Jonson thought of this type of Marlovian language as he notes in *Discoveries* (l.962), 'the Tamerlanes and Tamerchams of the late age, who had nothing in them but the scenical strutting, and furious vociferation, to warrant them to the ignorant gapers'. In my view, Jonson deliberately employs this distinctive style of language in his description of these militarily victorious kings, so that the masque audience or reader would readily associate them with the dramatic character of the over-reacher, the tyrant who is always ultimately destroyed. Furthermore, he does not need to state precisely, and dogmatically that Edward I, the Black Prince and Henry V all eventually met their deaths, man's ultimate fate, and that their ephemeral conquests were eventually claimed by other nations, because this moralising and ironic implication customarily accompanied such boasts and vaunting language – the masque audience was already in possession of this knowledge, gleaned from watching and reading the tragedies of blood that had been so popular in the past. In summary then, the main thesis of the *Barriers* is that the 'arts of peace' are also great acts and a public stage where the monarch can demonstrate his royal virtue; in this way Jonson rewrites the chivalric ideal, transferring its energy, motivation and moral force to the exercise of home government.

The list of exemplary monarchs predictably ends with King James himself, and the Lady of the Lake exhorts Meliadus/Henry, 'This is he, Meliadus, whom you / Must only serve and give yourself unto, / And by your diligent practice to obey / So wise a master, learn the art of sway'. As well as attempting to resolve potential conflict by integrating opposing mythical traditions, this masque also underscores the royal hierarchy which James surmounts. Pointedly, the Lady of the Lake declares that it is the Prince's duty to defer to the King and to learn from him the art of government, in readiness for the time when he will become the monarch; in the light of Roy Strong's analysis of the implicit challenge Henry posed to his father we may read these exhortations in the masque as an attempt to curtail temporarily Henry's ambitions and to put a stop to his incipient rivalry with his father, the King. The masque then moves on to the barriers themselves, and Merlin's announcement that Meliadus is ready for combat stirs Chivalry, who welcomes this resuscitation of knighthood. Merlin, however, yet again qualifies this eulogy, and insistently emphasises that the chivalric ideal needs to be recast to suit the present time:[35]

> Nay, stay your valour; 'tis a wisdom high
> In princes to use fortune reverently.
> He that in deeds of arms obeys his blood
> Doth often tempt his destiny beyond good.
>
> (ll.393-6)

And, in his closing speech, Merlin clearly demarcates 'cares in government' as the fitting concern of the King, leaving military exploits to less important members of the royal family. This is the kind of socially responsible approach to kingship that will make Britain the 'Mother of nations'.

One of the more notable aspects of the chivalric masques is that they stage an attempt to bridge the implicit gap between the King's real and idealised selves by reaching out of their symbolic fictions to the real King seated in the audience.[36] We have seen that in the *Barriers* Prince Henry adopts the role of Meliadus and is contained within the fiction of the masque, yet that fiction is violated by a direct reference urging Meliadus to emulate, 'Royal and mighty James'. Similarly, in *Oberon* the text reads:

> Melt earth to sea, sea flow to air
>   And air fly into fire,
> Whilst we in tunes to Arthur's chair
>   Bear Oberon's desire,
> Than which there nothing can be higher,
>   Save James, to whom it flies:
> But he the wonder is of tongues, of ears, of eyes.
>
> (ll.220-6)

In his seminal work, *The Jonsonian Masque*, Stephen Orgel interprets this move from the fiction of the masque out to the real King in the audience as a breach of artistic unity because the fictions of these masques do not establish a sufficient link between Meliadus/Oberon and King James.[37] The major difference between these and other masques lies in the fact that other masques do point towards the King but in his *metaphorical* capacity as a divine influence rather than as an individual seated in the audience; however, it may be that rather than labelling these masques as failures, it is possible to suggest that they represent an attempt to negotiate between the King's real and imagined selves and to link them in masque. This is a typical strategy of the chivalric masque, that is, calling up binary oppositions, but recasting the terms so that they move towards integration. Here, James is shown to be man, father, and divine ruler, and potential discrepancies between these roles are glossed over. Thus, what Orgel terms a breach of artistic unity in these masques is made more explicable by attending to the political motivation behind the direct address to the King. Moreover, this particular rhetorical strategy is also prompted by Jonson's attempts to develop the masque form; both the *Barriers* and *Oberon* represent an important transitional stage in the masque's evolution, straddling the earlier static, emblematic masques, and the later dramatic masques. *Blackness* clearly belongs to this earlier type, and is literally an emblematic presentation to the court of certain philosophical ideas; Jonson tells us how the daughters of Niger expressed emblematic motifs:

> Here the tritons sounded, and they [the masquers] danced on shore, every couple as they advanced severally presenting their fans, in one of which were inscribed their mixed names, in the other a mute hieroglyphic expressing their mixed qualities. Which manner of symbol I rather chose than imprese, as well for strangeness as relishing of antiquity, and more applying to that original doctrine of sculpture which the Egyptians are said first to have brought from the Ethiopians.
>
> (ll.236-42)

This masque represents a kind of animated iconography, whereas later masques such as *A Challenge at Tilt* (1613) and *The Irish Masque at Court* (1613/14) indicate a significant move towards the dramatic. In these masques the antimasque is well developed and increasingly dominant, allowing for chaos and disharmony in contrast with the masque proper, which represents values that resolve conflict. Thus, in *The Irish Masque* the Gentleman's song is part of a magical transformation that turns Patrick, Donnel, Dermock and Dennis from quarrelling buffoons into graceful courtiers. Yet experience had informed Jonson that the antics of quarrelling buffoons are of greater dramatic interest than the harmonious dancing of courtiers; thus, the *Barriers* and *Oberon* are partly shaped by his experimental insertion of dramatic content into a traditional emblematic form. For example, the unruly satyrs in *Oberon* resemble the Irish yokels, but the masque also incorporates the kind of emblematic elements that characterise *Blackness*, particularly in the presentation of Oberon in a chariot drawn by two white bears; Oberon does not speak or move out of the chariot but is presented as a living tableau. Moreover, the direct references to James in the chivalric masques involve an engagement with the audience that may be read as part of the masque's movement away from the emblematic towards the dramatic; for, the attempt to make a connection between events on the stage and the audience watching them is also a feature of Jonson's dramatic comedies.[38] For example, in the induction of *Bartholomew Fair* the scrivener addresses the audience and offers them a contract whereby the price of their ticket determines the legitimacy of their criticism of the play. Thus, the audience is encouraged to develop a detached critical awareness of the play and yet to feel intimately involved with it. Similarly, in the chivalric masques, the direct address to the King seated in the audience is a movement from stage to audience and may be seen as an attempt to encourage the courtly spectators to become involved and connected with the events depicted on stage (as ideally they were supposed to be) rather than being passive, unthinking viewers of the court spectacle.

While both the *Barriers* and *Oberon* constitute an intermediate stage in the masque's evolution, *Oberon* has an even greater dramatic emphasis than its predecessor; moreover, the unruly satyrs and bawdy comedy in this masque suggest that we may point to it as the first court entertainment to provide a dramatic antimasque.[39] In keeping with his lifelong cultivation of classical models, the type of amusing rogue that Jonson developed for both his antimasques and comic drama can be traced back to Lucian and Aristophanes. Jonson defines Oberon's harmonising power by setting it against the disruptive satyrs who are inclined to anarchy, and Aristophanes' plays feature the same kind of self-serving rogues; although we may enjoy the energy and imagination of such characters, their pursuit of self-interest is potentially damaging to the state. While the appearance of the masque causes the mavericks of the antimasque to vanish with a striking demonstration of royal power, the disruption caused by the antimasque figures is never really dealt with. Similarly, Jonson's dramatic rogues appear to elude the mechanics of justice; for example, although Volpone is sentenced by the Venetian authorities, he re-emerges in the epilogue to revel in the applause of the audience. Jonson was clearly attracted to characters exhibiting an anarchic impulse, possessing the energy and cunning that allows them to evade the orthodox rules binding the mass of people. We find such characters not only in the antimasques and comic drama, but also in Jonson's Roman tragedies; here, the self-serving rogues of the antimasque are placed within a dramatic context, where their anarchic impulses are played out to the bitter end, with dire consequences. Both the chivalric masques and the Roman plays employ historical myth as a context for these villains, but the first is essentially comic, as legislative authority is asserted in the masque and puts an end to the anarchy of the antimasque, whereas the Roman plays are largely tragic precisely because the ruling powers themselves are shown to be corrupt and a danger to civic peace and order. To some extent, the different perspectives of masque and Roman tragedy on political power and its relationship to anarchy are imposed by generic requirements; dramatic tragedy is grounded in the dissolution of social and family bonds, whereas the masque's *raison d'être* is an emphatic assertion of a structured and hierarchical society controlled by the monarch. Yet while such generic requirements are an imposition on the writer, they may also be seen as allowing Jonson to explore dual and potentially conflicting experiences of political authority; after all, he was a writer who alternately suffered and prospered according to the dictates of monarchs. At the closing stage of this chapter I want to continue this exploration of the connection between the chivalric masques and the Roman plays; I have argued that these masques constitute an early example of Jonson's attempt to dramatise the form, and it is precisely the later, dramatic antimasque that incorporated values counterbalancing the dominant discourse of masque. Perhaps more importantly, in terms of Jonson's personal agenda as a poet, his exploitation of historical myth in both the chivalric masques and the Roman plays also allows for a covert commentary on the political practices of the Jacobean Crown and the personal *mores* of the court.

Harsh and unendurable government – the Roman plays

Jonson also put to use the newly acquired renaissance knowledge of and fascination for classical culture in his drama for the public stage; themes similar to those in the chivalric masques run through the Roman plays, *Poetaster* (1601), *Sejanus* (1603) and *Catiline* (1611), although in the drama these themes are presented in a fundamentally different manner. The issues on which the earlier part of this chapter has focused can be loosely summarised as regal authority and its legitimation on the basis of a divinely ordained genealogy. Both the *Barriers* and *Oberon* fully exploit absolutist theories of divine right to justify the Stuart monarchy, but Jonson does not slavishly reproduce the chosen discourse of the Crown; this would, in any event, have been an impossible achievement because the Tudor synthesis of classical and chivalric myths broke down under pressure from the competition between King James and Prince Henry, leading to a polarisation of royal myth. As we have seen, in seeking to reintegrate these myths into a single tradition, Jonson manipulates them to qualify and comment on each other, provoking a dialectical exploration of what constitutes successful domestic and foreign policies. This shaping of myth is essentially optimistic, as the reconciliation of competing histories is shown to result in national peace and affluence, whereas in the Roman plays Jonson exploits classical myth to reveal that these are impossible goals in an environment where authority is rooted in corruption.

Although the philosophical idealism of the chivalric masques impinges on historical reality as they reach out of themselves to address the King in the audience, the historical element is overshadowed by the fantasy of the larger fictional structure. In the Roman plays, by contrast, historical realism is foremost, but as in the chivalric masques Jonson does not slavishly follow historical precedent. To suggest that Jonson manipulates his historical source material for the purposes of moral instruction is to place him firmly within the humanist literary tradition, a tradition that embraced history as a morally instructive text that no educational programme should omit.[40] Yet because the workings of history do not always witness the defeat of vice and the triumph of virtue, the poet was required to interpret history, that is, to select those facts that would be most supportive of the educative aim of his work, or 'truth of argument' as Jonson himself termed it (HS, IV, p.350). For *Sejanus* Jonson turned to the work of the Roman historian Tacitus, often regarded as the most truthful of Roman historians, and *Catiline* draws extensively on Sallust's *The Conspiracy of Catiline*. As J.W. Lever has evocatively shown us, the connection between Sallust's epitaph on Roman civilisation and much of renaissance Europe is frighteningly clear; perhaps most significantly, both cultures witnessed the increasing centralisation of power in the hands of an individual or individuals, resulting in the concentration of great wealth and influence in a small privileged group.[41] Certainly, this is the context in which the court masque evolved and it was the court's lavish display of wealth that partly lead to criticisms of excess and degeneracy prior to the Civil War. Jonson's satirical epigrams reveal that he was only too conscious that the idealism of masque was often far from the reality of the court and courtiers; these verses are poetic daggers, glinting with wit and satirically sharp; 'On Court-Worm' suggests the flavour of other epigrams with telling titles such as, 'To My Lord Ignorant', 'On Something that Walks Somewhere', and 'On Sir Cod the Perfumed':

> All men are worms: but this no man. In silk
> 'Twas brought to court first wrapped, and white as milk;
> Where afterwards, it grew a butterfly:
> Which was a caterpillar. So 'twill die.
>
> (*Epigrams*, XV)

The topical play *Catiline* shimmers with this vision of the Jacobean court as a place of excess and shallow display:

> Her [Rome's] women wear
> The spoils of nations in an ear
> Changed for the treasure of a shell,
> And in their loose attires, do swell
> More light than sails, when all winds play:
> Yet are the men more loose than they.
>
> (I. 555-60)

In a similar vein, the historian Sallust had recorded earlier the corrupting influence of wealth on the Roman state:

> To the men who had so easily endured toil and peril, anxiety and adversity, the leisure and riches which are generally regarded as so desirable proved a burden and a curse. Growing love of money, and the lust for power which followed it, engendered every kind of evil. Avarice destroyed honour, integrity, and every other virtue, and instead taught men to be proud and cruel, to neglect religion, and to hold nothing too sacred to sell ... At first these vices grew slowly and sometimes met with punishment; later on, when the disease had spread like a plague, Rome changed: her government, once so just and admirable, became harsh and unendurable.[42]

Joseph Allen Bryant Jr, however, has carefully charted Jonson's departures from Sallust and analysed their effects on the play. The most important alteration Jonson makes to his source material is the implication of Caesar in Catiline's plot, and it is useful to quote Bryant here on the effect of aligning Caesar with Catiline:

> What it does is to set Caesar and Catiline on the one hand against Cato and Cicero on the other, thus altering the balance of the original narrative and converting a relatively simple story of one man's plot into a study of the complex struggle between such forces as make for disintegration in a state and those forces which tend to preserve integrity. The original narrative is still there, of course: Cicero still detects the villainy of Catiline and leads the way to his removal and destruction. But in the context that Jonson gives it, this action is roughly analogous to a sick man's detection and treatment of an annoying symptom while the fatal cancer eats patiently away at the vital organ ... The reader cannot begin to understand either *Catiline* or *Sejanus* unless he is willing to bring a knowledge of history to the play and look before and after what he finds there.[43]

What is fascinating and daring in Jonson's manipulation of Sallust's account is that he is willing to implicate a 'divinely appointed' ruler in the corruption and deceit consuming Rome. The extreme danger of this strategy is apparent when we remember that James I claimed just this type of classical autocracy, and that Jonson's reflections on Caesar in this play could well have been read as implicit criticism of the reigning monarch. Jonson turns from the ideal possibilities of masque and allows a darker vision to conjure up a more pessimistic view of the modern renaissance state, and in this respect the Roman plays share common ground with the antimasque. Jonson's turn to Roman history in these plays is not only explicable in terms of his neo-classical sympathies, but also as part of his self-appointed role as social and moral arbiter, for the utilisation of ancient history allowed Jonson to comment obliquely on contemporary affairs, to underscore similarities between declining Rome and Stuart Britain. Critics who have examined the issue of censorship in the period tend to agree that this was a common practice in drama for the public stage, and that the reliance on ancient history was a protective measure against charges of sedition, for playwrights could always claim that they were commenting merely on the ancient world rather than on contemporary Britain. Elizabethan and Jacobean audiences, however, were skilled in drawing analogies and reading allegories, so the similarities between the two cultures were probably apparent to many.[44] Yet this protective mechanism did not always function efficiently, as Jonson found when he was arraigned for treason and popery in *Sejanus*.[45] Both the masque and the Roman tragedy present possible worlds that are an exaggeration of the state as it is; one is philosophically optimistic, the other horrifyingly dark. In both genres Jonson uses historical myth to comment upon the present, but in one case it is to extol, in the other it is to criticise the Jacobean state. In fact, as I have already suggested, the chivalric masques and Roman tragedies can be read together, as parts of a dialogic enquiry into the nature of authority.

Poetaster, *Sejanus* and *Catiline* constitute a dramatic triptych, each play presenting a view of the state that progressively darkens. Just like the court entertainment, *Poetaster* is a comedy precisely because the forces of chaos are controlled by divinely appointed structures of authority. Potential chaos is figured by the temporary reign of 'poetasters' and 'tumblers' such as Demetrius, Crispinus and Tucca; they attack the virtuous poet Horace and reign in their own antimasque-like inversion of the 'natural order', their warped values becoming the new prevailing order. This inversion of established structures is mirrored by a group of poets led by Ovid, who impiously impersonate the gods, and stultify their moral sense through an orgy of excess. That poets, who have previously proved themselves as honourable, should behave in this way is doubly alarming, and suggests that the larger degenerate atmosphere in which they exist is poisoning their better selves. Moreover, there is a disturbing connection between the poets in *Poetaster* and the sycophantic versifiers of *Sejanus*, who do not merely flout 'natural order', but are also intimately involved with its corruption. On reflection, we may conclude that in these plays Jonson was exploring the advantages and possible pitfalls of the court poet, a role on which he was embarking at the time of his composition of this public drama. In *Poetaster*, Jonson continually asserts through Horace that poets are the arbiters of society, a characteristically Jonsonian belief that crops up throughout his work, but perhaps most obviously in *Discoveries*.[46] In *Poetaster* the structure of justified authority is figured by the relationship between Caesar and Virgil, in which the poet's wisdom guides the Emperor's ineffable power, a function also adopted by Merlin in the *Barriers*. In this first Roman play, Jonson clearly projects an idealised image of his own role and influence, and implies that even absolute power should be conditional upon the wisdom of philosopher poets. At the close of the drama the combined influence of Caesar and Virgil exerts itself; Crispinus is cured of his 'filthy' words, Tucca recognised for the charlatan he is and Ovid banished. In this comedy right asserts itself over disorder, poet and Emperor are vindicated.

There is no such fruitful association, however, between poet and state rulers in *Sejanus*. Together with the people of Rome, the artists are silenced. Some of them, like Afer, even become flattering, sycophantic rhetoricians who help to nurture tyranny. The audience is encouraged to identify with those who are silenced and alienated from the powers controlling this nightmarish centralised state, and this identification is achieved by making the audience party to criticism of the regime by political commentators such as Sabinus. Jonson's conversations with Drummond reveal him to have been a superstitious man, so it is reasonable to assume that when he shows a state where the gods are ignored, he is intent in presenting a community in extreme moral decay. The most impious character of all is Sejanus himself, who makes a striking contrast with the masquers of an ideal platonic world, assiduously observing all the rites due to their representative of God on earth, King James. In *Sejanus* the deification and idolatry of political rulers seems to be a gross parody of legitimate religious experience and respect for divinely appointed rule, pointedly symbolising the extreme corruption of Rome. And yet, early modern discourse was often characterised by an ability to rewrite descriptive terms surrounding specific actions according to the current moral imperative; hence, greed and waste may be rewritten as liberality and magnificence. Accordingly, Jonson's audience may well have recognised that the homage paid to Sejanus and Tiberius, was not that distanced from the homage paid to the current monarch, and that this play constituted a veiled criticism of court flattery and extravagance. Rome itself, however, retains a sense of the old moral order, and her integrity is reasserted as the mob expresses an impersonal and merciless justice, and literally tears Sejanus limb from limb; however, while this symbolic and shocking act may be cathartic is some way, the renascent power structure represented by Tiberius is shown to be just as tainted as that of Sejanus. As a play, *Sejanus* confronts us with the conviction that power corrupts and the Machiavellian dictum that the skills needed to exert and retain authority are incompatible with normal virtue. Despite the destruction of Sejanus, the Emperor remains the sole ghastly manipulator of Rome but, importantly, the

Roman state still exists, although in a corrupt and parodic shadow of its former glory.

As the tragic sequel to *Sejanus*, *Catiline* represents the Armageddon of the super civilised state. In this play, the Roman state visibly disintegrates, a fact far more dangerous that even the nightmarish atmosphere of spies and treachery that marked Sejanus's control of Rome; whereas Sejanus is one corrupt individual, a weak Rome is prey to a thousand ambitious Catilines. It rests with Cicero to save Rome from Catiline, but this can only be a limited salvation, as an ordinary freedman, with more than ordinary political and rhetorical skills, directs the course of Rome. Any concept of her divinely appointed destiny has vanished together with any notion of a divinely appointed leader. Rome has been abandoned by the gods, and history tells us the sad fate of the declining state. The bleak vision of *Catiline* is the tragic, inverse image of the harmonious movements of chivalric masque, representing the glorious peace of the British nation directed by King James, its divinely appointed governor, and in *Oberon* Silenus salutes the King in an allusion to the Roman alternative shadowing the harmonies of masque:

> He's such a king as they
> Who're tyrans' subjects, or ne'er tasted peace,
> Would in their wishes, form for their release.
>
> (ll.264-6)

In Jonson's Roman plays the discordant antimasque elements of chaos and inversion of the recognised moral order expand, parody and devour the masque values of order and harmony. This process is most striking in the case of Afer, when the poet-philosopher becomes state toady. In attempting to reconcile the radically opposed views of authority and government that we find in the Roman plays and in the court masques, we may conclude that the emphatic idealism of masque compels the invocation of its binary opposite in drama as a logical extension of Jonson's exploration of state authority. It is undoubtedly significant that the last of these Roman plays was performed in 1611, the same year as the court performance of *Oberon*, the masque, which I argue, witnesses the first proper antimasque. Thus, the evolving antimasque appropriates those elements of disintegration that featured in the Roman plays, and juxtaposes them with the royal assertions of masque, producing a dialectic upon the nature of authority, upon which the main part of this book focuses. We may choose to see the Roman play and the antimasque as one half of a binary opposition, and the masque as the other; the antimasque, however, always falls short of the complete disintegration of the state as it is replaced by the masque in the progression of a single court entertainment, but no such divine intervention is available for Rome. Finally, it is instructive to remember that while Jonson had enjoyed the golden life at court, like many of the Roman poets he wrote about, he too had been imprisoned for murder, debt, treason, recusancy and Popery.

Reconciling Rome and London

Predictably perhaps, because of the very different handling of similar themes in Jonson's chivalric masques and Roman plays there has been some confused discussion on the topic of whether Jonson was a republican or a monarchist.[47] Clearly, it is clumsy to think of Jonson in such crudely polarised terms, as the plays and masques are linked by a number of factors, not least the use of historical myth. Instead of claiming Jonson for either the political left or right I would rather echo Graham Parry who seizes on the poet's ingenuity when he writes, 'One must admire the versatility and energy of a talent which maintained a variety of poetic roles so skilfully for so long'.[48] Many critics would, no doubt, assert that Jonson must have unreservedly supported his King because the chivalric masques culturally legitimate the monarchy in their representation of James as the descendant of the Trojan Brutus and the chivalric King Arthur, yet it is vital to remember that the requirements of the genre within which Jonson worked are at least as important as any personal support or criticism of the monarchy. This fact must partly explain how Jonson was able to criticise and praise the monarchy in the Roman plays and masques respectively. I am convinced that Jonson was more interested in examining the state than he was in defining it in any simple or monolithic way; moreover, the masques' function of panegyric is to improve as well as to praise, and they encourage the state to pursue a middle way, thereby undeserving of the charges of meretricious flattery that they have elicited. The eulogy of the chivalric masques and the criticism of the Roman plays are the complementary methods by which Jonson attempts to reform the state from within; while it castigates tyranny, the drama certainly does not advocate democracy, and although the masque celebrates monarchy it does not collude in the exercise of tyranny. Jonson endorsed a view of kingship where the monarch functions as a public servant, and his subjects perpetually enjoy 'the sweetness of his sway' (*Oberon*, 1.263). The emphasis Jonson placed on this belief is visible in *Discoveries* when he writes:

> A prince is the pastor of the people. He ought to shear, not to flea [flay] his sheep; to take their fleeces, but not their fells. Who were his enemies before, being a private man, become his children, now he is public.
>
> (ll.1550-4)

This view of the ideal absolutist and paternal ruler is embodied in the figure of Caesar in *Poetaster*; the Emperor has no inclinations towards tyranny and is happily advised by other wise and skilful men, Jonson shows us that poets are such men. We find the same concept of the benevolent monarch in the masque; here this view of kingship is placed within an abstract, philosophical context where James is the 'Roi Soleil' giving life to all his subjects. In opposition to the ideal monarch is the portrait of a hideous tyrant such as Tiberius; yet Jonson is no advocate of democracy, and the most chilling part of his Roman trilogy is *Catiline*, where the state is on the brink of lawlessness and collapse, lacking a strong leader to reinstate order; a similar crisis occurs with the mob's frenzied dismemberment of Sejanus. Despite the terror and corruption that distinguishes the state, Rome under Sejanus and Tiberius does retain a sense of order, even though that order is directed by the whim of a few warped individuals. Given the numerous statements in *Discoveries* endorsing the concept of rule by divine right, one must assume that in Jonson's world view tyranny is a political risk inherent in the government of a modern nation; furthermore, the warping of divinely appointed government into the tyranny of *Sejanus* and *Catiline* is brought on a nation by itself, as a result of its own impiety and moral decay. A view of divinely influenced and absolute power responsibly exercised on earth seems to encapsulate Jonson's concept of what the prevailing power structures of Stuart Britain should be; these are the fundamental and consistent political beliefs underlying the very different genres of chivalric masque and Roman drama.

Notes

1. In his essay, 'The Nature of Jonson's Roman History' (in, Kinney and Collins (1987), 207-22) Philip J. Ayres has carefully charted Jonson's use of and digression from historical sources in his Roman plays with the conclusion that Jonson is primarily a dramatist rather than an accurate historian.
2. See Sidney's 'The Defence of Poesy', 102-48 (p.107), in Dutton (1987).
3. See Sir Thomas Elyot's, *The Boke Named The Gouernor* 1531: 1883, 53-98. On the debate surrounding historiography at this time see Rackin (1990), 1-39.
4. Bacon asserts that historical fact should be clearly separated from its author's subjective opinions: 'I cannot likewise be ignorant of a form of writing which some grave and wise men have used, containing a scattered history of those actions which they have thought worthy of memory, with politic discourse and observation thereupon ... which kind of ruminated history I think more fit to 'be placed among books of policy ... than amongst books of history' (Bacon, *The Advancement of Learning* (1605: 1988), 71-8).
5. Whigham (1984), 40-2.
6. Strong (1967), 102-8 (104). Further references to this article are given after quotations in the text.

7. For a full account of the Woodstock entertainment see Yates (1957), 4-25 (12).
8. Peele, quoted by Strong (1967), 102.
9. Jonson's interest in European literature and thought is displayed in *Love Freed From Ignorance And Folly* (1611) and *The Vision of Delight* (1617) with allusions to Rabelais and the European tradition of the grotesque; see Chapter 3 of this book and Prescott (1984), 407-30. John Peacock comprehensively details Inigo Jones's debt to Italian and French sources for the sets of *Prince Henry's Barriers* and *Oberon The Fairy Prince*: Peacock (1995), 68-81, 282-93, 295-6.
10. For a fuller account of James's disgust at the crowds on his accession day see Goldberg (1983). *Julius Caesar* (1599), written by Shakespeare four years before James's ceremonial entrance into London, seems to suggest aptly the physiological impact of a leader's extreme distaste for the 'great unwashed' over whom he rules:

> As he [Caesar] refused it [the crown] the rabblement
> shouted and clapped their chopped hands, and
> threw up their sweaty night-caps, and uttered
> such a deal of stinking breath because Caesar
> had refused the crown, that it had almost choked
> Caesar; for he swounded and fell down at it.
>
> (I.ii.244-9)

11. Smuts (1987), 84. Further references to this book are given after quotations in the text.
12. For a study of the competition between King James and Prince Henry see Strong (1986), 71-85.
13. Jonson himself projected King James's anger at public commentary on his policies and actions in the masque, *News from the New World Discovered in the Moon* (1620).
14. Perhaps the most famous example of Elizabeth's anger at such an incident is her fury on discovering, in 1579, the Earl of Leicester's secret marriage to Lettice Knollys. See Neale (1934: 1979), 248-9.
15. There are a number of studies on the iconography surrounding Queen Elizabeth; e.g. Heich (1975); Yates (1975); Levin (1989); Strong (1987).
16. Miles (1986) suggests that the *Barriers* mirrors a 1588 masque written by King James for the Scottish Court. I have found a fragment of a masque that fits this description but its date is not certain. This masque is in the pastoral mode, but also includes chivalric sports such as tilting at the ring. King James's appropriation of aspects of the chivalric myth in this masque was probably prompted by the desire to establish his nation's strength, and to counter the effects of the factional feuding that had plagued Scotland. By 1610, however, the Arthurian chivalric myth was no longer suitable for an older British King who aspired to be Europe's mediator and peacebroker. See, Tait (1901).
17. *Tethys' Festival*, in Spencer and Wells (1967).
18. This accords with the explanation offered by Stephen Orgel for the move from the chivalric *Barriers* to the pacific *Oberon*: 'The martial side of the Prince's nature apparently disturbed King James, who vetoed a similar project for next year' (Orgel (1965), 67).
19. 'The style of kings,' – this phrase seems to have summed up a very important concept for King James, who used it to highlight the divine nature of a king on

earth, who in turn is answerable only to God. Just as we hope for justice and mercy from God, the earthly king should dispense such qualities to his people. A sonnet composed by James illustrates his vision of the 'stile of kings':

> God gives not Kings the style of Gods in vaine,
> For on his throne his Scepter do they swey:
> And as their subiects ought them obey,
> So Kings should feare and serve their God againe.

Sonnet prefacing the first book, *Basilikon Doron* (1599: 1969). Further references to this edition are given after quotations in the text.

20. Jonson himself represented King James as a model monarch who ruled with moderation, justice and mercy. See, for example, 'To King James' (*Epigrams*, XXXV):

> Who would not be thy subject, James, t'obey
> A prince, that rules by example, more than sway?
> Whose manners draw, more than thy powers constrain.
> And in this short time of thy happiest reign,
> Hast purged thy realms, as we have now no cause
> Left us of fear, but first our crimes, then laws.
> Like aids 'gainst treasons who hath found before?
> And than in them, how could we know God more?
> First thou preserved wert, our king to be,
> And since, the whole land was preserved for thee.

21. See note 12.
22. Strong (1967), 105.
23. See, for example, Ascham (1570: 1974), 68-9.
24. The lines quoted in the text also refer to England's union with France and Holland in a league organised by Henri IV of France to protect small Lutheran states from the growing aggression of the Roman Catholic Emperor; some months after the masque's performance, however, Henri IV was assassinated and the leaderless league dissolved.
25. As I have noted, although King James and Prince Henry appropriated classical and chivalric traditions respectively, for the Tudors, classical and native traditions were synthesised with the legend of the 'Pax Romana'. The birth of Christ was supposed to have occurred during Augustus's reign, which was significantly a time of universal peace. Holinshed writes, 'But whether for this respect or for that it pleased almighty God so to dispose the minds of men at that present, not onlie the Britains, but in manner all other nations were contented to be obedient to the Romane empire...'. For further detail see, Jones (1961). Shakepeare's play, *Cymbeline* may have been written around 1609/10 and so be contemporary with Jonson's chivalric masques of 1610/11. It is arguable that, like the *Barriers* and *Oberon*, this over-plotted play also sets out to synthesise 'classical' and 'British' historical myths. Such a similarity suggests that the nature of Britian's history was a topical issue exercising writers and audiences at this time.
26. This project of unification was objected to on several fronts; see my comments on *Hymenaei* in Chapter 3 for more detail on this.
27. Regarding the presence of neo-classical satyrs and folkloric fairies in *Oberon* Peacock (1995) notes, 'Since Jonson planned this masque as a serious pastiche of

98 Ben Jonson's Antimasques

a Greek satyr-play, the classicising design for the satyrs is appropriate, the quaint medievalising design for the fays is not at all' (p.141). Peacock is quite right to notice the presence of these two traditions in the masque, but rather than viewing the presence of the fairies and their costumes as an incoherent detail at odds with the neo-classical impetus of the masque, I would rather suggest that this masque, like *Prince Henry's Barrier's*, manifests an attempt on the part of Jones and Jonson to reconcile potentially oppositional mythic traditions and their political implications.

28. For more detail on Jonson's etymology, see Riggs (1989), 175.
29. Merlin's dismissal of the old chivalric ideal is demonstrated in the lines:

> No, let his actions speak him, and this shield
> Let down from heaven, that to his youth will yield
> Such copy of incitement: not the deeds
> Of antique knights, to catch their fellows' steeds,
> Or ladies' palfries rescue from the force
> Of a fell giant, or some score to unhorse.
> These were bold stories of our Arthur's age;
> But here are other acts; another stage
> And scene appears; it is not since as then:
> No giants, dwarfs or monsters here, but men.
> His arts must be to govern and give laws
> To peace no less than arms.
>
> (*Barriers*, ll.157-68)

30. Helgerson (1992), 42-3.
31. *Conversations With William Drummond*, in Parfitt (1988).
32. Strong (1986), 149.
33. For the designs for the gardens of Richmond Palace, see Strong (1986), 97-8. For illustrations of Oberon's palace and costume, see Strong (1986); Peacock (1995), 68-81, 282-93, 295-6.
34. On the mixed traditions in architecture see Gotch (1901); Girouard (1978); Evett (1990).
35. The rewriting of the chivalric ideal in this masque may be described as part of Jonson's wider rhetorical practice of *imitatio*. In *Discoveries* (ll.3057-73) he writes that, 'The third requisite in our poet, or maker, is imitation, to be able to convert the substance, or riches of another poet, to his own use ... Not to imitate serviley, as Horace saith, and catch at vices, for virtue: but, to draw forth out of the best, and choicest flowers, with the bee, and turn all to honey.'
36. The renaissance theory of the King's two bodies involved the monarch's dual status as mortal man and divine ruler. James's often less than decorous behaviour seems to have underlined a discrepancy between these two roles, or the King's real and ideal selves. The chivalric masques attempt to gloss over this discrepancy by reaching out from the masque where the monarch's divine power is figured, to the real monarch seated in the audience.
37. Orgel (1965), 89-91.
38. See, for example, the prologues to the 'comical satires': *Every Man In His Humour* (1598), *Cynthia's Revels* (1600), *Poetaster* (1601). At the opening of *Cynthia's Revels*, three of the boy actors squabble over who is to speak the prologue. In the course of their bickerings they articulate certain criticisms that

were levelled at popular drama. Firstly, (as in this case) that it was often acted by boys, 'rascally Tits', and secondly, that the theatre merely reworked stale plots and jests. These criticisms, however, are undermined when the critics are foregrounded as vain dilettantes. The prologue asserts that the poet's muse looks for those 'who can both censure, understand, define / What merit is'. In effect, this opening section presents the audience with a range of arguments for and against popular theatre, and places *Cynthia's Revels* within the context of contemporary drama. The audience is encouraged to make a discriminating judgement of this play, both on its own terms, and as an example of dramatic practice.

39. The antimasque of *The Masque of Queens* (1609) is often cited as the first example of the form, but it is a perfunctory prelude to the masque proper, and does not possess a developed subtext of dissent that features in later antimasques. Thus, I consider the antimasque of *Oberon* (1611) to be the first example of the antimasque proper, as its vicious satyrs and sylvans debunk the complacent orthodoxies of pastoral drama and poetry.

40. Ascham wrote that history 'Could bring excellent learning and breed staid judgment in taking any like matter in hand'. Similarly, Sir Thomas Elyot asserted, 'Surely if a noble man do thus seriously and diligently rede histories, I dare affirme there is no study or science for him of equal commodotie and pleasure, havynge regarde to every tyme and age'. Ascham (1570: 1974), 129; Elyot (1531: 1883), 1:91.

41. Lever (1971), 60. Sallust describes the Roman state as corrupted by money, greed and immorality, which promoted great wealth for a few and poverty for the many. This inequality bred the discontent that Catiline was able to exploit for his attempted coup, which, if successful, would have transformed the Republic into a tyranny. See Sallust (78BC-67BC: 1963), 151-228.

42. Sallust, 181.

43. Bryant (1954), 265-77 (p.271).

44. In the preface to his translation of *Orlando Furioso* (1591) Sir John Harrington usefully summarises the way in which analogy and allegory were understood in his day: 'The Ancient Poets have indeed wrapped as it were in their writings diverse and sundry meanings, which they call the senses or mysteries thereof. First of all for the literall sense ... they set downe in manner of an historie the acts and notable exploits of some persons worthy of memorie: then in the same fiction, as in a second rime and somewhat more fine, as it were nearer to the pith and marrow, they place the Morall sence profitable for the active life of man, approving virtuous actions and condemning the contrarie. Many time also under the selfe same words they comprehend some understanding of Naturall Philosophie, or sometimes of politik government, and now and then of divinitie: and these same sences that comprehend so excellent knowledge we call the Allegorie, which Plutarch defineth to be when one thing is told, and by that, another understood'. Strong (1984), 28-9.

45. Patterson (1984) describes a drama of dissent that employed 'functional ambiguity' in order to avoid censorship. However, she points out that in times of political stress this rhetorical practice could break down and result in the Crown taking steps to censor popular drama and its producers. Patterson's thesis is useful for understanding why Jonson was officially admonished for *Sejanus*.

46. 'He which can fain a Commonwealth (which is the Poet) can governe it with

Counsel, strengthen it with Lawes, correct it with Judgements, informe it with religion and Morals', *Discoveries*, ll.1034-7, in Parfitt (1988).
47. This debate is usually distilled into the question of whether Jonson's court entertainments are subversive or act to contain subversion. For the first position, see Dollimore (1989), 27; for the latter, Orgel (1965).
48. Parry (1981), 40

3
Present occasions and removed mysteries: the topicality of the antimasque

Thus far in this book I have argued for the pervasive presence of irony in Jonson's work, both offsetting and complementing the more orthodox praise of much of his poetry and masque. This is not to say that Jonson was hypocritically sniping at the Crown while presenting himself as its servant, or that he unequivocally celebrated this institution and its leading members, but rather to argue for a Jonsonian dialectic that has multiplicity and the availability of plural meanings as its distinguishing characteristics. It is this multidimensional aspect of Jonson's work that currently concerns many critics and, indeed, the holding in tension of complementary and contradictory perspectives in a single work is Jonson's great achievement as a literary artist. Bruce Thomas Boehrer's recent and impressive book chimes with many of my thoughts on Jonson, and he emphasises the semiotic fluidity of much of Jonson's writing. In relation to Jonson's notion of authorship, Boehrer writes, 'I would emphasize the simultaneity and interdependence of these various notions of authorship, each of which arises as a solution to a problem generated by one of the others, while in the process generating difficulties of its own, which render the previous attitudes indispensible in their turn'.[1] While it may seem erroneous to equate dialectic with the multiplicity argued for by Boehrer, the dialectic of masque, based on the presence of irony and panegyric, works to the same multivalent effect, resulting in a *conditional* endorsement of the monarchy.

I have described the *The Masque of Blackness* as a definitive example of the early masque form lacking a potentially ironic antimasque, yet still possessing those elements of ironic implication that the poet would go on to develop into the satirical antimasque. The delicate suggestion of subtextual meaning in *Blackness* is inflated in the developed antimasque, transforming the historical and formal significance of the masque entertainment as a whole. In this chapter I am especially interested in examining the historical pressures that shaped the antimasque, and will relate specific masques to their precise historical moments in order to demonstrate that the form is deeply implicated in its place and time. The pressures of history, however, are not solely responsible for the evolution of the antimasque, and I go on to consider the formal and artistic factors contributing to the development of the antimasque; moreover, the theoretical implications arising from this step in my argument demand an examination of the masque's reception at court. This is a particularly difficult issue and involves an interrogation of my claims regarding the ironic content of the masque from the perspective of its reception; for, if the antimasque destabilised the assertions of masque and the court, how did it remain acceptable to the court, the very body sponsoring and watching these entertainments? A further question arises regarding the expansion of the masques, because if the ironic content develops at the expense of the masque's orthodoxies, the court entertainment as a whole is thrown out of balance, and its pretensions to an intellectual dialectic jeopardised. This position also involves certain dangers for the poet, who becomes vulnerable to accusations of sedition. Certainly, the masques I examine in this chapter witness the expansion of the antimasque at the expense of the masque, thereby destabilising the traditional shape of the form and reshaping its semiotic structure.

Exponents of Cultural Materialism and New Historicism have expressed great interest in the masque as a form emphatically produced by its sociopolitical circumstances, and as I mentioned in the preface, many New Historicists take the view that the masque's aestheticisation of political realities into transcendent, supernatural truths pre-empts any controversial debate over the status of the monarchy, as it appears impossible and fruitless to question an hegemony directly resulting from divine, and consequently, natural law.[2] It should be clear by now that I consider this totalising and ultimately conservative view of masque to be an incomplete analysis, and it is typified by Stephen Orgel's summary of the relations between masque and *Realpolitik*:

> Masques were essential to the life of the court; their allegories gave higher meaning to the realities of politics and power ... a deep truth about the monarchy was realised and embodied in action, and the monarchs were revealed in roles that expressed the strongest renaissance beliefs about the nature of kingship and the obligations and perquisites of royalty.[3]

Orgel seizes on the obvious signification of masque, and ignores some of its subtler qualifications of the hegemonic view. While I may have reservations about Orgel's perspective on the interconnections between literature and history, his notable achievement has been the rescue of Jonsonian panegyric from the common charge of hypocritical flattery through his role in the development of a New Historicist viewpoint that was primarily concerned with the masque's occasion and ideological function rather than with the author, and by avoiding the trap of imposing anachronistic critical assumptions onto Renaissance culture. Whereas for earlier critics the masque's topical nature branded it as ephemeral and thus trivial, New Historicists locate the form's interest and value chiefly in its occasional nature, and in rejecting a view of literature as the passive mirror of history, New Historicism fully implicates literature in history and *vice-versa*. This challenge to the New Critical emphasis on the universal nature of literature involves an engagement with the occasional and specific political context of the masque, which is no longer treated as an embarrassment. As Jean E. Howard declares:

> Literature is *part* of history ... Rather than erasing the problem of textuality, one must enlarge it to see that *both* social and literary texts are opaque, self-divided and porous ... This move means according literature real power ... literature is an agent in constructing a culture's sense of reality.[4]

Viewed as social and ideological practice, texts are no longer condemned to be monolithic; as there are different historical pressures and ideological viewpoints (since ideology aims at, but can never achieve homogeneity), a text may be multiple and give voice to conflict and contradiction. It is this very multiplicity that gives rises to the dynamism that I have already argued for in Jonsonian masque, producing texts that are dialectic rather than simply ironic or panegyrical.

Unlike Orgel, Howard's version of the New Historicist view of the relationship between history and text allows for the dissenting irony of the antimasque and does not necessarily demand the triumph of royal propaganda at the expense of the ironic antimasque, alerting us to the fact that New Historicism itself may perhaps be more accurately described as a practice rather than as a consistent theory, although, as we have seen, it does rest on certain identifiable principles. It is probably too sweeping to apply Howard's thesis of multiplicity to all texts, but it seems particularly appropriate to masque, a form heavily laden with the pressure of monarchical propaganda. Another key American New Historicist, Stephen Greenblatt, suggests that the greater the pressure of propaganda in any text or event, the more likely it is to throw up alternative readings questioning the extreme absolutism of its discourse, and he articulates this idea in his acclaimed essay, 'Murdering Peasants':

> Identical signs can be interpreted as signifying both the radical irony of personal dissent and the harsh celebration of official order. This uncanny convergence is not, I would suggest, the theoretical condition of *all* signs, but the contingent condition of certain signs at particular historical moments,

moments in which the ruling elite, deeply threatened conjure up images of repression so harsh that they can double up as images of protest.

While Greenblatt is not discussing the dialectic between antimasque and masque here, but the double valuation of certain signs, the semiotic instability in both cases is similar; I suggest that the sheer weight of official propaganda in the masque necessarily implies satire as its binary opposite, a rhetorical version of what is popularly understood as Hegelian dialectic. As the influential Cultural Materialist critic, Jonathan Dollimore, emphatically asserts, although in support of a rather different point, official propaganda and its subversion are inextricably interrelated, as a subversive discourse must first be articulated before it can be silenced.[6]

The quotation from Greenblatt underscores another important historical factor for the development of the antimasque in addition to socio-political context, that of personal dissent. Infamously, Poststructuralism is characterised as erasing the role of the author, the reader's role becomes paramount, as 'there is nothing outside of the text'. However, this is at least a caricatured rendition of much recent literary theory, and it seems to me that within the bundle of theories that dominate contemporary criticism (such as Poststructuralism, New Historicism and Cultural Materialism etc.) there is a place for the 'author' as long as we remain wary of ascribing to the author complete authority over the text; yet while he/she may not have final authority or control over the meanings of a text, the personal agenda of the author is not to be ignored. This is particularly crucial in the case of Jonson, who promoted himself as an author with a clear moral programme, and insisted on his personal integrity as the guarantor of his poetry. With this critical *caveat* in mind, we can begin to consider the antimasque as an arena in which the poet produced the irony of dissent, questioning the official view of contemporary events. From the questioning implications of early masques such as *Blackness* and *Hymenaei* (both lacking a formal antimasque) we can trace a clear line of development towards the mature form of the antimasque which gives voice to more thematically and structurally developed strategies of dissent.

In an attempt to demonstrate my claims regarding the historicity of the masque and antimasque I will examine briefly three masques ranging through a period of ten years from 1606 to 1616. These particular masques lend themselves for consideration as they chart the rise of the antimasque out of latent implications of dissent that thread through the early masques. Earlier in this book I have argued for viewing the antimasque of *Oberon* (1611) as the first real example of the antimasque, which experiences an expansion that tellingly comes to a close with the end of King James's reign in 1626. The inflated domination of the antimasque is perhaps at its zenith with *The Masque of Owls* (1624), an entertainment constituted by an antimasque alone, the satirical consumption of the masque apparently complete; yet this particular entertainment is anomalous in that, although it was staged for Charles I, it was not performed at court. Moreover, at this point in time Charles was not yet King, so perhaps the absence of the monarch and the courtly context, with its wondrous sets, are factors partly explaining the disappearance of the masque on this occasion, and it may be argued that *Owls* is not actually a court masque in the strictest sense, and is thus the exception proving the rule that antimasque is always pursued by masque.

The masques that I examine in terms of their relationship to history are *Hymenaei* (1606), *Love Restored* (1612), and *Mercury Vindicated from the Alchemists at Court* (1616). *Hymenaei* is chosen as an example of the early court entertainment lacking an antimasque, but permeated with a muted irony similar to that in *Blackness*; *Love Restored* represents an important shift in the form, in that it is the second of Jonson's court entertainments after *Oberon* to be dominated by an antimasque which is overtly satirical on topical matters – the satire in this instance would appear to be directed at the detractors of royal policy, but a close reading reveals an ironic discourse pointing to the necessity for internal reform of the court. Finally, I discuss *Mercury Vindicated* as an example of the last stage of the antimasque's growth; this masque addresses directly behavioural modes at court, both above and below stairs. The in-depth analysis of particular masques in Chapter 4 continues my emphasis on the historical topicality of the form, and extrapolates this chapter's assertion of historical pressures shaping the politically dynamic and dialectic court entertainment.

Hymenaei

The notorious events surrounding the marriages of Frances Howard need little rehearsal, and *Hymenaei* was composed by Jonson to celebrate her first wedding to Robert Devereux, third Earl of Essex. Jonson's later embarrassment at having composed a masque in celebration of a marriage that scandalously collapsed is borne out by the fact that the folio text omits any mention of its precise occasion, except to label it as a marriage masque – somewhat unusual for a form known for its occasional nature. The happy couple were thirteen and fourteen years of age respectively, and while we may find their youth shocking, it is a clear indication that this was a dynastic marriage with a political motivation. Primarily, King James fostered this union as a way of healing the breach between two powerful families; in 1601 the second Earl of Essex was executed for attempted rebellion and the

Howard clan had largely contributed to his downfall. It seems that the King assumed that marital union between the parties would promote political accord within the court, although in retrospect we can see that this hope was more than a little naive, especially given the state of the King's own marriage. Moreover, hostility between the two families was fanned by religious differences; the leading members of the Northampton-Suffolk-Howard connection were known and accepted as Catholics, or at least as Catholic supporters, whereas the second Earl of Essex had championed a policy of militant Protestantism. King James's hopes for union were not merely limited to this marriage, but extended to the conjunction of Scotland and England and his aspiration to the title of King of Great Britain. However, this marriage of nations was not so easily achieved, arousing hostility from both the Scots and the English; despite the fact that in 1604 Francis Bacon failed to persuade Parliament to accept this union, James's exhibited an early sign of his high-handed and autocratic dealings with that institution and issued a proclamation announcing his assumption of the title 'King of Great Britain'; this was accompanied by the issue of new coins with appropriate emblems and the inscription, 'Quae Deus conjunxit nemo separet' – a ringing evocation of the marriage vow. Objections on both sides of the border were based partly on religious and legal differences; the Scots Presbyterians disliked James's attempted introduction of an Anglican style of worship in Scotland, while the English Parliament resented his efforts to replace a cherished system of common law with a Scots civil law based on Roman legal practices.[7]

This, then, was the historico-political moment at the time of *Hymenaei*'s performance. D.J. Gordon has definitively shown that the masque's trope of union draws extensively on Platonic and Pythagorean philosophy, although it may well be difficult for a contemporary reader to understand how Jonson was able to incorporate such apparently disparate elements as esoteric philosophy, classical customs, national and familial politics into a unified form, but as Gordon suggests:

> To relate present occasions to sublime and removed mysteries, to link Whitehall, the marriage of the Earl of Essex with Frances Howard, James and his cherished plan to the union of man, the universe of God: this for Jonson was the art of masque.[8]

The masque itself is modelled on a Roman marriage ceremony, and opens by bidding 'all profane away', and presents the symbolic figure of 'Union' as 'Mistress of these rites'. Hymen then acclaims a source of light, whose 'beams / Grace Union more than ours', somewhat predictably this source of light is 'The king and priest of peace'. Those accustomed to Jonsonian panegyric will immediately recognise King James in this representation, the priest of peace championing union against the objections of profane dissenters. The title 'priest of peace' pointedly refers to one aspect of James's project for national union: spiritual uniformity, which meant, in practice, an anglicising of Scottish worship. This particular masque subtext is reinforced by Leah Marcus's assertion that the classical altar dominating the set, was intended to be nothing less than the altar of the Anglican Church, the kind of church decoration James wished to impose on Scottish Presbyterians, but which they believed to be corrupt and corrupting.[9] Unlike Scottish religious dogma, Anglican theology acknowledged its basis in the Church of Rome, but in the belief that it had purged old practices of any vice, which, in any event, should be respected for their antiquity. As I have already mentioned, while this masque promotes an Anglican style of worship, it also upholds James's favoured system of Scottish civil law rooted in Roman law. Marcus tells us that, 'the King was known to prefer civil law over common law as more orderly, predictable, and useful in foreign affairs' (p.9). It is in this specific context that we can read the masque's symbolic figures of Reason and Order triumphing over the unruly and destructive humours and affections, elements that would later find a home in the antimasque. With such political occasions in mind we can see that a number of factors favoured Jonson's selection of Roman marriage rites as the setting for his masque; the emblematic impact of this framework is amply demonstrated by Reason, who informs us that Juno, the deity presiding over the rites, is also known as 'Unio', an anagram of her more commonly known title; Jonson's achievement here is the filtration of pressing political issues through a classical and philosophical trope based in Platonic and Pythagorean numerology – political expediency becomes divine necessity.

Thus far, it may well appear that my analysis of *Hymenaei* shows it to be little more than rigid state propaganda, yet I have suggested that this masque is typical of earlier entertainments in its latent implications of dissent; a close reading of the text throws up subtle discrepancies that fail to accord with the main thrust of its argument. In a verse to which I have already referred, Hymen sings:

> Tis so: this same is he
> The king and priest of peace!
> And that his empress, she
> That sits so crowned with her own increase!
>
> (ll.80-3)

These lines possess an unintended dramatic irony; Princess Mary, born in 1605, was a sickly child who, although still alive at the time of this masque's performance, died in the following year of 1607, and Princess Sophia, born in 1606, died the day following her birth. So the masque's celebration of Anne's fertility is shadowed by infant sickness and mortality. Despite the fact that Prince Henry was well at this time, Charles was reputed to be a sickly and slow child, although again ironically, it was Prince Henry, the darling of the nation, who was cut off in the prime of his youth in 1612. This history of infant sickness, relevant at the date of the masque's performance, and the later deaths force us to call into question the other assertions of the verse that James is 'The king and priest of peace'. We cannot fail to reflect that just as James's and Anne's hopes for the fruitful 'increase' of their family were disappointed, James's hopes for the spiritual and legal union of Scotland and England were thwarted. Jonson's assertion of 'truths' that are patently at odds with the historical context of the masque gives rise to other spiralling contradictions, destabilising royal propaganda and opening the way for a dialectic between royal claims and an historically based criticism of them.

While it seems quite obvious that *Hymenaei* celebrates a dynastic marriage, it seems equally obvious that some of the masque's language is particularly inappropriate for the occasion. At the end of Hymen's opening speech he declares, 'And view two noble maids / Of different sex to Union sacrificed'; albeit that these words accord with the masque's assumption of Roman ritual, they resonate with more contemporary implications; I have already shown how the masque's trope of union extends from this particular marriage to the union of politically hostile families at court and it is to this 'union' that the married couple are 'sacrificed' – individual preferences are subsumed by the requirements of *Realpolitik*. Given their age, it is hardly surprising that the couple are 'noble maids', and it was customary for such a young bride and groom to live separately with their parents until they were older. In these circumstances, the masque's numerous sexual references seem painfully tactless, for example, Reason explains the altar in the following terms:

> Nor is this altar but a sign
> Of one more soft and more divine,
> The genial bed, where Hymen keeps
> The solemn orgies, void of sleeps;
> And wildest Cupid, waking hovers
> With adoration twixt the lovers.

(ll.147-52)

Jonson's own notes to the masque demonstrate that such language has a clear classical precedent, and yet it may seem incongruous to the contemporary reader that the poet equates a religious altar with a bed witnessing the 'adoration' of Cupid. Perhaps Jonson is making an ironic point here, implying that this is what marriage should be like for the newly wed couple, rather than the dynastic yoking of two children.

The second part of *Hymenaei*, held on the night following the masque, is a jousting at barriers. Opposing sides support Truth and Opinion, and in the debate between these two figures Jonson continues his questioning of marriage as an institution, and more specifically, of the Howard-Essex marriage. In this debate Truth supports the married state, while Opinion champions the single life, but the audience must have experienced an acute difficulty in distinguishing between the two as they both appeared in the same costume signalling divinity and purity. Truth's arguments are often a reiteration of the sentiments expressed in the previous masque, whereas Opinion introduces some new ideas, so the jousting at barriers acts as an invitation to scrutinise the 'divine truths' of the earlier entertainment. Opinion radically challenges such 'truths', employing typically vivid and persuasive Jonsonian rhetoric:

> Untouched virginity, laugh out to see
> Freedom in fetters placed, and urged 'gainst thee.
> What griefs lie groaning on the nuptial bed?
> What dull satiety? In what sheets of lead
> Tumble and toss the restless married pair,
> Each offended with the other's air?
>
> (ll.685-70)

When Truth and Opinion look exactly the same, whom are we to believe? This problem of distinguishing correctly is made even more difficult when we remember the emphasis, running throughout Jonson's work as a whole, that appearances are often deceptive. Moreover, as we have seen, Opinion is given some very persuasive arguments sharpened with a satirical verve. Given that the masque and barriers are part of a wedding celebration one might assume that the poet urges us to concur with Truth, yet, as I have begun to suggest, this masque is not an unqualified celebration of marriage in all its symbolic manifestations. Conveniently, historical hindsight shows us that political pressures were at odds with individual preferences in this marriage, which ended in scandal and divorce in 1613, effectively bearing out Jonson's equivocation in this masque about the Essex-Howard union, and about marriage as an institution. Glancing at some of the poet's other statements on marriage, we may conclude that he would be more likely to agree with Opinion: he spent many years separated from his own wife whom he infamously described to Drummond as 'a shrew yet honest', and gives a blackly comic view of marriage in his satirical poem, 'On Giles and Joan':

> Who says that Giles and Joan at discord be?
> The observing neighbours no such mood can see.
> Indeed, poor Giles repents he married ever,
> But that his Joan doth too. And Giles would never
> By his free will, be in Joan's company.
> No more would Joan he should.
>
> (*Epigrams*, XLII)

So, despite the fact that the barriers result in Truth's favour, Truth is certainly not an unequivocal or clear-cut winner of the debate, but part of a wider discussion on marriage, focused in this instance on the Howard–Essex marriage; and this debate is part of the masque's process of contradiction that unsettles royal hegemony on the broader issue of union.

Love Restored

This masque was performed in 1612, a year of crippling dearth for the Crown; the financial crisis was further compounded by the death of James's supremely competent administrator, Robert Cecil, and with him died all hope for the Great Contract which would have ensured regular subsidies to James from Parliament in return for his surrendering of certain feudal rights. Cecil had attempted to resolve the financial problem with the imposition of 'Privy Seals', which were little more than forced loans, causing bitter resentment across the country, and many refused or were slow to pay. The economic embarrassment of the Crown was in painful contrast with the wealth of the City of London, which celebrated itself with a Lord Mayor's show entitled, 'Chruso-thriambos: The Triumphs of GOLD for the Honourable Company of Goldsmiths', an event which James doubtless found insulting, as the city in particular had shown great reluctance in contributing to the royal coffers.

Perhaps predictably in time of financial crisis, court entertainments were criticised for their costliness, and viewed as an unnecessary drain on revenue; this kind of criticism often merged with the widespread and outspoken Puritan attacks on masques, plays and country sports as occasions contributing to immorality.[10] King James sought to assert his authority against this criticism by placing such entertainments within royal sanction, a policy culminating in *The Book of Sports* of 1617. Here James proclaimed that a variety of sports were permissible on the Sabbath, and not blasphemous, as the extremist critics suggested. The royal assumption underlying this document was that if the state forbade such recreation, it risked provoking more dangerous forms of self-expression; through licensing revels and games, the Crown sought to protect and perpetuate the *status quo*.[11]

Added to the financial problems at court was hostility between English and Scottish courtiers; ill-feeling had intensified until it reached a crisis point in 1612. This year witnessed the infamous and violent quarrel between the Earl of Montgomery and Patrick Ramsay at Croydon races. The Englishman had struck the first blow, but it was widely believed that if the Scot had struck first, the incident would have exploded into a blood bath. Also in this year, the Scottish Lord Sanquhar arranged the murder of the English fencing master, Turner; the outcry was so great that a group of Scottish Lords who pleaded for Sanquhar's life could not move King James, who was only too aware that in order to maintain the stability of his position he had to be seen to maintain justice ruthlessly. Similar incidents appear to have sprung up everywhere at this time, demonstrating the jealousy and malice of the parties involved, and violent anti-Scottish feeling was common among the lawyers of the Inns of Court, as well as elsewhere. Events reached such a pitch that a Scottish court usher was forced to apologise to a lawyer whom he had injured when expelling him from the court at Whitehall, and the Scottish Murray family went as far as to murder a sergeant sent to arrest one of their number.

Love Restored is very different from *Hymenaei* in that the antimasque dominates the entertainment, and the masque appears to be tacked on, almost as an after thought. In this antimasque Jonson tackles the parsimony of Puritan critics of the Crown, and critics of royally sanctioned entertainment, as well as highlighting the poisonous hostility rife at court. These were all grave problems, and of an urgent topicality to the court and country, in contrast with the emblematic and philosophical emphasis of earlier masques such as *Blackness* (although, as we have seen, *Blackness* also has its topical aspects). Furthermore, *Love Restored* was the first masque that Jonson had written specifically for James; by this time Prince Henry had died and Queen Anne had hung up her dancing shoes. Given James's notorious taste for comic bawdy, the royal sense of humour should not be overlooked as a factor contributing to the nature and expansion of the Jonsonian antimasque.

The financial crisis of 1612 explains the modest scale of this masque; it cost a mere £180 to put on as opposed to the £1087 required to stage *Oberon* (1611). A further reason for the lack of spectacle in this entertainment was that Inigo Jones was occupied by designing another masque for Princess Elizabeth's wedding celebrations. We know that Jonson had his reservations about the spectacular nature of masque as a possible distraction from its philosophical essence, so it is no surprise that on this occasion he makes a virtue of necessity and exploits the lack of scenic effect to focus attention on certain philosophical threads running throughout the masque. The antimasque is somewhat unusual in that it opens parading its own artificiality; this may be viewed as a strategy endangering the court entertainment, as it underscores the ideological construction of the traditional masque vision and initiates a theme of self-reflexive criticism manifested in Plutus's disparaging comments on the frivolity and conspicuous consumption associated with masque.[12] Masquerado enters to proclaim that circumstances have prevented the performance, thereby implying that the court entertainment is a theatrical show rather than an extension of the reality of court life. He declares, 'A pretty fine speech was taken up o' the poet too, which if he never be paid for now, it's no matter; his wit costs him nothing'. These lines carry dual implications, first the wry humour of the poet who has perhaps not received payment in the ongoing financial crisis, and second, that in contrast with the usual trappings of masque (extravagant costumes, sets, etc.) his skill his literally priceless – it cannot be bought by himself or others; it is in this sense that his 'wit costs him nothing'. As Robin Goodfellow recounts his adventures trying to get into the masque, the splendour of masque is merely the sum of its parts, and these are broken down to be shown as meaningless externals. Against custom, Jonson does not allow such superficialities into his masque and they are kept off-stage, thereby flouting the trend for courtiers to indulge in costly displays devoid of any sound philosophical justification in the hope of winning favour and prestige.[13] In prioritising the poet's skill Jonson seeks to reform masque, however, it should not be assumed that in chastising excess, Jonson completely adopts the standpoint of Puritan critics. Plutus (disguised as Cupid) rehearses the well known moralising of Puritan rhetoric, and is initially seen as a figure of authority whose criticism often chimes with Jonson's views on the frivolity of masque. Yet, later on in the entertainment, Plutus is 'unmasked' by Robin Goodfellow and revealed to be nothing more than a hypocrite. As in the barriers of *Hymenaei*, there is an emphasis here on shape-changing and imposture, drawing attention to the difficulty of distinguishing true values from false ones, and highlighting Jonson's own equivocal stance on such matters. At his defeat Plutus growls, 'Alas! how bitterly the spirit of poverty spouts itself against my weal and felicity! But I feel it not. I cherish and make much of myself, flow forth in ease and delicacy, while that murmurs and starves'; like all true hypocrites, Plutus has tried to remove the excess of others in order to have it all for himself. As a country spirit, Robin Goodfellow is a wholesome antidote to the poisonous malice of Plutus, and he represents the honesty of country sports, the kind of festivities that critics like Plutus sought to abolish. Robin's geographical and moral distance from the court (he literally cannot get into it) and its corruption is surely significant and he is part of the masque's process of internal reformation, restoring it by imparting something of his rural integrity to a form which has become lost in its superficial excesses.

Love Restored seeks a *via media* between parsimony and meaningless display, polarised aspects of the same vice of greed. It powerfully suggests that this middle way can only be achieved with the aid of Love. The brief masque at the close of the entertainment presents Love and a vision of harmony:

> See, here are ten
> The spirits of court and flower of men,
> Led on by me, with flamed intents,
> To figure the ten ornaments
> That do each courtly presence grace.
> Nor will they rudely strive for place,
> One to precede the other, but
> As music in form them shall put,
> So will they keep their measures true.
>
> (ll.238-46)

Peace and prosperity will only be brought about when this harmony dispels the rivalling court factions; as we have seen this hostility is imaged by the conflict between Cupid and Plutus. The masque also seeks to heal over the divide between court and country, aptly demonstrated by the concerted attempt to prevent Robin Goodfellow from viewing the masque. The smooth lines quoted above are an example of what some critics term the masque's feebleness in verse and theme after the boisterous prose of the antimasque, but such a view fundamentally misunderstands the didactic thrust of this entertainment as a whole, for in this unusual masque the splendours of stage machinery have been stripped away leaving the masquers alone: they themselves must perform the 'motions' and not rely on elaborate machinery to create the miracle of masque. As the antimasque gives way to the masque there is an orthodox change in stylistic register and technique as vigorous prose becomes smooth verse, and conflict is erased by paeans to love, the royal virtue. Despite the usual transcendent language of the masque, Jonson offers a human solution to the crises of 1612, and in revealing the frailties of the court he implicates the King, because the court has become what it is under his leadership. With *Love Restored* Jonson appeals to the rational author of *Basilikon Doron* rather than to the lavish King who showered gifts on his favourites, and thus it is an entertainment that seeks to reform not only the court and the city, but also the King. The masque sets up a dialectic between Plutus's condemning view of ritual and sport and those like Masquerado who champion empty show, in this respect it is surely significant that in the absence of a masque Masquerado offer us a morris dance as a replacement. Neither extreme is acceptable, but an intermediary form of court entertainment, such as is attempted in this masque, can be a useful vehicle of didacticism and entertainment.

Mercury Vindicated from the Alchemists at Court

This masque was performed in 1616, a year of some note not only for the publication of Jonson's *Works*; scandal was electrifying the court and country with the trial of the Somersets. The tale has been told many times elsewhere, so I will merely rehearse the events; Frances Howard had successfully divorced the Earl of Essex and married Robert Carr, the Earl of Somerset. One of Somerset's close friends, Sir Thomas Overbury, voiced loud objections to the match and was imprisoned in the tower for his concern. Whilst there, Overbury died in mysterious circumstances that later came to light; the Somersets were accused of poisoning him. King James wanted the pair to plead guilty, thereby avoiding a trial that would drag his favourite and the court through a mire of scandalous rumour and speculation. However, the Somersets would not comply and the revelations of their trial shocked the prurient imaginations of the country. Mrs Turner, a confidante of Frances Howard, was said to have procured the poison from the quack Simon Forman. A list was obtained of court ladies who apparently used Forman's potions in their love affairs, but, tactfully, Lord Chief Justice Coke forbade the reading out of the list. Simultaneous with Somerset's spectacular fall from grace was George Villiers's mercurial rise as the court favourite. By 1617 Villiers had become an Earl in less than two years. His mother turned out to be a formidable matriarch, with the driving ambition to engineer brilliant marriages for even the remotest, most impoverished Villiers relations; and by 1616 she had become such a nuisance that she was sent away into the country. Aspiring courtiers soon realised the necessity of cultivating Buckingham, and those under his patronage soon filled the important government posts. To observing critics, Somerset's fall and Buckingham's rise seemed to illustrate graphically the immorality and greed of the court which respected the powerful *nouveaux riches* rather than ancient nobility.

Mercury Vindicated from the Alchemists at Court attacks the usual subjects of Jonson's satire, that is, greed, pretension, ambition, imposture and corruption. However, in focusing on these subjects at this time and in this context the masque also offers a critique of Buckingham's rise, his manipulation of the court and advancement of his own family. The chief protagonist of the entertainment is Mercury, who is tyrannised by Vulcan and forced to work against his nature. Thus the metamorphoses of this masque are unnatural; their perversion is signalled by the Cyclope who tends the fire torturing Mercury. As a one-eyed monster and slave of Vulcan, the Cyclope represents aberrant or even absent nature; he is part of the process of manipulating nature out of its natural shape.[14] Alchemy is a major trope for Villiers' rise, and this metaphor is exploited for its satirical potential because, traditionally, alchemy involved a transformation of irredeemably base metals into false gold.[15] Mercury introduces this metaphor with the exclamation:

> The whole household of 'em are become alchemists (since their trade of armour making failed them).
>
> (l.36)

James's pacific foreign policy meant that the aristocracy no longer distinguished itself in combat, but now achieved its position through court intrigue. The jostling for position and jealously guarded honour of a court that had no military outlet often resulted in duels and feuds. The antimasque reveals one court creature that thrived under the influence of Buckingham and his ilk:

> A master of the duel, a carrier of differences. To him went spirit of ale, a good quantity, with the amalgma of sugar and nutmegs, oil of oaths, sulfur of quarrel, strong waters, valor precipitate, vapored o'er the helm with tobacco, and the rosin of Mars with a dram o' the business, for that's the word of tincture, the business.
>
> (ll.132-7)

Precisely what is meant by 'the business' in this context is unclear, but it may be an allusion to the skill in intrigue and scheming that would be necessary for this 'master of the duel'. Unscrupulous ambition is contagious in this antimasque, even the below-stairs staff become involved in alchemy in the hope of future reward:

> A child o' the scullery steals all the coals for 'em too, and he is bid sleep secure ... For the pantry, they are at a certainty with me, and keep a tally: an ingot, a loaf or a wedge of some five pound weight.
>
> (ll.69-77)

The corruption of the court encourages corruption below stairs, and, indeed, G.P.V. Akrigg has shown that a large factor in James's ongoing financial crisis was the pilfering of servants.[16] However, this widespread corruption has more serious implications as it even challenges the King's position; Mercury declares that the alchemists,

> profess to outwork the sun in virtue and contend to the great act of generation, nay, almost creation.
>
> (ll.117-18)

Students of the masque will soon recognise the sun image as a common representation of the King and his power to transform vice into virtue, strife into peace, and to be the inspiring force of all life – an earthly simulacrum of divine authority. In championing those under his patronage, Buckingham challenges James's predominant position as the King who rewards with titles and offices; tellingly, Mercury condemns the creations of Vulcan as 'against the excellence of the sun and Nature, creatures more imperfect than the very flies and insects that are her trespasses and scapes'. Once again, the emphasis seems to be on imposture and the problem of distinguishing true from false creative power, the irony being that Buckingham himself is the King's creation. Thus, the antimasque acts as an urgent appeal for the restoration of Mercury's creative properties to James, and the reinforcement of courtly hierarchy where all are surmounted by the Sun King.

With the introduction of the masque Nature declares, 'How young and fresh I am tonight': she is in no need of the collaboration of alchemy to ensure her immortality. The masquers are urged to dance in harmony to prove that nature still reigns as mother. Love is the familiar invocation of masque, and perhaps in this short and jaunty masque Jonson suggests that Buckingham and his type could demonstrate more loyalty and love to the King and less to themselves.

In considering these three masques I have emphasised their historicity and how the weight of state propaganda found in masques such as *Hymenaei* gives rise to its satiric opposite. This can be seen as a further manifestation of the irony springing up in the discrepancy between the ideal and the real that I discussed earlier. In my view, Jonson exploits this problematic aspect of masque and develops it into the antimasque, such as we find in *Mercury Vindicated*. The historicity of the antimasque, however, is not confined to its mediation of state propaganda, but also relates to a considerable extent to the occasional and topical nature of the genre which tends itself to political comment and interpretation, whether or not this is favourable to the monarchy. The expanding antimasque seems to have been, in part, a response to those scandals that increasingly dominated the life of the Stuart court; for, if the poet is the moral arbiter of society, as Jonson often asserted, the onus is on him to underscore the errors of court and country in an attempt to reform them. Thus, a correlation may be detected between the perception of increasing degeneracy of the court, and the boldness of the antimasque's satirical content. However, as I emphasised earlier, the panegyric of masque is also corrective, so it needs to be explained in greater depth why the antimasque emerged as a distinct form and dominated the masque for a long and particular period of time. Scholars who are interested the ironic and satirical aspects of the antimasque often have to counter the question of why and how was such apparently subversive material acceptable to the court and King? As I hope is clear by now, I do not wholly accept the terms of this question, as Jonson was a poet who wished to reform from within, a project which is not compatible with subversion. Yet, this fact cannot gainsay the antimasque's ironic impetus; to return to the question outlined here, one answer can be found in King James's personal taste for bawdy humour, a taste which he apparently shared with Buckingham, and that was consequently fashionable at his court. Furthermore, the antimasque clearly responds to pressing issues of the day that Jonson wanted to tackle; yet these solutions cannot account completely for the growth and reception of the antimasque at court, which I hope to do in the remaining sections of this chapter.

To make readers understanders

I have already recapitulated the subversion/containment debate smouldering around the antimasque – Jonathan Dollimore's position is typical of the champions of subversion:

> The priority of masque over antimasque is reversed in order to collapse the former into the latter ... Sometimes a kind of poetic justice emerges from the dramatic 'antic' masque, but only as a perfunctory closure – that is, a formal restoration of formalist, providential/political orthodoxy after having destroyed its spirit.[17]

While the debate surrounding the antimasque has raged in the past, the conflicting methodologies appear to be at a stalemate, and the distinctions between them blurred. Leah Marcus, for example, apparently agrees with Dollimore's Cultural Materialist view of masque in suggesting that court artists, 'developed strategies for preserving their own "liberty", for saving their art from engulfment in the ethos of the court'. This largely accords with what I have said previously about Jonson's attempts to preserve his own critical 'voice'. However, at the same time as asserting the court artist's independence and integrity, Marcus sides with Orgel in suggesting that the main masque successfully diffuses the dissent of the antimasque and asserts the power and harmonious nature of the Stuart monarchy.[18] While providing a stimulating critique of Jonsonian masque, she fails to resolve these apparently conflicting views into a coherent theoretical position.

As I noted in the preface, Theodore B. Leinwand deplores the way in which this subversion/containment controversy has become petrified in monolithic and static, although contradictory, views of literature. His rejection of such critical polarities bears quoting again,

> Perhaps we can reconceive the binarisms of social process as other than conflict leading to one-sided victory. Compromise, negotiation, exchange, accommodation, give and take – these bases for social relations are as recognizable as those mentioned thus far.[19]

This view of the power relations implicit in texts as contingent and subject to change, clearly resonates with my views on the dynamic and dialectic nature of Jonsonian masque.

Many of the critics engaged in this debate on the function of the antimasque are working within the parameters of New Historicism, and while it is obvious that such an approach owes a great deal to a Marxist literary criticism, I would suggest that it is also Marxist critical theory that can help us out of the 'containment versus subversion' theoretical impasse.[20] In *A Theory Of Literary Production* (1966), Pierre Macherey stresses the polyvalent nature of the text, that is, its engagement in several, often conflicting, discourses at once; this means that, rather than viewing the masque as essentially or ultimately either conservative or subversive, we can see both discourses operating simultaneously within the masque. By extension, it may be asserted that this view applied to masque emphasises the lack of a point of closure where any dissenting discourse is suppressed. Macherey's emphasis on polyvalence, when it is applied to masque, correlates with Greenblatt's view quoted earlier: that 'the contingent condition of certain signs' may give them a double signification. For Greenblatt, this involves a radical form of equivocation that can encompass both the 'irony of personal dissent and the harsh celebration of official order'. The masque does not appear to embody a monolithic 'truth' but enacts differing ideologies that produce an interrogation of political and aesthetic reality. I do not suggest, however, that such an interrogation produces an answer or resolution, but rather that it remains open, dynamic and self-renewing. As Macherey asserts: 'The book is not an extension of meaning, it is generated from the incompatibility of several meanings, the strongest bond by which it is attached to reality, in a tense and ever renewed confrontation'.[21] This quotation is particularly relevant to masque because it suggests that such polyvalence arises not only from the textual process, but also from the relation of the text to its socio-political context. Furthermore, it could also be argued that, as a multi-media genre, the masque naturally lent itself to polyvalence.

The 'interrogation' of masque is conducted in terms of satire and panegyric. Satire corrects by heaping scorn on folly, whereas panegyric does so by presenting an ideal to be imitated. Significantly, both are intended to reform the monarchy rather than to undermine it or shore it up in its present state. So we might say that the relationship between Jonson's antimasque and masque forms an entertainment that is didactic and dialectic, attempting to reform the political system from within through a discussion of its faults and merits. My earlier treatment of the three masques *Hymenaei*, *Love Restored* and *Mercury Vindicated* demonstrated the historicism of these masques and also suggested that even the earliest masques, as well as those accompanied by an antimasque, embody a dialectic grounded in panegyric and satire aimed at just such reform. This dialectic does not move towards closure but defines areas of topical political debate; so, for example, *Hymenaei* reveals the many levels of union that King James was seeking to effect in 1606; the many incoherencies in this masque suggest the problematic nature of these political aims and resist the view of absolute power which the masque's dominant ideology seeks to promote.

Yet regardless of its didactic function, the dominance of the satiric antimasque over the eulogistic masque (lasting roughly from 1610 to 1625) has still to be accounted for when we remember that both poetic strategies are geared towards reform. One further explanation for the growth of the antimasque may have been Jonson's increasing confidence in his creation of the court festival, in that, as he became more expert in handling the form he was able to mould it to suit his own interest and tastes. The fact that the antimasque and Jonson's comic drama share many similarities is surely significant here. I suggest that a clearer understanding may be gained if the growth of the antimasque is considered in conjunction with Jonson's satirical comedies. It is often suggested that Jonson's comic talent as a dramatist was only fully realised when he shed the restrictive practice of writing 'humour' plays.[22] Although the characters in later comic plays such as *Volpone* and *The Alchemist* are 'humorous', they are more than mere symbol. The plurality of character and plot, and even the over plotting of these plays allows greater scope for alternative readings. The development of Jonson's technique in the comic plays obviously holds many parallels with the growth of the antimasque. Early masques, as Jonson came across them, still resembled the mummings that were their cultural precursors. In her seminal study, *The Court Masque* (1927), Enid Welsford has charted the origins of the English court masque, tracing its history in medieval 'mummings' or 'disguisings', which, in turn, stem from the earliest pagan festivals and rituals. These mummings were usually devoid of speech and involved a masked procession, with the participants in rich fancy dress, the costumes alone suggesting myth and allegory. The silent mummers often engaged in dice playing or 'mum-chance'. Sometimes a presenter would introduce a mumming in order to provide an aesthetic explanation for the splendour. It seems that, although Elizabethan masques did adopt certain aspects of French and Italian court entertainments, they still retained the silent, processional, and emblematic nature of the mediaeval mummings. Early masques such as those by Campion and Daniel exhibit much of this linear quality, although the symbolic allegory was expanded in action and marked by speeches. As yet, these entertainments did not mirror the developments being made in contemporary drama written for the public stage. It was Jonson who invested the Stuart masque with the dramatic interaction that is such an important and defining part of what we now regard as the antimasque.

Jonson's most obvious contribution to the masque was the introduction of plot and dramatic dialogue. Such elements increasingly characterised the Jonsonian antimasque and connections can be seen between this development and that of his comic drama. Antimasques such as that of *Mercury Vindicated* share with the comic drama a representation of the minutiae of mundane life in Stuart London, and this particular antimasque provides a below stairs view of the bread, coals and bloat-herring. Similarly, at the end of *The Alchemist* the audience is left with a view of 'a few cracked pots, and glasses'. The two genres share a certain absurdity and farcical quality as plots become so complicated that they threaten to devour themselves. In developing the comic aspect of the antimasque until it becomes almost a satirical mini-drama, Jonson remains true to his much quoted purpose of combining profit and pleasure in his didactic work – comic satire is funny as well as instructive. Jonson had learnt this lesson the hard way with his drama for the public stage; *Volpone* had entertained the audience, whereas his Roman plays, designed to be no less instructive, received a hostile reception as audiences appeared not have appreciated being lectured to at length by characters such as Cicero.[23] It seems that the exuberant comedy in Jonson's satire made the bitter pill of correction easier to swallow – a lesson that Jonson learnt on the stage and put into practice in his court entertainments. This must be partly the reason why satire dominated orthodox eulogy in many of Jonson's court festivals – the comic capers of Mercury and Vulcan in *Love Freed*, for example, make a more immediate impact on the imagination that the abstruse philosophical symbolism of the daughters of Niger in *Blackness*; although, as we have seen, if the iconology in the masque was tentatively appreciated, its disguise and governing trope of blackness had almost visceral impact. Although both masques are open to charges of indecorum on different grounds, it is important to remember that Jonson's project of reform was paramount and it is probable that he developed the strategy of reform that was most likely to succeed with his audience, and in James's court that form was comic satire. It is quite clear that the monarch enjoyed Jonson's often bawdy humour, and the court mirrored its monarch's taste.[24] With the accession of Charles I, however, masque regained its ascendancy over the antimasque, partly because the new monarch's taste did not encompass bawdy humour. Although masque poets after Jonson did create antimasques, these were chiefly pastiches that allowed courtiers to laugh at, not with, an outmoded aesthetic form which had become quaint and ridiculous, thus forfeiting any didactic edge it once possessed.[25] Shirley's *Triumph of Peace* (1633), commissioned by the Inns of Court, displays enfeebled antimasques where the Parliamentarians' attempt to appropriate a courtly form in order to speak their own concerns results partly in condescending laughter from the noble audience. As always, the court followed its most important cultural arbiter and Jonson adapted his late masques to accord with this new sense of aesthetic decorum. Although these late masques may appear to be uninteresting creations, flat and linear like those earlier masques and lacking Jonson's characteristically vigorous prose writing, Jonson was in fact maintaining the same poetic aims of combining profit and pleasure in his works, while changing tactic, rather than indulging in hypocritical flattery (although the desperate begging poems he wrote in this period in the hope of money or wine from the King cause the reader to wince). Jonson continued to create the court festival in a form that he calculated would receive the most favourable reception. For Charles and Henrietta-Maria, Neo-Platonism, in addition to the usual showy panegyric, appealed and made the didactic content of masque acceptable, albeit that didactic content was now more muted and tentative than it had been.

Satire and the authoritative community

At this stage in my argument, having asserted the satirically comic nature of the antimasque, I am now obliged to examine why the King and his court commissioned and welcomed entertainments from Jonson that the contemporary reader can interpret as critical of that very institution. The fact that the court continued to sponsor these entertainments undermines claims for the subversive nature of antimasque; it may be reasonably assumed that any subversive content would be quickly detected and suppressed, as was the case with Jonson's early satiric plays, *The Isle of Dogs* (1597, since lost), *Sejanus* (1603) and *Eastward Ho* (1606/6). On two of these occasions government authorities took such a dim view of what they interpreted as Jonson's dramatic subversion that he was imprisoned for his audacity. Yet, it is probably clear by now that, in my view, 'subversion' is too crude and simplistic a term to apply to the Jonsonian court entertainment; moreover, textual irony does not necessarily entail the rejection and overturning of the subject mocked, but rather, as in Jonson's case, can be part of a more complex procedure of reform or dialectical negotiation between representations supportive of the monarchy and those critical of it.

Although the court obviously enjoyed masque entertainment, there were objections, on the grounds of decorum, to some of Jonson's productions, as Dudley Carleton's comments on *Blackness* and *Pleasure Reconciled To Virtue* show.[26] Stanley Fish's theory of authoritative communities offers a compelling explanation of why the modern reader detects an ironic or satiric edge to the antimasque, whereas the court apparently often failed to, although it was sometimes objected to on the grounds of unseemliness; a charge far more serious than first appears, as decorum is concerned with maintaining the 'natural', or social, order. Fish writes:

> Norms are not embedded in the language (where they may be read out by anyone with sufficiently clear, that is, unbiased eyes) but inhere in an institutional structure within which one hears utterances as already organised with reference to certain assumed purposes and goals... interpretative strategies are not free, but what constrains them are the understood practices and assumptions of the institution and the rules and fixed meanings of a language system.[27]

According to this model of reading, interpretation is dictated by literary genre and social context. By extrapolation, we can state that the court was an institution trained in panegyric and the art of decoding it; because it had never previously encountered, and thus could not decode fully the ironic content of antimasque, the court received it as a simple clownish form of comedy, presented as an amusing prelude to the more serious and formal panegyric to follow. However, with the passage of time, the court acquired a familiarity with the workings of the antimasque, and its topicality; a self-conscious knowledge that is most obviously exploited with the knowing allusions in Shirley's *Triumph of Peace* (1633). Literary and social context are the crucial factors here as, after all, audiences had no problem recognising the satiric content of a play such as *Bartholomew Fair* when it was staged in the public theatre. Similarly, the court would have had little difficulty in recognising that the harmonies of masque symbolically enact an ordering of the earlier comic chaos, as it had experienced the masque's idealisation of political power in earlier entertainments. However, I have already asserted at length that the antimasque is a coherent structure of political dissent and much more significant than mere comic chaos. The contemporary reader is trained to consider the ambiguities, absences and elisions in texts and so will readily pick up structures of dissent that operate through such strategies (and perhaps, some would argue, impose a fashionable way of reading on a text whether it is appropriate or not). With the benefit of history and critical hindsight we can also read panegyric in a way that approaches an imitation of the court's reading of the form. Roland Barthes reiterates the Aristotelian concept of verisimilitude, suggesting that what is convincing in a work is that which does not contradict received opinion, 'for such works never contradict what the audience thinks possible, however, historically or scientifically impossible that might be'. Elsewhere he expands on this idea with the distinction between the 'work' which endorses received opinion (*doxa*) regarding culture and society, and the 'text' which is not contained by orthodox categories of literature, possessing a plural often contradictory, signification, and working to subvert the *doxa*. Barthes argues that, 'it may be said that the text is always *paradoxical*'.[28] The application of these distinctions is slightly complicated in the case of the Jonsonian masque, because, as I have already suggested, it is a text/event that is neither wholly 'work' nor 'text'. Yet, we can speculate that for the authoritative community of the court, the ironic or satirical antimasque did not exist because they approached the entertainment in its entirety as a 'work' rather than as a 'text'. Furthermore, it was only with prolonged exposure to the antimasque that the court audience began to accept that satire could transgress its orthodox boundaries and operate within the court entertainment, whereas the literary critic has long been interested in the power of texts to contradict their immediate social *milieu*.

The corrective effect of satire, however, depends on the ability to recognise and identify with the objects of satire, and the satire of the antimasque cannot correct if it is not recognised by the courtiers. One possible solution to this problem lies in the fact that Jonson's writings are permeated with the idea that he wrote for a few enlightened readers or 'understanders' rather than for the ignorant multitude. This topos is succinctly expressed in the preface to *The Alchemist*:

TO THE READER

If thou beest more, thou art an Understander, and then I trust thee. If thou art one that tak'st up, and but a Pretender, beware of what hands thou receiv'st thy commodity; for thou wert never more fair in the way to be cozened (than in this Age) in Poetry, especially in Plays: wherein now the concupiscence of dances and antics so reigneth, as to run away from Nature and be afraid of her, is the only point of art that tickles the spectators.

The point is that only a few will truly 'understand' the play and profit from it, the less enlightened 'pretenders' will still enjoy the comic stage business but completely miss the more serious moral implications, an important dimension of Jonson's comic drama. This unthinking enjoyment is also caricatured by the poet in the text of his accession day entertainments for King James where he writes, 'And for the multitude, no doubt but that their grounded judgements, said it was fine, and were satisfied'.[29] This distinction between 'understanders' and the dull multitude is also present in the masque texts, despite the apparent ideological homogeneity of the audience (although we should bear in mind that Jonson makes this distinction in the published version of the masque text which would have been open to interpretation by a much wider range of readers). In the preface to *Love's Triumph Through Callipolis* (1631) Jonson writes the epigraph, 'To make the Spectators Understanders'. Similarly, in a note to a much earlier masque, *Hymenaei* (1606), Jonson accompanies an explanation of the allegory with the jibe, 'And for the allegory, though here it be very clear and such as might well escape a candle, yet because there are some must complain of darkness that have but thick eyes, I am contented to hold them this light'. Although this comment does not apply to the ironic or satirical nature of the antimasque (*Hymenaei* does not have an antimasque) he acknowledges that the true significance of his work will be beyond most of his readers, as, presumably, it was for many in the original court audience. In this instance he decides to aid such poor understanding, but the phrase, 'I am contented to ...' indicates a grudging accommodation of such dullards and implies that Jonson will not always be 'contented' to make allowances. (It is worth noting here that a recurring trope in Jonson's poetry is the faculty of understanding, which is endowed with an almost three-dimensional power; see, for example, *Epigrams,* CII, 'To William, Earl of Pembroke'.) If, as Jonson implies, the refined or subtextual meaning of much of his masque was beyond the comprehension of many in the court audience, this may explain why, often as not, the audience did not object to the satirical barbs that were directed at it. But there still remain some few 'understanders' in all audiences that Jonson relies on to profit from the didacticism of his masques as well as his drama and poetry.

My theorising on the satirical antimasque is straightforward thus far, and may be summarised with the assertion that different communities of readers (for the individual usually generates signification within the parameters of a given community) produce different 'texts', although they may scrutinise the same arrangement of words on a page or actions on a stage. Moreover, the generic codes and conventions shape the reading of texts in that an audience is likely to respond differently to satiric elements according to the context of dramatic comedy or that of masque. However, an important qualification to this statement, and Fish's theory of reading, is that within a given community there may be readers who depart from the majority consensus and manage to read across generic constraints to produce readings that 'go against the grain'. Such readers might be Jonson's 'understanders'.

Although unorthodox readers exist within every community, they are not usually of sufficient numbers to undermine radically the textual readings of the majority. Problems arise, however, if the majority community produces a reading of the author's work that is at odds with its own interests; for example, when those who are usually oblivious to the satirical barbs aimed at them in plays or masques become aware of them. Such new awareness may be the result of a significant change in the community structure or cultural context. A reading that 'goes against the grain' cannot, however, be produced out of nowhere, and will be 'detected' only if the reader is so inclined. And yet why would a cultural majority produce a reading from a text that would seem to undermine its own position? History may help us to resolve this question; in *Conversations* it is recorded that in 1605/6 'he [Jonson] was delated by Sir James Murray to the king for writing something against the Scots in a play, *Eastward Ho*, and voluntarily imprisoned himself' (1.270). This accusation arose at a time when many Londoners were beginning to resent the influx of Scots to court and city, and were incensed in their belief that the Scots were appropriating as much of the Crown's wealth for themselves as possible. This resentment expressed itself in the form of satirical doggerel, and jokes on the stage at the expense of the Scots. As one of King James's favoured Scottish courtiers James Murray must have been acutely conscious of these barbs and keen to stamp them out – hence his prompt reporting of Jonson for slander. Scots like Murray had risen under the new Stuart regime from economic weakness and, from a London perspective, cultural marginality, to become a dominant group at court. The context and structure of the court significantly changed at this time. Jokes that were acceptable to an older, more established Elizabethan power base became subversive for the newly aggrandised Scots. Jonson responded to this shift in power and patronage and directly represented the effects of the new regime in his drama. In doing so, he touched on popular perceptions of the Scots' accumulation of London's wealth and domination of political power. The fact that such people had recently acquired a power that had yet to be consolidated (some historians might say it never was) ensured a sensitivity to any satiric reference to their new status. Satire is largely grounded in topical issues; a more established regime may have ignored the kind of jokes Jonson wrote into his plays, and, as it became established, these jokes would lose their satirical bite. However, the recent cultural shift in the aristocracy and court elite meant that these jokes could be viewed as subversive, and Jonson was imprisoned for *Eastward Ho*.

These experiences must have taught Jonson that drama or poetry which relates to the socio-political context and addresses contemporary issues in a dialectical manner can be dangerous for the author. The Murray incident shows that the politically powerful are capable of reading a text in a way that undermines their own authority, while ignoring any indications within the same text that shore up their current status. In this authoritarian climate the author may become the target of the state's displeasure. In my view, much of Jonson's work is dialectical in its polyvalence; to adopt Joseph Loewenstein's term, it possesses a 'semiotic plenitude', or what we might label as rhetorical instability – Jonson's ability to fashion texts that apparently simultaneously enact contradictory ideologies.[30] Dialectical texts are often oblique in their suggestion of meaning; while this allows scope for covert criticism, an inappropriate signification is more easily produced when a text is non-specific as to how it should be read; this very danger is illustrated in *Poetaster* (1600/1). The authoritative poet figure in this play, Horace, is accused by the tribune Asinius Lupus of composing an emblem representing an intended threat against Caesar. Horace explains that the emblem was intended for Maecenas and not for Caesar, therefore the eagle that Lupus sees in the emblem (the eagle being a traditional symbol for Caesar) is in fact a vulture. Lupus leaps on this discovery as an even greater slander against Caesar, but Horace insists that the emblem was not intended for Caesar, and represents a vulture and a wolf. Lupus interrupts, reinterpreting this as a slander against himself, on account of his last name. Horace then goes on to explain that the vulture and the wolf are attacking an ass. Lupus declares that this is an even greater insult on account of his first name. Maecenas continues the exposure of Lupus's foolishness by explaining that the ass is intended to have the signification that the ancient Egyptians attached to it, that is, 'Patience, frugalite, and fortitude; / For none of which, we can suspect you, tribune' (V.iii.103-4).[31] Despite the sharp comedy of this scene, it is a real possibility that if the authoritative Maecenas had not been present to defend Horace, Lupus's wilful 'misreading' of the emblem could have resulted in a verdict finding Horace guilty of treason against Caesar, and a serious, if not mortal, penalty. In this play Jonson bluntly shows us how individual perspective moulds the production of meaning, a realisation that must be the basis for any dialectical investigation; yet he also reveals that this kind of writing is perilous indeed, especially when commentators simplify the dialectical text for their own ends. For his part in *Eastward Ho* Jonson was fortunate enough to be merely imprisoned, 'as there were rumours that they [the authors] should then have their ears cut and noses' or worse (*Conversations*, l.274). However, the indefinite nature of dialectical signification also leaves scope for the author's defence against or evasion of charges of sedition. Annabel Patterson's study of censorship has led her to develop a theory of '*functional* ambiguity, in which the indeterminacy inveterate to language was fully and knowingly exploited by authors and readers alike'.[32] This means that, while Horace is vulnerable to attack from Lupus because of the ambiguous nature of the emblem, he is also able to take refuge in its ambiguity; the multi-referential symbolism of the emblem ensures a protective indeterminacy preventing Asinius from incontrovertibly proving that it is deliberately and directly subversive. Horace evades the charges against him with the backing of Maecenas, just as Jonson himself, with the help of a powerful statesman sympathetic to his plight, evaded charges of subversion for his plays, *The Isle of Dogs*, *Sejanus* and *Eastward Ho*.

These are some of the advantages and dangers lying in wait for the composer of the dialectical text. In a note to *The Masque of Queens* Jonson asserts implicitly his belief in the capability of a few 'understanders' and declares that, 'a writer should always trust somewhat to the capacity of the spectator, especially at these spectacles, where men, beside enquiring eyes, are understood to bring quick ears, and not the sluggish ones of porters and mechanics' (l.95). Jonson clearly places the onus on the spectator to 'read' the masque well, and the implication is that a good reading may always be offset by one that is superficial (as demonstrated by Carleton's remarks on *Blackness*) or finds treasonable or objectionable content in the text/event. In his creation of masque Jonson was never accused of treason, but he was accused of aesthetic unseemliness and a lack of poetic skill; these are serious charges to level at a writer who set himself up not only as a dramatist and poet but also as a cultural arbiter of what constituted good poetry and drama. Moreover, Jonson sought to legislate over moral matters, as well as literary matters; his efforts appear to have been largely successful resulting in an impressive reputation, but one that could be seriously damaged if such accusations of artistic failure stuck. As a commonly cited example of damaging 'misreadings' we have Carleton's comments on *Blackness*; in the first chapter of this book I discussed at length the poetics and philosophy behind this masque, yet Carleton could only (infamously) comment on it as:

> Too light and Curtezan-like for such great ones. Instead of Vizzards, their Faces and Armes up to the Elbows, were painted black, which was Disguise sufficient, for they were hard to be known; but it became them nothing so

well as their red and white, and you cannot imagine a more ugly Sight, than a troop of lean-cheek'd Moors ... [The Spanish ambassador danced with] the Queen, and forgot not to kiss her Hand, though there was danger it would have left a mark on his Lips.[33]

Carleton views Jonson's masque as an example of dangerous aesthetic indecorum, breaching the boundaries of race, class and gender. Its incipient danger is indicated by the trope of infection employed when Carleton suggests that the Spanish ambassador's lips could have been stained by contact with the Queen's hand. Although he proves himself capable of thinking in metaphor, and he balks at the hint of miscegenation present in the Queen's disguise, he appears unable to pick up the erudite symbolism of the masque itself. The charge of indecorum was also levelled at the antimasque; after the unfavourable reception of *Pleasure Reconciled to Virtue* (1618) Jonson rewrote it as the more absurd and nonsensically comic *For The Honour Of Wales*. This version had a new antimasque, but repeated the original masque. Sir Edward Harwood damns the first antimasque with faint praise when he records that it was 'not ill-liked'. Sir Gerard Herbert also commented on the two 1618 masques in a letter to Carleton, clearly agreeing with the general consensus of opinion when he writes that the second masque, 'was much better liked than tweluth night; by reason of the newe conceits & ante maskes & pleasant merry speeches made to the kinge'.[34] But why should Jonson's audience take such a violent dislike to his creation for the festivities in 1618? It seems to have been felt that an antimasque featuring mischievous pygmies and dancing bottles, symbolising drunkenness, was an inappropriate context in which to present Prince Charles in his first court masque. Such a view seizes on the indecorum inherent in the antimasque, but fails to consider how its relation to the masque gives rise to a view of order and harmony; for Hercules has to learn that pleasure is reconcilable with virtue, and the delights and benefits of order are figured by the intricate dances led by Daedalus. It seems that on this occasion Jonson's dialectic approach to masque backfires on him in the way I suggested earlier, with the authoritative audience only picking up those antimasque elements of irony and disorder, and failing to appreciate the masque's resumption of order. It may also be the case that 1618 witnesses the point where Jonson's expansion of the antimasque was perceived to overwhelm the masque to an unacceptable degree; under pressure, the important philosophical content inherent in the first antimasque, gives way in the second to knockabout humour at the expense of the Welsh.

Despite these misreadings of masque, it was in Jonson's interest to preserve the 'semiotic plenitude' of the court entertainment; this allowed him to develop his own critical voice, while the indeterminacy of these texts acted as a protective mechanism against accusations of subversion or treason. In a recent essay Joseph Loewenstein draws attention to what he considers to be the unusual appearance of masque texts. He notes a 'typographic chatter' and explains this as:

> The dense play of roman and italic type (sometimes further unsettled by Greek), the visual interruptions worked by the stage directions (both tabular registers and prose descriptions, the latter of sometimes Shavian length), and, above all, the printed marginalia, with their pointed clog of abbreviation and textual reference – the combined effect of all this is to produce a textual coruscation that disrupts the easy symmetries of verse array.[35]

Loewenstein views this manipulation of the texts as a strategy for preserving the 'semiotic plenitude' of the masque performance, preventing the prioritising of one meaning over another, and directing the reader to an appreciation of the masque's dynamic nature. In this way Jonson seeks to prevent superficial readings like Carleton's, or readings that produce treason or subversion from the text, as typified by Asinius Lupus. Paradoxically, it seems that Jonson preserves the dynamism of his masque in the stasis of print. For, as Loewenstein argues, the poet orders his printed text in such a way as to question the very notion of stable meaning: 'the typography of these texts achieves something analogous to the semiotic dazzle of masque performance'. Jonson seems to have considered the contemporary 'understanders' of his work outnumbered by 'pretenders' such as Carleton. However, the masque texts continue the didactic project. Those able to respond to the masque's 'semiotic plenitude' will cease to be 'pretenders' and become 'understanders'.

Notes

1. Boehrer (1997), 35.
2. Early critics of masque also commented on its occasion, Herford, Percy and Evelyn Simpson (1925–52), extensively list such occasions. Although the work of Herford and Simpson has been fundamental for the current wave of Jonson studies, much of it has been surpassed by more recent work such as Orgel (1965); (1975). Marcus (1986), demonstrates a New Historicist view of the relationship between masque and its occasion. Dollimore (1989), suggests a Cultural Materialist approach to this topic.
3. Orgel (1965), 33.
4. Howard (1987), 3–31 (15).
5. Greenblatt (1992d), 99–126 (110).
6. Dollimore (1989), xxi. Dollimore makes this point in connection with renaissance drama, and its relationship with the state.
7. Much of the historical material in this chapter is taken from Akrigg (1962).

8. Gordon (1975), 157-84. Further references to this text are given after quotations in the text.
9. Marcus (1981) 7-17 (7). Further references to this essay are given after quotations in the text.
10. Lucy Hutchinson certainly considered court entertainments as part of a general decline into immorality in the reign of James I. She wrote, 'To keep the people in their deplorable security till vengeance overtooke them, they were entertain'd with masks, stageplays, and sorts of ruder sports, Then began Murther, incest, Adultery, drunkeness, swearing, fornication . . .' etc., Hutchinson (1806: 1973), 42. Stephen Orgel writes, 'Hostile critics saw in the royal histrionics only frivolity or hypocrisy, and even sympathetic observers regularly referred to masques as "vanities" . . . these works are totally self-regarding. They are designed to be so' Orgel (1965), 59.
11. On Stuart censorship see, Burt (1987), 529-59.
12. Foregrounding the artificiality of a work is a device that Jonson used successfully in his plays, for example, in the prologues of *Cynthia's Revels* and *Bartholomew Fair*. In doing so, Jonson encouraged his audience to develop a critical awareness of the drama they were about to see, rather than being passive, unthinking spectators.
13. Despite Sir Frances Bacon's well known dismissal of masques as 'toys', there is evidence to suggest that he also sought to win royal favour by financing such events. C. E. McGee and John C. Meagher note that the antimasque and masque of the anonymous *Masque of Flowers* (1614) were described as, 'Francis Bacon's First Masque' and 'Francis Bacon's Second Masque'. McGee and Meagher (1988), 17-128 (26). Perhaps it is worth noting that this particular masque seems to fit Bacon's dismissive description of the form: it lacks any apparently significant philosophical discourse, apart from the obvious one of using spectacle to glorify the monarchy.
14. Throughout his work Jonson draws on two traditions of the Cyclops. The latter is that of the Cyclops who assist Vulcan at his forge. An earlier tradition, however, is the tale of the Cyclops Polyphemus who captured Ulysses. To effect his release Ulysses plied Polyphemus with wine and then burned out his only eye. Both Euripides and Homer tell how when the satyrs or other cylops asked Polyphemus who had injured him, he replied, 'Outis' (Nobody), this being the name Ulysses used when Polyphemus took him captive. Both myths suggest that the Cyclops 'tortures' Mercury under the direction of Vulcan; see Wheeler (1938), 76. This image of mercury being manipulated to create 'unnatural' forms chimes with Jonson's regular criticism of art that runs away from nature, or makes it afraid. See, for example, the preface to *The Alchemist* and the induction to *Bartholomew Fair*, ll.112-18.
15. Donne, as well as Jonson, found the ideas surrounding alchemy compelling metaphors for human experience, although both writers expressed a scepticism about the process itself. Alchemy involves paradox, in the sense that disparate, and often mundane, elements are distilled into the single precious commodity of gold. The trope of reduction from complexity to unity in the production of a single element is also present. However, this alchemical gold may be viewed as an illusion and 'flashily false'. Jonson's contempt for the promises and illusions of alchemists is expressed in the epigram. 'To Alchymists',

> If all you boast of your great art be true;
> Sure, willing povertie lives most in you.
>
> (*Epigrams*, VI)

Mercury Vindicated demonstrates Jonson's view of alchemy as a distortion of nature, which he uses as a metaphor for the decline in the literature and society of his time. Yet, his play, *The Alchemist* also displays his fascination with alchemy as a trope of transformation; in this play, a belief in alchemy (albeit misplaced) enables a temporary transformation of dreams into reality, although this 'reality' is, of course, just an extension of the alchemical illusion.

16. 'For a picture of what went on, one may turn to an undated report in the Public Record Office. It paints a dark picture of conditions at court. Even the most inferior servants in the Lord Steward's departments, the grooms and their "children", have their own servants coming into the palace and secretly conveying away wood, coal, butter, fruit, spices etc. The royal bakers are making lightweight loaves and misappropriating what they save. The pantry officers are disposing improperly both of the fine bread and the coarse. The officers of the buttery are selling the King's drink for their own profit. The cooks in the kitchen are selling off the best of the meat delivered to them so that only half of that is served on the King's tables...' etc. Akrigg (1962), p.89. A letter to a government official signed by Thomas Chaloner reveal that in the ongoing financial crisis tradesmen were not paid for their services to the royal household and faced ruin: 'And let me entreat your favour to mr palmer the princes Imbroderer, who is ready to perish for want of money, all his friends & creditors having in his distress left him'; PRO, LS13/280.
17. Dollimore (1989), 27.
18. Marcus (1986); see the chapters on Ben Jonson.
19. Leinwand (1990), 477–90 (479).
20. In addition to Leinwand, there are other critics who seek to move away from the containment/subversion impasse. Stallybrass and White (1986) also examine texts through a model based on negotiation and exchange and look for intersection or 'hybridisation'. More recently, Chedgzoy (1995) distances herself from the containment subversion debate, preferring to focus on contemporary appropriations of Shakespeare, and how Shakespeare can be made to speak for a variety of concerns at the present time, rather then being the preserve of the high art/ heritage establishment.
21. Macherey (1978), 79.
22. These plays concentrate on individual 'humours' or follies – the didactic structure of the play prevents any interesting development of character beyond the boundary of a particular folly. See Watson (1987).
23. In his preface to 'The Reader In Ordinarie' at the beginning of *Catiline*, Jonson records the poor reception of the play, especially the public's dislike of the character, Cicero, 'Though you commend the first two Actes with the people, because they are the worst; and dislike the Oration of Cicero, in regard you read some pieces of it at Schoole and understande them not yet; I shall finde the way to forgive you.'
24. A taste for bawdy satire was not confined to James I and his court circle, as the favourable reception of Jonson's comedies for the public stage shows.
25. Lucy Hutchinson gives a contemporary account of the change in court taste and behaviour initiated by the accession of Charles I: 'The face of the Court was

much chang'd in the change of a King, for King Charles was temperate and chast and serious; so that the fooles and bawds, mimicks and catamites of the former court grew out of fashion, and the nobility and courtiers, who did not quite abandon their debosheries, had yet that reverence to the King to retire into corners to practise them. Men of learning and ingenuity in all arts were in esteeme, and reciev'd encouragement from the king, who was a most excellent judge and a greate lover of paintings, carvings, gravings, and many other ingenuities less offensive then the bawdry and prophane abusive witt which was the only exercise of the other court' Hutchinson (1973), 46.

26. HS (1925-52), vol.X, 448, 449, 553.
27. Fish (1980), 306.
28. Barthes (1987), 34; (1977), 155-64 (157-8).
29. HS (1925-52), vol.VII, 91.
30. Loewenstein (1991), 168-91.
31. For a more detailed consideration of this incident, see Young (1992), 17-36.
32. Patterson (1984), 18.
33. *Ben Jonson. The Complete Masques*, ed. Orgel (1965), 4. In fact, Jonson often devoted his polemic to refuting such charges – evidently he felt it necessary to defend his reputations as both critic and poet/dramatist.
34. HS (1925-52), vol.X, 576-7.
35. Loewenstein (1991), 180.

4
Jonson's consuming satire and the carnivalesque antimasque

In the previous chapter I attempted to demonstrate the interactive relationship between history and the antimasque, examining how historical pressures shaped and gave rise to the form. In referring to the historicist debate surrounding the antimasque, I have been at pains to avoid any essentialist conclusions as to how the court entertainment operates, and tried to show that it is rather a dynamic, conditional text/event that relies on dialectically based strategies of accommodation, equivocation and negotiation. I have also emphasised that the polyvalence, or rhetorical instability, manifested in the masque is part of a wider tendency found in Jonson's other plays and poetry, while the dramatic and exuberant nature of the antimasque is partly indebted to his comic drama. By endowing the masque with a measure of polyvalence, Jonson liberates himself as author and carves a space for an independent critique of the state, evading charges of either hypocritical flattery or subversion. Perhaps one of Jonson's most important contributions to the genre of court masque is this negotiation of a critical space in which the author may assert and maintain his poetic integrity and independence. This chapter builds on the theoretical position of the previous one, and examines two antimasques in great depth as part of the wider project of illuminating the ways in which certain antimasques are expanded to such a degree that they threaten to consume their accompanying masques.

Thus far, I have been underscoring what Peter Stallybrass and Allon White term 'the dialogic emphasis' of Jonson's works;[1] in a manner similar to Hegelian dialectic, poetics may end in synthesis with the rhetoric of politics, panegyric often implies its polar opposite of satire, didactic exhortation can become controlled mockery; and perhaps most obviously, in Jonsonian terms, this dialogic or dialectic model informs the construction of the antimasque/ masque entertainment. Having already suggested that the irony or satire of the antimasque forms an important counterbalance to the panegyric of masque, I wish now to extend the terms of this debate into the polarised yet complementary areas of the 'grotesque' and the 'classical'; these are, of course, the political, social and aesthetic categories identified by Mikhail

Bakhtin, and have become increasingly *de rigeur* for any analysis of Renaissance culture, and Jonson in particular. However, while Bakhtin's work does indeed shed much light on Jonson's twin impulses of bawdy comedy and neoclassicism, I am wary of applying Bakhtin's theories too thickly and indiscriminately to Jonson's masques and play, and there are key moments in the argument of this chapter where I depart from Bakhtin in the interests of Jonson. It would be easy to assume a clear dichotomy between the grotesque antimasque and the classical masque, yet this is not so; boundaries between masque and antimasque grow blurred as the form develops and, although they appear to be separate discourses, they seep into one another. Bakhtin describes the carnival's discursive exchanges as, 'a complex intersection of languages, dialects, idioms and jargons' which give rise to 'an intense ideological struggle'.[2] For this study of masque, such a description also suggests the way in which the low language of the antimasque jostles against the courtly utterances and ideology of the masque in entertainments such as *The Irish Masque At Court* (1613/14) and *Mercury Vindicated From The Alchemists At Court* (1616). Bakhtin depicts language as a philosophical discourse expressing social values, and similarly, the dialogic intersection of languages in the court masque can be viewed as social competition, an ideological struggle between social groups; for example, in *The Irish Masque* the Irish 'imbashators' of the antimasque press their own claims in the low language of Jacobean stage-Irish jargon against and in spite of the derogatory scorn poured on them by the standardised eloquence of the court gentleman who dominates the following masque.

As I have indicated, much recent discussion of the grotesque has been motivated by Bakhtin's work on the carnival in his book *Rabelais And His World*, and debate is still centred on Bakhtin's model no matter how far it takes issue with his main tenets. Jonson's *Bartholomew Fair* (1614) has been rich plunder for Bakhtinian critics as it appears to embody so much of what has been defined as grotesque or carnivalesque.[3] In the first part of this chapter I will examine *Bartholomew Fair* in the light of these critical assumptions to arrive at a formula of the Jonsonian grotesque and its relationship with the classical. This will lead to a discussion of the two masques *Love Freed From Ignorance And Folly* (1611) and *The Irish Masque At Court* (1613). I shall try to show that these masques share the complex relationship of the grotesque and the classical exhibited by *Bartholomew Fair*. In these entertainments the grotesque of the antimasque envelops and threatens to take over the classical masque, and, as the orthodox structuring of the form is put under pressure, the masque itself almost disappears, but is always reasserted, if only as an afterthought, as the formal rules of the Stuart court entertainment dictate that antimasque must be followed by masque. As Alan Fisher remarks in reference to Jonson's deployment of mock-heroic, 'Jonson ... gives us standoffs, not resolutions: when his high meets low they jostle and brawl like enemy entourages meeting in a narrow street'.[4] While any brawling in the court entertainment may be limited to the antimasque, Fisher cogently suggests the way in which Jonsonian poetics remain open, embracing multiplicity and resisting the impulse for a conclusive resolution to the tensions between high and low, panegyric and satire, masque and antimasque. Although the orthodox form of the masque is conventionally reinstated, it has been destabilised, by the encroaching antimasque which transforms Jonson's royal entertainments into comic mini-dramas.

Before going on to discuss Jonsonian grotesque in *Bartholomew Fair* it would be useful to recapitulate on the Bakhtinian model of the fair that most discussion uses as a starting point and also Bakhtin's formulation of the terms 'classical' and 'grotesque', exploring how they might be adapted to describe particular Jonsonian texts. Bakhtin's festive market place is a kind of primitive and socialist utopia where all rank and hierarchy is abandoned. People are the carnival, 'carnival is not a spectacle seen by the people: they live in it, and everyone participates because its very idea embraces all the people'. The carnival has a special time of its own and a 'universal spirit':

> The carnival is far distant from the negative and formal parody of modern times. Folk humour denies, but it revives and renews at the same time. Bare negation is completely alien to folk culture.[5]

The kind of negative parody rejected by Bakhtin in favour of the fair's spirit of rejuvenation is that typified generally by Swiftian satire, where what is undesirable in society is reviled, but there is a failure to offer any positive alternative. For Bakhtin, the carnival spirit has a wider application than just to the fair, and often embodies an irreverent, laughing double of officially sanctioned ritual. He writes, 'nearly every Church feast had its comic folk aspect, which was also traditionally recognised'. The festive abuse and degradation characterising carnival is also a process of regeneration, whereby structures are broken down into their component parts so that they may be reconstituted again; the body returns to earth to be born anew in a perpetual cycle. The grotesque carnival is an affirmation of the body in its universal role, the emphasis on open orifices in the carnival excesses of eating, defecation etc. foregrounds the body's interconnection with the outer world: 'The material bodily principle is contained not within the biological individual, not in the bourgeois ego, but in the people, a people who are continually growing and renewed. This is why all that is bodily becomes grandiose, exaggerated, immeasurable' (p.11).

Bakhtin clearly makes a connection between the private and the universal in renaissance texts:

> However divided, atomised, individualised were the 'private bodies', Renaissance realism did not cut off the umbilical cord which tied them to the fruitful womb of the earth ... The private and the universal were still blended in a contradictory unity.
>
> (p.23)

Bakhtin's phrase 'a contradictory unity' seems to suggest neatly here one result of the discursive exchanges in some of Jonson's plays and masques. In *Bartholomew Fair*, social groups that later in history would become polarised (and were perhaps already polarised in the 'real' London of 1614), are intimately involved with each other. The petty bourgeois visitors to the fair become involved with it and the socially inferior fair traders in a way they neither expect nor readily accept. In the court masques of this chapter, the clear boundary between antimasque and masque is also blurred as the two forms collapse into each other. That increasingly polarised social groups and cultural productions should paradoxically arrive at a synthesis is indeed 'a contradictory unity'.

Despite my adoption of Bakhtin's key terms and concepts thus far, I am wary of imposing rigorously his model of the carnival on Jonsonian texts. Neil Rhodes has pointed out why the critic should resist such an imposition on *Bartholomew Fair*, noting that for Bakhtin the carnival is saturnalian not satirical, and that he rejects 'modern' satire here on the grounds that it lacks an impulse for rejuvenation.[6] Rhodes emphasises, however, that a connection between satire and saturnalia is typical of an Elizabethan manifestation of the grotesque: 'in the sixteenth and early seventeenth centuries satire, saturnalia, and, indeed, the sermon were forms which frequently interlocked, and it is from the uneasiness of their mutual relationship that the Elizabethan grotesque is generated'. Rhodes shows an early modern discourse of the grotesque distinguished by an intense physicality of language where sign and signified are closely allied. Such language develops a tonal uncertainty as it combines obscene images in a humorous fashion, heaping macabre synonyms together in a breathless stream of words, which is all the more startling for its radical break with the Euphuistic tradition.[7]

Bartholomew Fair and the antimasque

The above analysis of Elizabethan rhetorical practice undeniably mirrors the linguistic exchanges in *Bartholomew Fair*, where insults spark and crackle through the text, testament to the imaginative and rhetorical creativity shared by Jonson and some of his contemporaries such as Donne and Nashe. While the saturnalian elements of the fair are obviously manifested with Ursula's gargantuan proportions and the subversive impetus of the fair as a whole, satire is also an integral part of the play. Hypocrites are exposed and the weakness of flesh revealed, but there is no permanent moral rehabilitation of Overdo or Busy, and Bakhtin's emphasis on bodily regeneration is missing. The overwhelming physicality associated with the satirical realism of the fair disables what I have argued in Chapter 1 to be the didactic and reformative edge of Jonson's satirical poetry and antimasque; and this must be one of the greatest differences between Jonson's antimasque and his comic drama, although the latter is marked by the regenerative impulse shared by antimasque and masque, it also significantly resists it. The questionable availability of moral regeneration does not exclude didacticism from the comic satire, but the overwhelming impression is of the poet telling us how it is; the 'understanding' audience may learn and benefit from Jonson's raucous laughter, but there is little hope that the subjects of his comic satire, the types characterised by Overdo and Busy, will ever learn to be anything other than what they are. Hence, Jonson's dramatic comedies are marked by the twin impulses of satiric amusement and moral despondency.

Having asserted the differences between *Bartholomew Fair* and the antimasque, the Bakhtinian critic must acknowledge that there are many striking parallels between them, one of the most outstanding of which is the literalism inherent in both literary forms. This literalism involves an emphasis on the body or material objects that works to undermine the more tenuous claims of philosophical or metaphysical rhetoric. Whereas Jonson's panegyrical poetry or masque is often rational or contemplative as it fixes on the mental or spiritual qualities of its subject, the antimasque and comic drama form a great contrast with an exuberant literalism which constantly seeks to undermine those who pretend to a metaphysical outlook. Justice Overdo is a character type who might have found a place in Jonson's verse panegyric where he would probably be praised as an impartial lawgiver whose concern for the ethical aspects of the law is admirable. Overdo, however, appears in *Bartholomew Fair* and this context affords him very different treatment. In the play he sets out with the lofty aims of instituting justice and moral behaviour at the fair, and he seeks to discover its 'enormities' by visiting it in disguise; he merely succeeds, however, in being seated on the hard bench of the stocks, and the receiving end of the fair's festive abuse. His spiritual aims are overturned by the fair's effect on his anatomy, indeed, the literalism or comic realism of the fair is closely linked with physicality. Overdo valiantly attempts to reject his experience of what

Bakhtin describes as 'the material bodily principle' by sublimating his pain in stoic rhetoric, he exclaims, 'I do not feel it, I do not think of it, it is a thing without me. Adam, thou art above these batteries, these contumelies'. Quarlous, one of the visitors to the fair recognises this as part of the fair's saturnalian inversion, 'What's here? A Stoic i' the stocks? The fool is turned philosopher' (4.6.81). In this saturnalian world, nothing remains what it seems; Overdo's disguise transforms him from a justice into a fool and rogue fit for the stocks and public humiliation. This process of stripping away or inverting identity is an integral part of the play's satirical project, whereby Overdo and his peers are revealed to be flawed, and the hierarchy which they seek to protect spurious and hypocritical. In this play satire and saturnalia combine to produce a Jonsonian version of the grotesque, emphasising the body as a means of stripping away hypocrisy and inverting the social hierarchy. For example, Rabbi Busy's enthusiastic and physical response to the smell of roast pig (he snuffs the air like a hound) reveals his puritan and ascetic rhetoric to be merely a veil over his extreme physical sensuality. The grotesque discourse of the fair is grounded in a literalism marked by incongruous lists of synonyms and bizarre images, loosely tied together by the image of the fair itself.[8] Although Jonson's non-dramatic poetry and court masques are geared towards legislating for reform through satire and panegyric, the fair denies orthodox legislation of any sort, whether social, religious or legal, as boldly demonstrated by the overturning of Quarlous, Busy and Overdo.

The extensive critical disagreement over a definition of the grotesque suggests that no one blanket definition will serve different cultures, genres or periods; for example, Bakhtin shows that Romantic grotesque is substantially different from medieval grotesque.[9] However, he defines the saturnalian carnival as an irreverent mimicry of licensed ritual such as religious celebration, depending on an emphasis on the open, porous body (forever drinking, sweating etc.), as opposed to the closed, distanced nature of the bourgeois self. In defining the grotesque, Bakhtin cites the classical as its polar opposite:

> All signs of its [the classical] unfinished character, of its growth and proliferation were eliminated; its protuberances and offshoots were removed, its convexities (signs of new sprouts and buds) smoothed out, its apertures closed.
>
> (p.29)

Bakhtin goes on to develop this image by aligning it with the classical statue, a smooth unified object, devoid of any trace of its production, whole and complete. Such an object's perfection is also determined by its separateness from the outside world; it appears to be untouched by it and is completely self-contained. Stallybrass and White admit that Bakhtin's use of the key terms, 'classical' and 'grotesque' is often ambiguous, but they go on to offer a clear summary of what they consider is meant by these words,

> The classical statue has no openings or orifices whereas grotesque costume and masks emphasise the gaping mouth, the protuberant belly and buttocks, the feet and the genitals. In this way the grotesque body stands in opposition to the bourgeois individualist conception of the body, which finds its image and legitimation in the classical. The grotesque body is emphasised as a mobile, split, multiple self, a subject of pleasure in processes of exchange; and it is never closed off from either its social or ecosystemic context. The classical body on the other hand keeps its distance.[10]

Jonson's credentials as a grotesque writer are surely established by poems such as 'On Groin' or 'On Gut', and probably the most important aspect of Jonsonian grotesque is an absurdist combination of classical and grotesque elements in a single text, as I will try to show below. Clearly, these descriptive analyses of the classical indicate analogies with the court masque as a neoclassical ritual which also obscures it processes of production as it proclaims itself a reflection of the monarch's identity. If we turn to consider *Bartholomew Fair* in the light of these terms, it seems that, in manner similar to the distanced and self-contained classical statue, the bourgeois visitors to the fair insist in their social distance from the fair people. However, as opposed to the intangible assertions of class, the fair has an insistent physicality which embraces and absorbs the visitors in spite of their social and physical reservations. Mistress Overdo and Win become prostitutes and are discovered by Justice Overdo vomiting violently after drinking to excess. A similar transformation and absorption happens to all the outside visitors to the fair. In Jonson's carnival, grotesque realism is linked with the saturnalian; the fair inverts the received humanist and neo-classical hierarchy of mind over body and the body itself becomes the site of identity. At the fair, the outstanding example over body determining identity is, of course, Ursula, whose name puns on the Latin for 'little bear' and whose size fashions her character. Her fatness is a major symbol for the fair, and the emphasis on her constant eating, drinking, sweating and urinating suggests the outpouring and uncontained nature of the grotesque body.

Bakhtin's formulation of 'a contradictory unity' of the private body and universal earth in renaissance realism can be used in this study to suggest that the fair's absorption of the bourgeois individualist outsiders is a process marked by tension and resistance. One of the ways in which the play manifests this resistance is in the initial tension between grotesque desire and classical revulsion. The symbolically charged pig is a reification of such tension. Despite the fact that the pig's association with excrement and rubbish has ensured its demonisation in modern discourse,[11] Jonson places the pig (and Ursula the pig woman) at the centre of his play where they embody the wider conflict between the classical and the grotesque. Littlewit longs to eat pig at the fair but obviously feels it unseemly to be seen there. To preserve his reputation he prevails on his wife to feign a pregnant craving for pig. As the pregnant woman with incontinent appetite, in Bakhtinian terms all womb and mouth, Win has the discourse of the grotesque imposed on her, while her husband assumes the classical mantle of guide and protector, more fitting with his social position of proctor. This process of desire, denial and then a hypocritical feeding of desire is one that marks others of Littlewit's family. The most outstanding hypocrite, of course, is the puritan Zeal-of-the-land Busy. When consulted on the propriety of eating pig at the fair, Busy describes such a desire as 'the disease of longing, it is a disease, a carnal disease, or appetite incident to women: and as it is carnal, and incident, it is natural, very natural'. Busy colludes in and intensifies the association between the apparently pregnant Win and what Bakhtin terms 'the lower bodily stratum'. At the same time as reviling this aspect of the grotesque, Busy legitimates desire for the pig and declares it to be natural; his manipulation of puritan discourse is recognised and welcomed by his co-religionist Dame Purecraft who exclaims, 'think to make it as lawful as you can' (1.6.54). Busy makes it lawful by distinguishing between 'Bartholomew pig' and nourishing meat; one is idolatrous, the other permissible. The difference is achieved by the way in which the pig is approached, as Busy says,

> We may be religious in the midst of the profane, so it be eaten with a reformed mouth, with sobriety, and humbleness, not gorged in with gluttony, or greediness.
>
> (1.6.64)

The emphasis on appearance is telling; Busy literally 'pigs out' at the fair but cloaks the real nature of his greed in puritan rhetoric, yet Jonson does not want his audience fooled and so he shows Busy becoming a beast himself as he snuffs the air for scent of roast pig,

> It may offer itself, by other means, to the sense, as by way of steam, which I think it doth. (*Busy scents after it like a hound*)
>
> (3.2.70)

Under his desire for the food of the fair, Busy takes on a bestial physicality, thereby revealing his gluttony, this foregrounding of the body being the effect of the fair's grotesque impulse. Moreover, if revulsion bears the impress of desire, once desire and the body have been sated, the revulsion regains its former virulence:

Pur. Brother Zeal-of-the-land! What shall we do? My daughter Win-the-fight is fallen into her fit of longing again.

Bus. For more pig? There is no more, is there?

Pur. To see some sights, i' the fair.

Bus. Sister, let her fly the impurity of the place, swiftly, lest she partake the pitch thereof. Thou art the seat of the Beast, O Smithfield, and I will leave thee. Idolatry peepeth out on every side of thee.

Kno.[Aside] An excellent right hypocrite! Now his belly is full he falls a-railing and kicking, the jade ... two and a half he eat [ate] to his share. And he has drunk a pailful, he eats with his eyes as well as his teeth.

(3.6.34)

Busy's body determines his attitude to the eating of pork, when his stomach is empty he is all too ready to rationalise it and make it acceptable, and when his stomach is full he can revile it from a position of satiety. My reason for discussing the pig's centrally symbolic position in this play is to emphasise its role in bringing to the fore the resistance of the classical to the discourse of the grotesque prior to a synthesis of the two. Some of the visitors to the fair express a reluctance to become involved with it, although they are eventually embraced by it and witness the erosion of cultural barriers which they sought to maintain. This initial resistance of the classical to the grotesque is a discursive difference that can be figured in various but analogous sets of binary oppositions; medieval versus renaissance, popular versus elite, festive social equality versus atomised hierarchy, the fat of the fair versus meagre Lent and, in the terms of this book, antimasque versus masque. Much of the tension in Jonson's play is occasioned by the conflict between its medieval roots and the renaissance present, and as such represents a wider socio-economic conflict that reverberated even in the court at Whitehall.[12] *Bartholomew Fair* succeeds in breaking down such binary oppositions, but, as Stallybrass and White are keen to remind the reader, we should be wary of eliding the literary fair with historical actuality.

Although the fair traders are in competition with one another there is a strong sense of them as a community, and this community spirit is incontrovertibly displayed in the rush to aid Ursula when she is injured. Similarly, when visitors to the fair ridicule Leatherhead, his competitor, Joan Trash, angrily leaps to his defence. Conversely, however, the visitors to the fair embody a different but influential social impulse; they are individualists, mini-capitalists whose goal of furthering their own social and economic position results in ruthless competition. For example, Winwife and Quarlous are apparently good friends, but when they both compete for the heiress Grace neither hesitates in duping or deceiving the other. As his name suggests, Winwife gets the girl, but Quarlous has no hesitation in duping the couple out of Grace's portion; this triumph is far more than a consolation prize as the play makes it almost painfully clear that Grace's money, rather than her person, was always the real goal of these two friendly rivals. Moreover, as Dame Purecraft confesses, the religious sect that is supposed to be a model community is revealed to be a collection of greedy hypocrites who thrive on cheating each other (5.2.43). Neither do the visitors to the fair participate in it in precisely the way that Bakhtin suggests (except perhaps for Bartholomew Cokes). They come with the intention to view, and like Littlewit, are only too conscious that the fair is socially beneath them. Quarlous and Winwife epitomise the *petit bourgeois* voyeur, whose status depends on maintaining a distance between his gaze and its object. Grace Wellborn is also acutely conscious of her social distance from the fair and protests that, 'there's none go thither of any quality or fashion' (1.5.118), but of course, therein lies its secret and prurient fascination for the middle classes. Quarlous and Winwife constantly assert that they are only attending the fair in the hope that the fool Bartholomew Cokes will provide some sport. Act 2 provides an example of their aloof and arrogant attitude when they are invited to drink by the fair traders:

Kno: Master Winwife, you are proud (methinks) you do not talk, nor drink, are you proud?

Winw: Not of the company I am in, sir, nor the place, I assure you.

(2.5.45)

Bartholomew Fair witnesses the assertion of rank and individualism at the expense of the community as a whole, and immediately undermines this assertion. Despite themselves, the visitors to the fair are gradually drawn in by it and in some cases are assimilated into its festive anarchy and amorality. The reluctance with which some of the visitors experience this assimilation is clearly expressed when Winwife articulates his indignation at being offered the common goods of the fair and his companion Quarlous perceptively retorts, 'Why, they know no better ware than they have, not better customers then come. And our very being here makes us fit to be demanded, as well as others' (2.5.13). However, there is a sense that perhaps this assimilation of the visitors by the fair is a temporary accommodation for the duration of the fair only rather than a permanent social assimilation. The history of capitalism and the mercantile classes tells us that in actuality the Quarlouses of this world became the ideological majority, and Bartholomew Fair itself declined and disappeared in the nineteenth century. However, in Jonson's play of the fair social categories are eroded, and the socially high mingle with the socially low. Moreover, the distinctions between the cultural expressions of these social groups are also questioned, as the play probes its own nature in relation to the masque. The low mimetic realism of the fair destabilises and consumes events such as the court masque that are traditionally seen as high mimetic art. While the masque and its neo-classical context would appear to be the binary opposite of the fair, this is another rigid polarity that the fair erodes, and the uncontainable low mimetic realism of the fair is part of its grotesque impulse, as I will go on to discuss below.

In relating earlier the distinction between the classical and the grotesque to that between the masque and antimasque, I suggested that the dichotomy between these two sets of terms is less secure than it at first appears. Contrary to expectation, there are plenty of clues in the text of *Bartholomew Fair* suggesting parallels between the grotesque fair and the masque proper, rather than with the antimasque. In 2.5.3 Quarlous and Winwife make comic analogies between the fair and masque:

Lea. What do you lack gentlemen, what is't you lack? A fine horse? A lion? A bull? A dog, or a cat? An excellent fine Bartholomew bird? Or an instrument? What is't you lack?

Qua. Slid! Here's Orpheus among the beasts, with his fiddle.

Tra. Will you buy any comfortable bread, gentlemen?

Qua. And Ceres selling her daughter's picture, in gingerwork!

Thomas Cartelli has drawn comparisons between *The Tempest* and *Bartholomew Fair* and this exchange might be seen as further evidence of Jonson's imaginative engagement with Shakespearean drama (*The Tempest* is generally dated to 1610 or 1611, making reference to it by *Bartholomew Fair* (1614) chronologically possible; furthermore, there is a clear reference to this play in the induction to *Bartholomew Fair*).[13] In the above quotation Quarlous and Winwife describe Joan Trash in terms of *The Tempest* masque; in this masque Ceres appears as part of a wedding celebration and she symbolises abundance but in conjunction with chastity. Prospero calls on her to exhort Miranda to be chaste until marriage and his masque operates on the principle of control and restraint, whereas Bartholomew Fair's traders seek to feed and profit from indiscriminate appetite. If Shakespeare's play contains a dramatic representation of the Jonsonian court masque, Jonson, in turn, uses Shakespeare's masque as an intermediary to undermine bathetically his own version of the form. This destabilising impulse of *Bartholomew Fair* makes it analogous with the antimasque; both structures use parody or satiric realism to offset and question the philosophical and political claims of masque itself. The fair and the antimasque both appropriate the language of the metaphysical masque and mingle it with a low mimetic realism that debunks the metaphysical in favour of the literal, and this appropriation is both saturnalian and satirical. The culturally low comes to dominate the culturally high and represents it as a hollow sham; the rhetoric of the court masquers and visitors to the fair is virtually consumed by the grotesque body and literalism of the antimasque and the fair itself. This process is aptly imaged by Ceres' descent from her position as a goddess in Prospero's masque, to selling gingerbread at Bartholomew Fair.

At the same time, however, as the fair undermines the claims of masque (thereby sharing some of the functions of the antimasque) it also, paradoxically, stresses its status as masque. Later on in 2.5 Knockem equates Ursula's tent with the courtly setting of masque, 'This is Ursula's mansion, how like you her bower? here you may ha' your punk and your pig in state' – here the words 'mansion', 'bower' and 'state' point towards the architectural and pastoral qualities of the masque which mystically present the divine 'truths' of state.[14] The comedy in these comparisons arises in the discrepancy between the fair and the terms in which it is described; another example of Jonson's exploitation of the ironic gap between actuality and the ideality of the terms used to describe it which I discussed in Chapter 1. One of the striking factors about *Bartholomew Fair* is that it not only stages a comic clash between the antimasque of the fair and the masque proper, grotesque and classical etc., but the grotesque fair (however comically) also claims the status of classical masque and underlines similarities between the two occasions. Both are spectacles, both imaginatively heightened versions of reality, both ephemeral and yet claiming a significance that dictates their recurrence at special times of the year. Bakhtin recognised the close connection between the fair and more courtly forms of entertainment:

> The court festivals with their masquerades, processions, allegories, and fireworks owed their existence in part to the carnival tradition. Court poets, especially in Italy, produced these festivities and were connoisseurs of their field. They understood its philosophical and utopian contents.

So it appears that the masque is directly descended from the fair, and that there is good reason for using the apparently inappropriate language of masque to describe its festivities. In some of the Jonsonian court masques such as *Love Freed* and *The Irish Masque*, the barrier between grotesque and classical, antimasque and masque, appetite and authority is fundamentally destabilised; in *Bartholomew Fair* it is broken down.

The play's process of eliding the two cultural models is continued by Bartholomew Cokes. He is the ultimate spectator and rushes from booth to booth, prompted by his insatiable curiosity and appetite for the fair. Like the courtier at a masque where the antimasque is provided by professional actors, Cokes is socially superior to those who entertain him. In 3.4 Leatherhead's wares inspire Cokes to have a wedding masque, 'What a masque I shall furnish out, for forty shillings (twenty pounds Scotch) and a banquet of gingerbread? There's a stately thing! Numps? Sister? And my wedding gloves too? (I never thought on afore). All my wedding gloves, gingerbread? Oh me! What a device will there be?' (3.4.137). Cokes sees no essential difference between the requirements of masque and the products of the fair with which he will supply them. His masque will clearly be the sum of external parts, fiddles, gloves and gingerbread. The motivating philosophy behind masque that Jonson stressed so emphatically in the prefaces and notes to his court masques is irrelevant for Cokes, and his attitude to this courtly form of entertainment shadows Jonson's often-voiced fear that masque might degenerate into an empty show lacking an informing philosophy. Cokes seeks to transfer the display of the fair to his masque and continue his role of spectator, and the masque becomes the fair as it is modelled into the kind of comic spectacle that amuses Cokes.

This erosion of the masque proper is symptomatic of the fair's grotesque impulse to appropriate 'high' culture and to re-present it as part of the fair's saturnalian satire. Perhaps the outstanding example of this process is the puppet show in Act 5 where classical myths are updated to mirror early modern London. Littlewit modestly describes his rewriting of the myths to Cokes,

> I have only made it a little easy, and modern for the times, sir, that's all: as for the Hellespont I imagine our Thames here; and then Leander, I make a dyer's son, about Puddle Wharf: and Hero a wench o' the Bankside, who going over one morning, to old Fish Street; Leander spies her land at Trig Stairs, and falls in love with her. Now do I introduce Cupid, having metamorphosed himself into a drawer, and he strikes Hero in love with a pint of sherry.
>
> (5.3.100)

That Littlewit attempts to cover up his authorship of the puppet show implies a consciousness that his play has more to do with the grotesque than the classical. He draws on the stories of Hero and Leander, and Damon and Pythias; both these classical tales had been retold recently in versions by Marlowe and Edwards. Although Marlowe's poem is highly erotic, both these retellings drew on the highminded qualities of the protagonists that the original classical myths had emphasised. The puppet show debunks such lofty aims and behaviour and replaces them with a grotesque literalism and emphasis on the body. It is significant, I think, that *Bartholomew Fair* implicitly alludes to these poems by Marlowe and Edwards because such allusion foregrounds these stories as source material for contemporary high art, and immediately rejects such art in favour of Littlewit's irreverent telling of these myths. Platonic love is replaced by drunken lust, and characterised by smutty puns. For example, the classical myth of Hero and Leander tells how Hero kept a light shining in her window to guide Leander in his swim across the Hellespont. Littlewit reduces this light, a symbol, of platonic love, to a phallic pun:

> *Pup.L.* But lest the Thames should be dark, my goose, my dear friend, let thy window be provided of a candle's end.
>
> *Pup.H.* Fear not, my gander, I protest, I should handle my matters very ill, if I had not a whole candle.
>
> (5.4.280)

As high culture is collapsed into low culture, the boundary between what is normally recognised as reality and art, or the worlds of fact and fiction, is also eroded. As I showed in Chapter 1, Jonson's didactic intention in poetry and masque largely depends on preserving such distinctions, whereas in *Bartholomew Fair* they are drawn upon only to collapse under the pressure of the fair's satirical anarchy, which apparently lacks the didactic impetus of the satire in Jonson's masques and poetry. The puppet master, Leatherhead, not only addresses the puppets but is also addressed by them. Moreover, the illusion of the puppets as living beings is not only perpetrated by Leatherhead for the purposes of the show, but also immediately accepted by some members of the audience outside of the show itself. Coke's foolishness demands that he is such a spectator; but perhaps more surprisingly, Rabbi Busy launches into a debate with one of the puppets as if it were a rational, animate self. It might be more reasonably expected that Busy would lecture the fair in general on the profanity of the puppet show rather than seeking an interactive debate with the puppets themselves. In condemning the puppet show, Busy draws on the traditional arguments levied against the theatre, but in defence of his show, Leatherhead declares that it is 'licensed by authority', however, Busy's assertion of his own spiritual authority entails his rejection of all secular authority. He addresses and condemns the puppets as real versions of what they represent (that is, as male actors who take on female roles and costume in keeping with Jacobean stage practice), thereby demonstrating that he shares something of the fair's literalism. Busy exclaims,

> My main argument against you, is, that you are an abomination: for the male among you putteth on the apparel of the female, and the female of the male.
> (5.5.83)

The puppet Dionysius turns this literalism against Busy by taking it one step further and insisting that they are neither male nor female, and the puppet arrives at a paradoxical position where he insists in the debate on his status as a rational self, but confutes Busy by showing that his objections cannot apply to an inanimate object such as a puppet. The puppet Dionysius visually reinforces this part of his argument by revealing what lies underneath his garment; of course, there is nothing there. The puppet is animate, but merely a representation of the human actor, rather than the real thing. However, the puppet's twisting of the logic of literalism defeats Busy who resignedly declares, ' Let it go on. For I am changed, and will become a beholder with you'. The fair's grotesque literalism thus triumphs over Busy and his attempt to manipulate it. As the arch Puritan is assimilated by the fair, Justice Overdo reveals his true identity and asserts that he will 'take enormity by the forehead'. Overdo stages a last attempt to preserve the social and cultural categories that he sees the fair eroding; a futile attempt which he is forced to relinquish upon the discovery of his wife vomiting after drinking to excess. This spectacle serves to remind him of his frail, corporeal humanity and prompts him to invite all of the fair to his home for a celebratory feast. The law is overturned by festive anarchy, a process mirrored in the court masques immediately preceding *Bartholomew Fair*. In these instances, elements of the grotesque embodied in the antimasque virtually overwhelm the classically and symbolically rigorous masque and turn the whole entertainment into a sort of comic mini-drama. Yet it is important to remember that the masque is always reinstated after the antimasque and thus never completely consumed in the way that Busy and Overdo are consumed by the fair.

The carnivalesque antimasque: *Love Freed From Ignorance And Folly* and *The Irish Masque At Court*

Bartholomew Fair was first performed in 1614, and the two masques I consider in the second part of this chapter can be seen as part of the same impetus eroding established barriers between antimasque and masque, grotesque and classical, that I discussed in relation to *Bartholomew Fair*. The first of these is *Love Freed From Ignorance and Folly* (1611) followed by *The Irish Masque At Court* (1613/14). In her essay, 'The Stuart Masque And Pantagruel's Dreams', Anne Lake Prescott has set a precedent for discussing the masque and antimasque (and their relationship) in the context of a grotesque discourse filtered through an old folk tradition. In alluding to the influence of the grotesque on the antimasque, she refers specifically to *Les Songes Drolatiques* by Richard Breton, published in London in 1565. This was a form of popular poetry and emblem book attributed to Rabelais, featuring grotesque and surreal figures. Prescott suggests a link between these Rabelaisian figures and certain antimasque characters, and she argues that despite the heavy classical influences in masque, 'it seems unlikely that Jones and his collaborators, especially Ben Jonson, could have composed antimasques of any vigor had their imaginations not extended into other less fashionable realms of image and behaviour, including realms as psychologically compelling as they were morally (and perhaps by now aesthetically) disreputable'.[15] Prescott places both Jonson and Jones in a tradition of the grotesque, which she describes in terms that are equally applicable to *Bartholomew Fair*.

Following Prescott in exploring the grotesque in relation to the antimasque, I would suggest that such grotesque images or figures are involved in a broader conflict between the realms of the antimasque and masque. The title of the first masque in question (*Love Freed From Ignorance And Folly*) points directly to its dominant tensions. Love is the classically based virtue which the abstract philosophy of masque embraces, and love is under attack from ignorance and folly, some of the dominant characteristics of the antimasque and the fair. The structure of the court entertainment demands that the masque triumph over the antimasque, but this is not achieved until the elements of ignorance and folly have posed a significant and credible threat to the *status quo*. Although the values of the antimasque are ultimately banished, they have dominated the entertainment, encroaching on the masque to a point where the masque's resolution seems to be a perfunctory afterthought. As antimasque attempts to displace masque from the centre of the court festivity, the delicate balance of the established antimasque/masque interaction is disturbed. Earlier masques are marked by a brief antimasque which merely heralds or acts as a foil to the masque proper. In *Love Freed*, however, the antimasque threatens to consume the masque.

The antimasque is introduced with 'a strange music of wild instruments', a direct challenge to the harmonious music and dance distinguishing the masque. A Sphinx appears leading Love bound; Jonson's gloss on the text explains the significance of the Sphinx: 'By this sphinx was understood ignorance, who is always the enemy of love and beauty and lies still in wait to entrap them'. What is interesting about this Sphinx is that it is not lying in wait to entrap but has already succeeded in entrapping Love, thereby revealing Love to be weak and impotent. There are good political reasons why Jonson chose to represent Love this way: since Love is the creative spirit most often associated with the King in masque, in demonstrating Love's weakness the antimasque suggests that the monarchy's weakness may lead to disempowerment at the hands of dissenting factions. Certainly, in formal terms it appears that the antimasque (represented by the Sphinx) has successfully disempowered the masque (represented by Love). Moreover, the Sphinx's actions reveal Love and the high mimetic art of the masque to be vulnerable and weak. In rejecting the metaphysical rhetoric of Love in favour of a grotesque discourse, the Sphinx initiates the same kind of grotesque inversion of the dominant discursive hierarchy that disabled Busy in *Bartholomew Fair*. Love's rhetoric is shown to be impotent he manages to answer the Sphinx's riddle only with the aid of the muses' priests) before the triumphant physical power of the Sphinx and her follies. Love is bound and imprisoned, and the follies celebrate their triumph with a dance. Although the text gives the reader the bare information that, 'The Follies dance', we can assume that this dance is a tamed, Stuart version of the frenzied dances of the *Bacchae*, which Jonson had evoked in earlier antimasques such as *The Masque of Queens*, where the anarchic impulse of the antimasque is gesturally expressed in wild and bizarre dances, inverting traditional dance movements, 'doing all things contrary to the custom of men'. Just like the witches in *Queens*, the Follies perform a grotesque inversion of the humanist hierarchy of mind over body and replace it with an uncontrollable physicality that usurps rationality.

The plot of this entertainment indicates that the forces represented by the masque must have been subject to independent degeneration before they became vulnerable to the antimasque. Love goes on to describe how he and the Daughters of the Morn were captured by the Sphinx. Jonson's gloss, in this instance, is lengthy and detailed:

> The meaning of this is that these ladies, being the perfect issue of all beauty and all worldly grace, were carried by love to celebrate the majesty and wisdom of the king, figured in the sun, and seated in these extreme parts of

150 Ben Jonson's Antimasques

> the world, where they were rudely received by ignorance on their first approach, to the hazard of their affection, it being her nature to hinder all noble actions; but that the love which brought them thither was not willing to forsake them, no more than they were to abandon it, yet was it enough perplexed, in that the monster ignorance still covets to enwrap itself in dark and obscure terms, and betray that way, whereas true love affects to express itself with all clearness and simplicity.
>
> (ll.90-114)

This note is lengthy compared with other glosses incorporated into the main text of the masque, and it purports to elucidate the allegory of the masque, but the reader is compelled to question Jonson's claims for clarity and simplicity. Rather, it seems that Jonson adopts the strategy of the monster ignorance and wraps his masque in 'dark and obscure terms'. It may be that Jonson offers us this complicated allegory as a means of deflecting overtly critical scrutiny of the antimasque's political content, thereby demonstrating how the classical allegory of masque may be manipulated by the devious antimasque; this is achieved by the antimasque's appropriation of the allegorical and philosophical language of the masque in an apparent explanation of its plot.[16] The note's focus on the philosophical nature of the antimasque ignores, and directs attention away from its grotesque discourse which employs parody and satiric realism to question the 'truths' of masque. The antimasque colonises the masque and utilises its discourse as a mode of defence against accusations of political subversion, yet this defensive action is not wholly devious as Jonson was certainly not intent on bringing down the masque and its attendant values, but as I have been at pains to express, he was engaged in a more sophisticated intellectualising of the court entertainment and its politics. The appropriation of discourse is, of course, a typical strategy of the grotesque; we have seen it at work in *Bartholomew Fair* where the puppet Dionysius manipulates Busy's own literalising logic against him, and Winwife's puppet show draws on classical myth only to rewrite it in the language of the fair. The grotesque of the fair and this antimasque is primarily a discursive structure, that expands to take over the language of high mimetic art, and masque in particular.

The process of querying the masque is continued by the representation of Love as persistently foolish and ignorant. Such a representation is striking because Love is normally a symbolic figure associated with kingship in masque, where it is shown to be omnipotent and divine. Certainly the treatment of Love in *Love Freed* is akin to the saturnalian inversion which turns figures of authority into figures of ridicule in *Bartholomew Fair*. The Sphinx offers to free the captives if Love can answer a riddle and Love reveals his foolishness by offering absurd solutions, including a one-eyed mistress! The forces of the antimasque exult, as the representatives of the masque bow under their pressure:

> *Sphinx.* Nay, your railing will not save you;
> Cupid, I of right must have you.
> Come my fruitful issue forth,
> Dance and show a gladness worth
> Such a captive as is Love,
> And your mother's triumph prove.
>
> (l.204)
>
> *The Follies dance, which were twelve she-fools.*

This moment seems to witness a triumphant carnival inversion as antimasque overturns masque, the physical energy of this wordless dance gesturally refutes the power of Love's rhetoric and the world of masque to which he belongs. The follies are clearly related to the Rabelasian figures which Anne Lake Prescott detects in some of Jonson's antimasques, figures that physically and behaviourally manifest an inversion of the presumed natural order, and exist in the realm of the 'topsy-turvey' world.[17] It is no accident either that the Sphinx and her she-fools are specifically female, since this is a further manifestation of a saturnalian and grotesque inversion of the early modern dominant discursive order; in this topsy-turvey world, the body reigns over the mind, female over male, and antimasque threatens masque. The destruction of Love is prevented, however, by the appearance of the muses' priests, figures doubtless intended by Jonson to represent the didactic poet as the repository of wisdom and integrity. The priests instruct Love as to the correct answer of the riddle, but this belated assertion of masque values seems somewhat unconvincing as it is only brought about by the intervention of the priests; however, we may choose to view this development as a further assertion of Jonson's dearly held belief that monarchical love can only be effective under guidance from instructing poets.

The discursive exchanges of the classical and the grotesque are associated with certain socio-political values, and mediate a wider ideological conflict, to which I will now turn. Like the masques examined in earlier chapters, *Love Freed* is fully implicated in its historical moment, and the expanded antimasque allows for a discussion of the roles of Parliament and King, and the state of the contemporary monarchy. The Sphinx in this masque resembles Plutus in Jonson's following masque, *Love Restored* (1612). Both have an abrupt, almost vicious manner and they are isolated misanthropists who are ultimately defeated. It has been established that the figure of Plutus is a characterisation of the Puritan, and it could be said that in this masque the Sphinx embodies the Puritan/Parliamentarian dissent distinguishing

1611.[18] It may seem anomalous that the Sphinx/Puritan is part of the antimasque's grotesque impulse, whereas in *Bartholomew Fair* Busy, the Puritan, is part of the authoritarian hierarchy which the grotesque impulse of *Bartholomew Fair* erodes. This shift in roles for the Puritan figure is possible because although the discursive strategies of the play and the court entertainment are similar in certain respects, they are not the same. However, both texts draw on a cultural grid where the carnival mob is socially lower than the puritan and the petty bourgeoisie, and they, in turn, are lower than the aristocracy. *Bartholomew Fair* taps into the first part of this grid, where Busy and his colleagues claim authoritarian roles over the fair mob. In the court masque the focus on this cultural grid shifts upwards and Busy etc. are socially lower than the aristocracy involved in the masque. In Jonson's plays and masques the grotesque defines itself against that which is culturally or socially higher. So, although the discursive networks of the fair and the court masque are not identical, they both operate within the same hierarchical social grid. As a representative of the masque, Love automatically possesses a classical and aristocratic status which is threatened by the Sphinx's grotesque impulse to assimilate it.

At the Sphinx's entrance she curses Love's authoritarian rule:

> Come, sir tyran, lordly Love,
> You that awe the gods above,
> As their creatures here below,
> With the scepter called your bow ...
> no sooner you do draw
> Forth a shaft, but is a law.
>
> (ll.1-11)

Love possesses the kingly attributes of a sceptre and the power to make arbitrary laws, and as such we could regard him as a figurative representation of the monarch. The traditional bands that blind Love's eyes (because Love is blind, of course) are a symbol of the ignorance and folly that lead to his downfall. As the Sphinx scoffs:

> The bands
> Of your eyes now tie your hands.
>
> (l.16)

According to the Sphinx, Love is not only authoritarian and foolish, but also treacherous:

> All the triumphs, all the spoils
> Gotten by your arts and toils
> Over foe and over friend,
> O'er your mother, here must end.
>
> (ll.18-21)

The last reference is obviously an allusion to Venus, Love's mother, although there is no suggestion as to how Love triumphed at the expense of his mother. However, it would be quite clear to a Stuart court audience that James deliberately distanced himself from his mother, while emphasising his relationship with Elizabeth I and his potential as her legitimate successor. Mary Queen of Scots had been viewed by the Elizabethan crown as a threat to the recently negotiated Protestant settlement. James had abandoned his mother and her Catholicism to the executioner, reinforcing his claims, as a staunch Protestant, to the English throne. So, by implication, the masque's examination of the relationship between a royal mother and son hints that not only is the King tyrannical and fallible, but also scrutinises his claim to the throne. More importantly, this repudiation of the mother by the son is a grotesque inversion of what was commonly accepted as a 'natural' and religious hierarchy where parent is respected by child. The monarch's version of the grotesque, however, is sublimated because to acknowledge it would be to encourage a dangerous and destabilising effect on the hierarchical structure which he now dominates. The dominant class exploits the grotesque to further its own ends and gain its prestigious position, and then attempts to repress this process on order to stabilise and secure its own position. This repression and sublimation of the grotesque by the dominant classes is a strategy emphasised by Stallybrass and White:

> The bourgeois subject continuously defined and re-defined itself through the exclusion of what it marked out as 'low' – as dirty, repulsive, noisy, contaminating, yet that very act of exclusion was constitutive of its identity. The low was internalised under the sign of negation and disgust.[19]

Although Stallybrass and White refer to the bourgeois subject here, this description is also valid for the aristocratic subject's definition of the self against the lower bourgeoisie. The cultural process is similar, even though the focus has shifted up the social grid.

It is this unstable and contradictory aspect of Love's position that the Sphinx seizes upon and attacks. She bluntly reveals that Love has profited from an empowering process that he seeks not only to deny others but that he also refuses to acknowledge. Naturally, Love defends himself against this attack and asserts that civilisation would end without him. He justifies his power with a mixture of mysticism and pragmatism:

> I rather strive
> How to keep the world alive,
> And uphold it; without me
> All again would chaos be.

(ll.24–7)

154 Ben Jonson's Antimasques

This explanation obscures what the Sphinx has shown to be the material basis for the monarch's position. Instead, Love refocuses this dispute on the Stuart monarchy's belief in the mystery of rule by divine right, when the King is appointed by God to be governor on earth. This rationale implies that without a king there can be no order, and 'all again would chaos be'. Certainly, recent history had shown that the lack of a strong king meant bloody struggles for power, and Love capitalises on this anxiety, thus deflecting attention away from the weaknesses of his rule.

The antimasque provides us with a critique of a contemporary power struggle between the monarch and the puritan bourgeoisie and employs the arguments of both sides, although neither is completely vindicated. The Sphinx is ultimately defeated and her version of the grotesque impulse resisted because, in the terms of the court masque, her brand of democracy is destructive. Yet Love is also shown to be fallible; his error is rooted in his overreaching and inflated idea of his position as monarch. Love sublimates his relation to the grotesque, glorifying in his role as protector to the Daughters of the Morn. Love represents himself as a willing sacrifice, a Christ-like figure, for whom, 'it is no small content, / Falling, to fall innocent'. He claims the lofty and spiritual status of the neo-classical monarch that the literalism and bodily energy of the Sphinx seek to undermine and reveal to be a sham. For example, Love believes that he is the wisest candidate to answer the Sphinx's riddle, and yet persistently gets it wrong; clearly, Love and the monarch he represents do not possess the wisdom that they claim. As I suggested earlier, it is significant that Love can only answer this riddle after heavy prompting from the muses' priests; Love is obviously not divine himself but in need of higher guidance. This guidance emanates from the muses, that is, the poet who serves as a medium for their divine wisdom.[20] The weakness of Love here is interesting when we remember James's many declarations of his status as God's regent on earth which worried some of his subjects, who thought that his claims to divinity were an expression of James's view of monarchy as a self-contained autocracy, and that he was seeking to dismantle the powers of the House of Commons enshrined in common law. Although Love and the classical values of masque are reinstated in this court entertainment, the destabilising effect of the antimasque has revealed Love's historical involvement with the grotesque which he seeks to deny, as well as his failure to live up to the classical ideals of the masque to which he belongs. It is only the rigid and pre-ordained structure of the court masque and the poet's deliberate and overt declaration of his presence in the guise of the muses' priests that stops Love and the masque from being engulfed by the anarchic forces of the Sphinx.

While Love resembles the fallible personality of King James as an individual, the presence of Phoebus (another manifestation of the Sun King) alludes to the Renaissance view of the divinity of kingship, entailing the immortality of the monarchy sustained by a divinely moulded genealogy.[21] The Daughters of the Morn (the monarch's subjects) have to travel to catch a sight of Phoebus:

> And they would look as far
> As they could discern his car,
> Grieving that they might not ever
> See him.
>
> (ll.74-7)

It may well be that these lines contain an example of that punning word play that Renaissance writers so delighted in, albeit late twentieth-century readers may find it puerile to some extent; the Daughters of the Morn grieve because their attempts to view Phoebus are frustrated by his car blocking their view, perhaps a playful, oblique allusion to the influence of Robert Carr over the monarch at this time. As with all of James's favourites, Carr's position became so inflated that his monopoly of the King's attention prompted resentment from many quarters; concomitant with his increasing fascination with Carr was James's neglect of state affairs and public ritual, serving to compound a general perception that the monarchy was becoming increasingly distanced from the people. Love's description of the abode of Phoebus certainly indicates that he resides far apart from his subjects, and, in fact, the Daughters of the Morn subject themselves to considerable hardship in their arduous journey to his remote western palace; they,

> Hither to the west,
> Where, they heard, as in the east,
> He a palace, no less bright,
> Had, to feast in every night
> With the Ocean, where he rested
> Safe and all in state invested.
>
> (ll.84-9)

While there was a long tradition of Britain's identity as the fabled western isles of classical and neoclassical literature, this myth is invoked here not with an emphasis on the west as the locus for a continuing golden age, but on Phoebus's palace in the west as far distant from his subjects in the east. This perception of a dangerous distance between the monarch and his subjects has its counterpart in historical actuality, for whereas Elizabeth made many royal progresses in order to see and be seen by her subjects, James's preference was for absenting himself from London to go hunting in places such as Newmarket and Royston with a select group of his favourites. The dangerous implications of this newly imposed distance are imaged by the fact that the Daughters are captured on their journey by the vindictive Sphinx, and indeed the classical distance insisted on by the ruler becomes a dangerous void into which the Sphinx moves. I have already noted the Sphinx's significance in terms of Parliamentary and Puritan dissent, a counter discourse most notable among the mercantile classes of the capital; James's absence unfortuitously coincided with the expansion of this social group and its acquisition of a political status commensurate with its economic power.[22] In these circumstances it is hardly surprising that the instinctively obedient Daughters are captured by the Sphinx, and their vulnerability is at least partly the fault of Phoebus's absence. Jonson manipulates the emblematic significance of the antimasque's plot in order to comment obliquely on some of the more disturbing developments in Jacobean society, and offers an analysis of their root causes and possible results.

The antimasque ends and the masque proper draws the entertainment to a close when the muses' priests appear to instruct Love with the correct answer to the riddle; divinity is on the side of monarchy as the poet instructs the autocrat. Moreover, the security of the established church is seen to be bound up with that of the state. The priests declare:

> We court, we praise, we more than love,
> We are not grieved to serve.
>
> (ll.308-9)

Subjects of the Crown are also shown to subscribe to the contemporary hegemony, as the Graces of the masque sing:

> A crown, a crown for Love's bright head
>   Without whose happy wit
> All form and beauty had been dead,
>   And we had died with it.
>
> (ll.269-72)

The classicism of this masque is destabilised by the grotesque Sphinx but it is not completely consumed, and Jonson shows us through the Graces and the Daughters of the Morn that most of Phoebus' subjects are content to pay homage to their ruler in return for his protection and the preservation of society. It is possible to remark that *Love Freed* acts as a reminder to the Crown that the principle of monarchy is the only sure defence against civil strife and a dangerously democratic puritanism, and the chaotic consequences of letting everyone have a say are vividly imaged for us in *Bartholomew Fair*. But this masque's reinstatement of classical values does not entail an unqualified eulogy of the contemporary hegemony, rather the King's weaknesses have been pointed to and the damaging effect they may have on the body politic itself. One implication may be that unless there is some reformation there will always be the Sphinx threatening to overthrow Love and his autocratic rule, and it is in this sense that Jonson's masque is both didactic and dialectic, entering into a discussion of the state of the monarchy and underlining the urgent need for reformation from within, and an attempt to pre-empt violent and radical change imposed from without.

The Sphinx's actions are part of a growing tendency of the antimasque's threat to consume the masque, albeit this threat is never fulfilled, and related to the saturnalian and satiric inversion of accepted hierarchies dominating *Bartholomew Fair*. Clearly, these formal changes in structure that expand the antimasque at the expense of the masque have strong political implications. The expansion of the antimasque and its grotesque impulse allows for a dramatised discourse questioning the 'truths' of masque; the court masque as a whole is no longer a ritualised and contained affirmation of state ideology but an occasion exploring exactly what that ideology means, its strengths and weaknesses. An example of this type of probing analysis is Love's eventual success ensured by instruction from the muses's priests and the didactic implication here must certainly be the typically Jonsonian dictum that the ruling powers can only continue effectively if they allow themselves to be guided by wiser philosopher-poets. The expansion of the antimasque and its dialectical engagement with the masque proper is continued and developed in the following masques, *Love Restored* (1612), *A Challenge At Tilt*, (1613/14), *The Irish Masque At Court* (1613/14) and *Mercury Vindicated from the Alchemists at Court* (1616). The Jonsonian court entertainment continues to be dominated by the expanded antimasque until 1625 (the year of James I's death), thereafter it resumes its earlier form where the masque dominates. The last examples of Jonsonian masque witness the increasing marginalisation and trivialisation of the antimasque and the suppression of its grotesque impulse as the masque regains its dominant position. The antimasque, however, did not disappear with Jonson's death, but limped on in Caroline incarnations, but largely transformed from its earlier vigour and interrogatory power into a comic pastiche of itself. While there is no doubt that Shirley's *Triumph of Peace* (1633) certainly articulates unrest at certain aspects of royal policy, and perhaps more directly than Jonson ever did, it does so by putting on an antic guise and laughing self-reflexively at the antimasque as an outmoded and crude entertainment now out of place in the sophisticated elegancies of the Caroline court. These developments are connected with the growth of political absolutism in Caroline government which I will discuss in the following chapter.

The Irish Masque At Court is of special interest for a study of the erosion of cultural and discursive barriers between antimasque/masque and grotesque/classical as it was performed in December 1613 and January 1614, the same year as *Bartholomew Fair*. David Lindley has reconstructed the socio-political background to this masque in some detail so I will merely summarise his findings here.[23] The masque was staged as part of the celebrations for France Howard's notorious second marriage to Robert Carr and was so popular that it had a second performance. The other occasion that the masque engages with is the state of disunity in Ireland. By 1613 the plantation of Ulster was under way, and in 1612 a new Irish Parliament was called, with new seats created to be manipulated by the King in furthering his own supporters. These attempts to stabilise the Parliament in the King's favour led to more disruption with the Catholic faction withdrawing. Throughout 1613 fears grew that this dissent would develop into rebellion, and as part of an attempt to forestall such a disaster a number of Irish delegates came to England to put their case to the King. Part of their goal was to convince the King of their loyalty. James, however, refused to take such protestations at face value and forced the Catholics to declare in favour of either the Pope or the King. The result of this was that two members of the delegation were imprisoned and one prosecuted. David Lindley demonstrates that Jonson's masque engages with these political circumstances and describes the entertainment as a complacent 'picture of Irish submission to English culture'. Such a view clearly jars with what I have argued to be the consistently dialectical nature of Jonson's court festivals, where the distinguishing characteristic of the antimasque is its engagement with and questioning of the official ideology belonging to the masque proper. It also overlooks the fact that the formal expansion of the antimasque was a crucial enabling factor in the development of Jonson's critical voice in the court festival.

One of David Lindley's objections to the masque is what he sees as a disempowering of Irish claims by representing dissent as an aspect of comically rude servants, rather than the concern of Irish gentlemen, as was the historical case. Thus, Lindley regards the antimasque as belittling the causes of dissent against the Crown. Alternatively, it may be that Jonson used the comedy of the Irish rustics to protect himself from accusations of subversion. These Irishmen do, in fact, voice their cultural claims, but obliquely through the medium of comedy and, if under pressure, the poet could always claim that such assertions were humorously ironic. Such deviousness appears to be characteristic of Jonsonian antimasque and allows for a play of meaning that is far more complex than a mere submission to royal hegemony.[24]

In viewing this masque as essentially conservative Lindley addresses the containment/subversion debate that exercises so many critics of early modern texts and culture. Part of that debate has been specifically concerned with Bakhtin's formulation of carnival. Terry Eagleton points to what he considers to be an obvious flaw in Bakhtin's concept of the uncontainable and celebratory carnival urge to overturn received structures of authority:

> Carnival, after all, is a *licensed* affair in every sense, a permissible rupture of hegemony, a contained, popular blow-off as disturbing and relatively ineffectual as a revolutionary work of art. As Shakespeare's Olivia remarks, there is no slander in an allowed fool.[25]

Carnival seems to be subject to the same arguments surrounding the nature of the antimasque; opposing sides champion these texts/events as either subversive or conservative. However, Stallybrass and White recognise that this is a monolithic definition of a complex cultural and discursive process:

> It actually makes little sense to fight out the issue of whether or not carnivals are *intrinsically* radical or conservative, for to do so automatically involves a false essentializing of carnivalesque transgression ... It is in fact striking how frequently violent social clashes apparently 'coincided' with carnival.[26]

Rather than imposing the rigid binarism of the subversion/containment debate on carnival or antimasque it may be more useful to describe them as discursive 'negotiations'[27] or to recall the theory of Pierre Macherey discussed in Chapter 3 which describes texts as polyvalent and self-divided. This seems especially relevant to masque which, by its very nature, is implicated in a fluid and complex historical situation. The assertion of polyvalence is a critical move recognising that the balance of power in any text/event is contingent and often contradictory. By focusing on particular texts, and by thinking of such texts as an ongoing process of negotiation between ideologies, we should avoid a false essentialized view of how they operate.

This controversy demonstrates the fluid, indeterminate nature of the relationship between masque and antimasque, capable of both radical and conservative interpretations. Jonson's dialectic is fundamentally equivocal, and in *The Irish Masque*, this involves satire being directed at both the court masque and its sponsors, as well as at the Irish rustics. In the analysis below, I hope to show how Jonson's satire works on more than one level in this masque.

Upon his entrance Donnel declares, 'Ish it te fashion to beat te imbashators here, ant knock 'em o' te heads phit te phoit stick?'. Lindley glosses this reference thus: 'The antimasque contains a number of references to the white stick of the Lord Chamberlain, employed in trying to debar the footmen from the hall ... The reducing of the Irish to comic figures, sneered at for their lower class indecorum, enables the "white stick" to be used as an acceptable manifestation of royal power, obscuring and rendering comfortable the real force James was prepared to exercise.' Lindley emphasises the conservative function of the antimasque and suggests that dissent is represented merely to be ridiculed and disempowered. However, if the antimasque is considered in relation to the grotesque of carnival, it could be argued that the emphasis on the white stick and the beatings it administers foregrounds Bakhtin's 'material bodily principle' at the expense of the masque's moralising rhetoric. This focus on the body is part of the literalising emphasis of grotesque discourse, as I discussed earlier, and, delivered here in the vigorous speech of stage Irish, decentralises the metaphysical rhetoric of the masque from its symbolically central position; so, the antimasque's emphasis on the beatings given the Irishmen can be viewed not only as an example of the court entertainment's conservative strategy, but also as part of a grotesque impulse threatening to consume the philosophical certainties of masque. Having said that, it is appropriate to reassert here that, in contrast with the grotesque's assimilation of the classical occurring in *Bartholomew Fair*, the antimasque questions and destabilises the masque in order to promote reformation from within the court itself, rather than to negate or consume the masque. Such a consumption can never be completed because the structure of the court entertainment demands that the masque always be reinstated after the antimasque. The antimasque's didactic and reformative impulse (conspicuously lacking in *Bartholomew Fair*) is related to the regenerative nature of carnival that Bakhtin underlines, and is analogous with the reformative didacticism of Jonson's verse satire and panegyric, discussed in Chapter 1. But the renewal of the court through satire is complicated in this instance because the antimasque satirises the rough Irishmen overtly, and the court only by implication.

Returning to Donnel's comment on the white stick with these thoughts in mind, the incident might equally be seen as underlining the physical violence and political pressure brought to bear on the Irishmen, and not necessarily as a comic justification of royal policy in this area. Donnel pointedly describes his countrymen as 'imbashators', implying that they are men of status on an important political mission who should not be bullied and brow-beaten by the English authorities. While the comic deformation of standard English may be seen as undermining the seriousness of the Irishmen's claims, it is important to remember, as I stated earlier, that the oblique assertion of cultural claims through the medium of comedy is a characteristic Jonsonian strategy for self-defence against accusations of writing against the state. Jonson's dialogue brings the real circumstances of the 'imbashators' to the fore; they may be comic and rude but they are also treated unjustly by the government.

The disturbance caused by the Irishmen is increased when they search for the King:

Dermock. Phair is te king?

Donnel. Phich is te king?

Dennis. Tat ish te king.

This failure to recognise the King can be seen as an example of the foolishness of the Irishmen who cannot recognise the King despite his regal magnificence and central position in the audience. And yet, there is also a Jonsonian play of meaning in this moment that may suggest that the Irishmen do not recognise the authority of the King for the same reasons that some of the real delegates refused to prioritise the King's authority over the Pope's on doctrinal grounds. Furthermore, James cannot be recognised as King because he does not behave like one; his own *Basilikon Doron* had asserted that a king should rule with mercy and justice, yet we have seen how the King departed from his own model of monarchical rule in his attempts to manipulate the Irish Parliament, and produce more Protestant members than Catholic. Furthermore, the Irish delegates had personally experienced the willingness of their King to use physical violence and threats in order to achieve his ends.

The comic business of the scene is increased as the Irishmen squabble among themselves, their quarrels clearly representing the disunited state of their own Parliament. Their speech belongs to the genre of Elizabethan grotesque identified by Rhodes, where incongruous images are heaped together, sentences are interrupted and broken off, and words babbled out in an overwhelming stream of language.[28] For example, in the course of the argument, Dennis swears,

> If I speak, te divel take me! I vill give tee leave to cram my mout phit shamrocks and butter and vaytercreshes instead of pearsh and peepsh.
>
> (ll.42-4)

These Irishmen exist in the real world, the pressure of which is imaged in the minutiae of every day life that accompanies them. They think in terms of shamrocks, butter, watercress, cows and garrans (horses). The grotesque particularity of the real world presses against the mysteries of the masque and demands notice; it may even invite a literalising rather than a symbolic reading of the masque itself. This literary manifestation of the things of everyday life is a characteristic shared by *Bartholomew Fair*, where, the varied and disordered objects of life have a similar effect in undermining traditional structures of authority. Bartholomew Cokes's masque becomes a mere display (emptied of the philosophical complexities accompanying orthodox masque), a display of all the incongruous and useless things he buys at the fair.

In addition to its role as an aspect of the grotesque, the language spoken by the Irishmen also has an historico-political significance. The comic brogue that Jonson gives the footmen to speak is in keeping with Elizabethan and Jacobean stage practice. They resemble Whit in *Bartholomew Fair* who shares their anarchic enthusiasm for life. The dialogue is a clear indicator that these are comic Irishmen, yet Jonson forces more comedy out of their language difference by having them declare the obvious, 'We be Irishmen, an't pleash thee'. This emphasis on cultural difference, however, is not merely comic exploitation of the Other as crude and uncivil but also points to important religious differences. The footmen constantly swear by 'Got' and, more unusually, one of them exclaims, 'Sacrament of Creesh'. The prominence of the religious sacrament in their everyday discourse marks them out as Catholics. The Protestant communities of Northern Europe regarded five of the seven Catholic sacraments as idolatrous blasphemy and rigorously suppressed them. So Jonson points here to a difference of much greater significance than mere dialect. This is the religious bone of contention that will prevent James's absorption of Ireland, an absorption which the harmony and unity of the following masque foreshadows in an extravagant wish-fulfilment of the state. Yet despite the antimasque's emphasis upon religious differences the footmen themselves fervently declare their loyalty to the King:

Dermock. Tou hasht very good shubshects in Ireland.

Dennis. A great good many o' great good shubshects.

Donnel. Tat love ty mayesty heartily.

Dennis. Ant vill run trough fire ant vater for tee, over te bog and te bank, be te graish o' Got and graish o'king.

(ll.91–5)

No doubt these lines comically parody the protestations of loyalty made by the real Irish delegates. But the antimasque also suggests that the conflicting claims of church and state cannot be reconciled. In the last line quoted it is clear that Dennis gives God's grace precedence over the King's grace. King James was looking for a reversal in that order of loyalties, provoking a conflict to which the antimasque alludes and which resulted in imprisonment for some of the real Irish delegates. Dennis's implicit inversion of the hegemonic structure of early Stuart Britain where the state controlled and dominated the church results in an irreversible questioning of the possibility of the harmonious integration of Ireland into Britain.

Although on one level of satire we are invited to laugh at the Irishmen, the antimasque, it may be argued, not only questions the masque but ridicules and debases it. Jonson can be accused of bawdy and cheap humour at the expense of the footmen when they repeatedly mispronounce 'sit' as 'shit' – a grotesque emphasis on what Bakhtin terms the 'lower bodily stratum'. The point is, however, that the Irish gentlemen are ready to enter and perform a masque after, 'Tey have shit a great phoile i' te cold, an't be' – creating a graphic juxtaposition of the grotesque antimasque and the neoclassical masque. The footmen are conscious of the spare nature of their masque and previously apologised for it:

Donnel. And tey tell ty mayesty, tey have ne'er a great fish now, nor a shea-monster, to save teir cloysh alive now.

Patrick. Nor a devoish vit a cloud to fesh 'em out o' te bottom o'te vayter.
(ll.70–4)

Stephen Orgel's note to these lines suggests that they are a satiric reference to the two other masques commissioned to celebrate the Howard–Carr marriage by Samuel Daniel and Thomas Campion.[29] That be as it may, Jonson's own *Masque of Blackness* was also distinguished by special effects designed to evoke a magical sea-scape inhabited by strange marine creatures. With this in mind, it is possible to argue that Jonson is not only poking fun at his competitors but also at himself and the scenic display of the masque form. This would chime with the often commented on debate between Inigo Jones and Jonson where both prioritised their respective skills of visual design and poetry, usually at the expense of the other.[30] However, it is also possible that as well as engaging in a critique of the masque's spectacle, Jonson also mocks the Irishmen as a type of ignorant spectator who fails to appreciate the serious and arcane significance of the masque.[31] Like Cokes, the footmen think that the most important requirement of masque is a series of eye catching scenic effects. Although this simplistic view of masque may be represented ironically, the dramatic vigour and literalising impetus of the antimasque remains intact and attempts to compress the mysteries of the masque into mere display. As necessity forces the Irish gentlemen to reject the traditional splendours of the Stuart court masque (they have lost their costumes *en route* to Whitehall), they prepare to dance in their mantles, which is in itself an important assertion of national culture, as the mantle was a distinguishing part of Irish dress that English officials sought to replace with the English cloak as part of their 'civilising' of Ireland.[32] This assertion of national identity is accompanied by a belittling of the most important member of the Stuart court after the King. As the footmen refer to the wedding they have come to celebrate they describe Carr as 'Robin' and remark on 'he tat vears te biggesht feather in ty court, King Yamish'. If size of feather denotes status, this too must be Carr. In debasing Carr's position the footmen also debase the court and its rituals, however, the satire in this court entertainment works in at least two directions, and the Irishmen's ignorance may also mean that, once again, they cannot appreciate the significance of the masque and the role of the masquers.

The masque proper opens as a gentleman appears to silence the footmen. He addresses the masquers in smooth poetry as opposed to the vigorous prose dialogue of the footmen and the masquers perform to the music of an Irish bard. The masque's mystery is reasserted and as the gentlemen dance their Irish mantles fall away, revealing rich masquing costumes. Irish becomes English in a smooth and miraculous transformation. Lindley writes that the figure of the bard in the masque is an appropriation of Irish culture and absorption of that nation into 'Britain'. He sums up this process in these terms: 'The assertion of civility is symbolised by the movement from servant to gentleman; prose to verse; dialect to "standard" English, and, of course, antimasque to masque'. This is all quite true, but does not sufficiently take into account the pressure of the expanded antimasque and its available implications that destabilise the 'truths' of the masque proper. In clearly proposing a conservative view of this masque, Lindley implicitly declares his opposition to a Cultural Materialist view of court masque as a subversive form, thereby returning us to the unhelpful binarism that dominates and petrifies masque criticism. Conversely, in this book I have tried to avoid essentialising the masque and to adopt instead a dialectical approach emphasising that the political and the philosophical are combined in the explicitly ideological court masque which is polythematic as well as polyvalent. It is this aspect of the Jonsonian masque that makes it such a richly rewarding cultural event to study.

Some conclusions on the expansion of the antimasque

In attempting to describe the way in which the antimasque and the fair destabilise or empty out the discourse of the masque, I have implied that the development of the antimasque is a logical culmination of Jonson's dialogic approach and oblique criticism of the monarchy. However, in the development of the antimasque there are other factors to be taken account of, such as the pressure of political events. Clearly, the reasons behind the growth of the antimasque are complex, and are not easily separated from each other but are interrelated in a way that can often seem confusing. For these reasons, the following summary account of the growth of the antimasque does not pretend to be definitive.

The cultural historian Roy Strong makes a link between the masque's form and content and the rise of Stuart absolutism, although it may be more accurate to describe this link in terms of the Stuart monarchs' continuing and intensifying, but ultimately unsuccessful, efforts to secure complete absolutism. On form Strong writes:

> It can be no coincidence either that perspective scenery was used for court performances only, and that its introduction into England coincided with the serious promotion of the Divine Right of Kings. Perspectives made the ruler the emblematic and ethical centre of every court production and emphasised the hierarchical gradations of life.[33]

By extrapolation, the expansion of the antimasque may also be viewed as part the Stuart monarchy's ideological goal of uncontested absolutism; this is seen to be the case according to the typically New Historicist analysis of the antimasque, whereby the powers of the masque and the monarchy are emphatically demonstrated by the fact that they seem to dispel magically the vigorous dissent of the antimasque. Thus, the antimasque plays a crucial role in the representation of the monarchy's absolute power, because dissent needs first to be represented in the antimasque before the powers manifested in the masque can deal with it. The masque presents a stylised and ideologically authoritative version of actuality where the spectators see for themselves the powers and effects of the monarchy. But if, on the one hand, the antimasque is implicated the masque's absolutism, on the other it also destabilises the metaphysical assertions of the masque, as I have shown earlier in this chapter; the whole court entertainment becomes polyvalent as royal hegemony is embodied, but only to be questioned by the expanded antimasque. The latter point of view might appear to negate the antimasque's implication in the absolutism of the masque, but in keeping with the dialogic impetus of the Jonsonian masque there appears to be a basis for both views (although, as I have suggested in this chapter, these alternatives are not always equally balanced. The court entertainments discussed here witness a marginalisation of the masque as it retreats under pressure from the antimasque). Strong underscores the fact that the dialogic impetus of the Jonsonian masque only disappeared under Charles I as royal claims to absolutism became more intense (for example during the twelve-year period of personal rule):

> By about 1630 these extremes of obscurity in allusion [in masque] were in retreat, giving way to a bolder, more easily read repertory. It cannot be a coincidence that this happened simultaneously with another development, the abandonment of a complex, polycentric vision which allowed for other viewpoints and readings, in favour of a unified monocular one which had no room for alternatives.[34]

So it seems that the expanded Jacobean antimasque served two masters, royal absolutism and the poet's articulation of dissent. This is a paradox brought about by the fact that the increasingly absolutist ways of the state encouraged the growth of the antimasque, but, taken to their logical conclusion in the reign of Charles I, largely destroyed it. However, as I have already suggested, the fact that the court entertainment can accommodate readings destabilising the masque indicates that 'absolutism' is not an accurate term to describe the ideology of masque; the fact that alternative readings are implicit in the court entertainment means that masque (and its ideology) did not enjoy an absolute or uncontested hegemony. It seems that the Jacobean assertion of 'divine right' allowed for the invocation of its binary opposite in the antimasque, and this may have been possible because of the Crown's belief in an unshakeable *status quo*. It is surely no accident that Jonson stopped writing court masques a very few years after Charles's accession to the throne. In the face of increasing political instability the new monarch required of masque an uncompromising form of panegyric where royal truths are asserted and not open to debate, for it was parliamentary debate on the state of the monarchical government that visibly undermined it. As the characteristic Jonsonian masque was dialogic there was no place for it under the new regime. Jonson did write two Caroline masques but they are very different from earlier masques as they are styled to meet the needs of the new King, as I will discuss in the following chapter.

Another motivating factor behind the growth of the antimasque may have been the poet's desire to address the actual nature of the court. As Stephen Orgel has pointed out, the masque presented courtiers in their idealised roles, that is, the masque is a philosophical ideal of what the courtiers should be.[35] As the masque traditionally precluded comment on the historical reality of court life, Jonson developed the antimasque to accommodate what he saw as his role as social commentator, pointing out the faults of this elite part of society with a view to its reform. Again, this element of mimetic realism may be seen as a feature of the grotesque and an importation from comedies such as *Bartholomew Fair*. The satirical basis of this mimetic realism is obvious in a masque such as *Mercury Vindicated* where the dramatic antimasque reflects the actual corruption and overweening ambition of prominent courtiers by presenting Mercury as a creative spirit (often a quality associated with the King in masque) enslaved by Vulcan and producing deformed creatures. The dramatic antimasque allows Jonson to comment critically on what is wrong with the government and the court, whereas the masque is largely restricted to an idealising reflection upon the monarchical hierarchy (although latent ironies are present in the apparently most orthodox masques). In developing the antimasque, Jonson makes room for his own critical voice to be heard and the comic and dramatic form of the antimasque can also be understood as a result of his instinct for theatrical drama. The antimasque often shares with Jonson's satirical comedy for the public stage a fast and furious pace, absurdities and caricatures which provoke hilarity, but which also function as moral fables and the overwhelming message of both these literary modes is that everyone has the potential of becoming like the comic villains of drama or the absurd grotesques of antimasque if we do not pause to reflect, or undergo a neoclassical self-criticism.

My discussion of the carnivalesque aspects of the antimasque has led to a consideration of its expansion into comic mini-drama. In both his drama and court entertainments of 1613/14 Jonson erodes the barriers between the culturally high and the culturally low. Of course, this erosion is never complete in the court entertainment as the masque always re-establishes itself, but not before the absolutism of its discourse has been ineradicably questioned. It is this power of certain mature Jonsonian court entertainments to question and discuss the royal hegemony that they themselves express (and would not exist without) that makes them intriguing texts to study. Earlier masques such as *Blackness* gesture towards the more fully worked out dialectical structures of later masques, where the critical impulse is fully developed in the way I have described. It may be that these distinctive characteristics of the mature Jonsonian court entertainment place him in a wider European frame, an insight drawn from the fact that Terence Cave's comments on the major French writers of the Renaissance seem particularly apt in respect of the mature Jonsonian antimasque:

> The major French Renaissance texts are characteristically reflexive, dialogic, and open-ended. Written in the shadow of an impossible ideal, they proliferate in order to question themselves and lay bare their own mechanisms.[36]

Notes

1. Stallybrass and White (1986), 66, and the section 'Smithfield And Authorship Ben Jonson'.
2. Bakhtin (1986), 470-1.

3. Bakhtin's ideas have permeated much recent criticism of *Bartholomew Fair*. For a materialist slant, see Haynes (1984), 645-68. For a feminist shaping of Bakhtinian criticism, see Paster (1987), 43-65.
4. Fisher (1997), 59-84 (62).
5. Bakhtin (1986), 7. Further references to this edition are given after quotations in the text.
6. We should not be too ready to follow Bakhtin in dismissing all satire as a reductive literary form. Such a definition is far too simplistic to describe Jonson's use of satire. I showed in Chapter 1 that both Jonson's verse panegyric and his verse satire are didactic and geared towards reform. This regenerative impulse, however, is muted in the dramatic comedies, and especially in *Bartholomew Fair*.
7. Rhodes (1980), 7.
8. On the Elizabethan discourse of the grotesque, and with particular reference to *Bartholomew Fair*, see Rhodes (1980), 3-155.
9. Bakhtin associates the festive abuse and focus upon the low in medieval grotesque with regeneration and cycles of renewal, and differentiates this from a Romantic manifestation of the grotesque where there is an emphasis on horror and the alienated individual. An example of this type of grotesque may be found in Wordsworth's reflections on Bartholomew Fair in *The Prelude*:

> All freaks of Nature, all Promethean thoughts
> Of Man; his dulness, madness, and their feats,
> All jumbled up together to make up
> This Parliament of Monsters. Tents and Booths
> Meanwhile, as if the whole were one vast Mill,
> Are vomiting, receiving on all sides,
> Men, Women, three-years' children, Babes in arms.
>
> (VII:679-94)

10. Stallybrass and White (1986), 22.
11. The pig is commonly used to describe those we consider to be greedy or bigoted. The pig is also traditionally reviled by Judaism as unclean and Christian discourse adopted this symbolism, hence the Prodigal Son in the depths of his despair lives with pigs and shares their food. However, the pig itself provides sustaining food - unlike other farm animals the pig is only worth its meat. Early Renaissance agricultural tracts praised the pig for being the farmer's ally, manuring the land and disposing of waste. The Bartholomew pig focuses ideological conflict, it is food and excrement, useful and a pest, classical and grotesque, Renaissance and Medieval.
12. The socio-economic order of the medieval period was unsettled in the early seventeenth century with the growth in wealth of the middle classes and yeoman farmers. This was brought about primarily by inflation; those who produced goods for sale gained political power commensurate with their new wealth. As an illustration of this social mobility Christopher Hill quotes Dekker in *The Honest Whore* (1604) II.i:

> *Castruchio*: What an ass is that lord, to borrow money of a citizen!
> *Belafont*: Nay, God's my pity, what an ass is that citizen to lend money to a lord!

There are many other references of this type in drama of the period where the

young aristocratic ass squanders his patrimony on the ephemeral pleasures of London. Depopulation of the countryside in favour of the new industrial centres was accompanied by the passing of land from the crown and peerage to the gentry, as Fynes Moryson disdainfully observed, 'Gentlemen disdaining traffic and living in idleness do in this course daily sell their patrimonies... The buyers are for the most part citizens and vulgar men.' As the bourgeoisie ousted the aristocracy from economic pre-eminence, they sought to differentiate themselves from the masses; this tendency is imaged in the scornful and superior attitude expressed by Quarlous etc. towards the traders in *Bartholomew Fair*. See Hill (1989), 11-15.
13. Cartelli (1983), 151-72.
14. Rhodes (1980), 142. Rhodes points out that the word 'mansion' also links the fair with the old morality drama where mansions were fixed symbolic centres for Everyman to negotiate his way through.
15. Prescott (1984), 407-30 (407).
16. In this connection it is useful to note the historical context of this entertainment. By 1611, the King's relations with Parliament had reached a low point. The Crown suffered from increasing debt, inefficiency and corruption in its machinery of government. In an attempt to improve efficiency and revenues, the Secretary of State, Robert Cecil, drew up the Great Contract in 1610. The proposal was that the Crown would surrender its feudal rights in return for an annual grant and immediate subsidy. The proposal failed, as Parliament was angered by the amount demanded. The King, wary of surrendering his sovereignty, raised the stakes too high until the terms of the contract were unacceptable. The failure of the Great Contract led to the dissolution of Parliament in 1611. Among the disgruntled members of Parliament were those we could crudely label as the Puritan faction. The Hampton Court Conference of 1604 on religious matters had raised the hopes of moderate Puritans, yet most of the few concessions granted were never honoured. In addition to such religious and parliamentarian unrest there was concern caused by James's adoption of his favourite, Robert Carr. By 1611, Carr was in the ascendant. It could be said that James's poor judgement is reflected in his appointment of his inexperienced favourite to be Cecil's successor as acting Secretary of State. In a few years Carr would fall from favour embroiled in scandal associated with murder, magic and infidelity. The major text used for this historical material is Akrigg (1962).
17. For a description of the topos of the 'topsy-turvey world' or 'the world turned upside down' see Stallybrass and White (1986), 56-9.
18. Marcus (1986), 32
19. Stallybrass and White (1986), 191.
20. Jonson's claim for the unique status of the poet as advisor to kings is well known. In l.3016 of his *Discoveries* Jonson noted, 'Solus rex, aut poeta, non quotannis nascitur' – Only kings and poets are not born every year. Parfitt (1988), 447.
21. In Chapter 1 I suggested that the figures of Niger, Oceanus and Sol in *The Masque of Blackness* (1605) are all characterisations of the different facets of King James. Similarly, the presence of Hercules in *Pleasure Reconciled To Virtue* (1618) suggests the multiple nature of the King, as Hercules was renowned for being a drunkard as well as for his heroic strength and fortitude.
22. Paradoxically, while the Puritans/Sphinx represent potential subversion of the monarchy, they also represent another focus of authority (just as Rabbi Busy

claims an authoritative status in *Bartholomew Fair*). This dual role can be explained by a shift in focus up or down the social grid that I have already discussed in this chapter. However, the Puritan insistence on a spiritual hierarchy produces a different but related discourse where the social grid remains the same but with substituted cultural categories. In this reformulation of the social grid the Puritans claimed religious authority (in God's name) over and above the King, which also served to weaken the monarch's secular authority. Identity is still constructed here in terms of inferiority and superiority in a hierarchical model.
23. Lindley (1987), 248-64.
24. At the end of Chapter 3 I discussed this type of indeterminacy or polyvalence which is apparent in much of Jonson's work, with reference to Annabel Patterson's theory of 'functional ambiguity'.
25. Eagleton (1981), 148.
26. Stallybrass and White (1986), 14.
27. I adopt this term from Theodore B. Leinwand's essay, 'Negotiation and New Historicism'. In this excellent essay Leinwand reviews the subversion/containment debate and rejects it as a reductive binarism. In its place he posits a more complex view of the negotiations that take place in a text. These texts are historically contingent and reflect a moment in the constantly shifting balance of power. He sees texts as both potentially subversive and conservative, with the emphasis on either of these terms depending on the moment of the text's historical production; Leinwand (1990), 477-90.
28. Rhodes (1980), 3-155.
29. *Ben Jonson: The Complete Masques*, ed. Stephen Orgel (1975), 484.
30. On the debate regarding the respective merits of Jonson's poetry and Jones's architecture see D. J. Gordon (1949), 152-78; and Evans (1992), 3-37 (note 18).
31. Jonson's scorn for those who failed to comprehend the symbolism of these ritual occasions is illustrated in his note to the printed text of his part in King James's accession day festivities: 'Neither was it becomming, or could it stand with the dignitie of these shewes (after the most miserable and desperate shift of the Puppits) to require a truch-man, or (with the ignorant Painter) one to write, *This is a dog*; or *This is a hare*: but so presented, as upon the view, they might, without cloud, or obscurity declare themselves to the sharpe and learned: And for the multitude; no doubt but their grounded judgements did gaze, said it was fine, and were satisfied'; HS (1925-52), vol.VII, 91.
32. In this period, Ireland's 'improvement' was often represented in terms of its increasing Anglicism, and its insufficiency as rooted in native Irishness; see, for example, Fynes Moryson's description of dietary habits: 'Many of the English-Irish have by little and little been infected with the Irish filthiness, and that in the very cities, excepting Dublin, and some of the better sort in Waterford, where, the English continually lodging in their houses, they more retain the English diet'; Moryson (1603?: 1890), 413-30 (419).
33. Strong (1984), 156.
34. Strong (1984), 32.
35. Orgel, *The Illusion of Power* (1975a), 39.
36. Cave (1979), 182.

5
Heavenly love and the collapse of the court masque

Jonson wrote his two final court masques in 1631 after a fall from favour lasting six years. These two masques depart from those written for the Jacobean court in several ways, and these changes may be linked with the new political and aesthetic climate of the Caroline court. Through his promotion of the arts Charles asserted his view of kingship. In 1629 he commissioned Rubens to paint the ceiling of the Banqueting House at Whitehall, and the design (which was probably worked out by Charles himself in conjunction with Inigo Jones) featured the heavenly apotheosis of James I, a graphic emphasis of the Stuart belief in the divine sanction of their rule. Charles appeared to grasp immediately how the arts might be manipulated to reinforce the power of the State, and his own absolutist claims; the Whitehall ceiling depicted a King who possessed all essential wisdom, and thereby powerfully self-sufficient and in no need of any outside counsel. Charles was interested in all manner of the arts, he amassed a great collection of fine art, encouraged composers, and purportedly wrote plays that were attributed to other writers. It is likely then, that Charles would have been interested in the court masque for aesthetic as well as ideological reasons. Even if Charles did not actually compose the texts of these late masques, it seems probable that his views and tastes powerfully informed their content, although we should not underestimate Henrietta Maria's influence in this sphere. Royal taste largely accounts for the fact that the theatricals and masques of the Caroline court were pastoral in style, and largely omitted the political strains of the Jacobean entertainments. Jonson's last masques appear to be shaped by this intensified atmosphere of royal absolutism, and the court masque as a genre seems to collapse into a monologic representation of royal authority. However, despite this collapse and the enfeebling of the antimasque, ironic tensions and contradictions remain latent within the masque itself, in a manner similar to the early masques. This may be attributable to the fact that ideology, no matter how absolute, is never completely self-contained, and, moreover, that Jonson's critical impulse was extremely developed by the time he wrote these masques, thus making it unlikely that this impulse would be completely extinguished, even under these conditions of intensified royal absolutism.

The masques of 1631 constitute the last, declining phase of the Jonsonian court entertainment and, in particular, the enfeeblement of the antimasque. The antimasque itself had grown out of latent ironies in the early masques, and developed into a dominant component of the Jacobean court entertainment, encompassing strategies of dissent that offset and questioned the ideology manifest in the masque proper. The Caroline entertainments witness the decline of the expanded antimasque, which is enfeebled and stripped of its capacity to articulate dissent. However, it bears repeating that, despite the enfeebled nature of the Caroline masque, even these, the most orthodox of court entertainments, express anomalies and contradictions in the masque itself which qualify its main assertions.

Through the pastoral fantasies represented by these masques, the King declared for himself and his court an unassailable and self-contained status, a claim which Parliament had previously resented and interpreted as an illegal and tyrannical assault upon their rights enshrined in common law. Although Parliament was dissolved throughout the 1630s, the period during which these entertainments were staged, the grievances of 1629 did not evaporate and were shown to be of concern to the next Parliament of 1640, following the twelve years of Charles's personal rule. Despite the King's attempt to quash Parliament's articulation of political dissent, widespread discontent rapidly increased. In 1626 Parliament attempted to impeach Buckingham; the attempt failed but it coalesced public resentment at the power and influence enjoyed by the royal favourite and may have indirectly contributed to his assassination two years later. Charles found Parliament so intractable that he dissolved it in 1629 for twelve years, and it was during this period that Jonson wrote his last masques. Religious and political discontent increased sharply during 1633/4 with the appointment of the Arminian, Laud, as Archbishop of Canterbury, and the introduction of Ship Money tax, which was widely resisted and lead to the infamous trial of John Hampden. Parliament was so incensed by these developments that, in 1640, it successfully impeached the Lord Treasurer, Strafford, and Archbishop Laud, both of whom were later executed. This political strife soon exploded into Civil War; Charles could no longer look to the pastoral fantasies of the court (including Jonson's last masques) for a definitive representation of himself as monarch, and was forced to turn his attention outward, to the contentions of the real world pressing in upon the court.[1]

As I suggested earlier, Jonson's last masques, *Love's Triumph Through Callipolis* and *Chloridia* appear to share in the conspiracy of silence on political matters characterising royal productions of their particular historical moment. The fact that they seem to operate as a monologic articulation of royal policy, lacking the dialogism of earlier masques may be accounted for when we remember that, in addition to the new political and aesthetic climate at court, Jonson's enforced estrangement from court circles meant that he was probably keen to produce entertainments that would meet with approval and fit in with the fashionable cult of neo-platonic love fostered under Charles and Henrietta Maria. In this chapter I will offer a reading of the first of these masques and then go on to suggest in more detail how it differs formally from earlier masques.

Love's Triumph Through Callipolis

Love's Triumph Through Callipolis is the first of a pair of masques performed in the New Year of 1631; it was performed by the King and his gentlemen, and was followed by *Chloridia*, an accompanying entertainment in which the Queen and her ladies performed. The preface to *Love's Triumph* designates Ben Jonson and Inigo Jones as the 'inventors'; D. J. Gordon has written on the significance of this term and the great importance attached to it. Briefly, the conceit of 'invention' encompassed the authorship of the masque's informing philosophy; the inventor had a status superior to that of a mere writer, designer or musician, whose skills were employed in realising the 'inventor's' overall vision.[2] The competition between Jonson and Jones in this respect has been summarised by Orgel and Strong as, 'The question of what constituted the 'invention' of the work; of whether spectacle was an expression of the text, or text an explanation of the spectacle'.[3] It is notable that after his quarrels with Jones, and the court's displeasure with him in favour of Jones, Jonson should retain the top billing in this partnership. Orgel and Strong emphasise that the preface raises Jones to the status of co-inventor with Jonson, but it is significant that Jonson's name still has priority over Jones's in the printed text. This may be accounted for by the textual authority of the writer; whereas Jones would be concerned with creating the spectacle of the masque, terminating at the end of the night, Jonson not only wrote the poetry but also prepared the texts for publication and posterity.[4] In managing the text for the press Jonson can still assert an authorial supremacy over the architect, although this may not strictly mirror their ongoing power struggle at court in which Jones often seems to have been the victor.

The epigraph at the head of the masque text reads, '*Quandos magis dignos licuit spectare triumphos* ?', this is an allusion to Martial and translated in the Orgel edition of the complete masques as, 'When could one behold more worthy triumphs'. This quotation may be an example of what Neil Rhodes describes as rhetorical 'bravery', that is, a confident assertion of the power of the poetry and spectacle of the masque to move the spectator or reader of the text.[5] However, it may also be another example of the covert irony that is present elsewhere in Jonson's poetry. The Latin word 'spectare' seems to emphasise the cognate English word 'spectacle', which can be used in the pejorative sense of a visual splendour that is superficial and empty of any deeper meaning, just as Jonson's famous 'Expostulation with Inigo Jones' dismisses and denigrates Jones for his 'mighty shows' made out of 'inch board' and 'slit deal'. 'Triumphos' is the final word of this quotation which, obviously, means 'triumphs' in English. In his book *Art and Power* Roy Strong discusses the triumphal entry of military victors into the vanquished city (Mantegna's *Triumphs of Caesar* are an early modern pictorial representation of this) as a cultural precursor to the monarch's entrance into a city that is already part of the nation-state and where the city authorities fete their own monarch.[6] These events shared an emphasis on visual display and spectacle, and much of their significance is derived from the fact that existing power relations were made publicly visible through a symbolic demonstration in which the city fathers acknowledged the superiority of the monarch. The epigraph's last word, 'triumphos' calls on all these associations, linking with 'spectare' and 'spectacle', and exploiting the ambivalent resonance of that term. These associations are not arbitrary, and Jonson may have deliberately incorporated them in the beginning of the masque text in an indirect defence of his own philosophically based art. Such a defence incorporates an implicit attack on Jones's creation of spectacle as empty and meretricious set decoration (although it was now as important as masque poetry, as Jones's title of 'co-inventor' demonstrates). The semantic instability of the Martial quotation may be read ironically, and interpreted as the poet's vigorous self-defence, just before his failing powers and influence were finally extinguished.[7]

The preface to this masque is often quoted when critics attempt to explain a Jonsonian 'theory' of masque. Jonson writes that 'public spectacles, either have been or ought to be the mirror of man's life' and 'carry a mixture of profit with them no less than delight'. Didacticism combined with entertainment is easily recognised as one of Jonson core poetic tenets (see Chapter 1); the mirror image, however, seems to have generated some confusion. It has been cited as evidence for the ideality of the Jonsonian court masque, that the courtiers are important in their symbolic roles, not as who they really are.[8] But surely, the most obvious fact about a mirror is that it provides an accurate reflection, rather than being an agent of transformation, as the argument above appears to assume. It is worth noting, however, the seventeenth-century mirrors were often full of what we would describe as imperfections and presented slightly distorted images of the subject. In fact such subtle distortions were often held to be fascinating in their own right, and were incorporated as a design feature, illustrated by Parmigianino's *Self-portrait in a convex mirror* (1524).[9] These distortions, however, do not present a complete transformation of the subject but alter the perspective in subtle ways. Similarly, masque offers a manipulated perspective that idealises the courtiers, who perform in a ritualised spectacle; this is not an accurate, realist mirroring of actuality but neither is it a wholesale transformation. Like the mirror, the distortions of the masque encompass glimpsed possibilities of an alternative image or self that may be strived for by the courtly masquers and audience in their everyday lives. The responsibility for the transformation of the self is placed with the courtiers themselves, rather than immediately conferred by participation in the masque. Thus, masque retains the didactic edge that Jonson emphasises in this preface by withholding the courtiers' ideal status, but, at the same time, presenting them with a suggestion of the ideal. The gap between the ideality of the masque and the actuality of the court is didactic, and it is up to the courtiers to cross it. This figurative sense of a perspective on the self is paralleled by the use of lines of perspective in the traditional masque set. This use of physical perspective idealises the social hierarchy which the King surmounted, and represents a philosophical and pseudo-empirical justification of the absolutism which Charles claimed. Like the image of King James painted on the Banqueting House ceiling, the monarch's central position in the masque audience (where all lines of perspective meet) demonstrates that he sees, and thus knows, everything.[10] Yet, the certainties of the perspective set, are often destabilised by the anxieties manifested in the masque text, as I hope to show below. In *Love's Triumph*, the traditional lines of perspective meet at Henrietta Maria seated at the forefront of the audience, occupying the King's usual position. The royal persona is still all-seeing but, importantly, female rather than male. The Queen's adoption of the King's usual position in the audience may be partly explained in pragmatic terms, in that this space was unoccupied by the King who was directly involved in this entertainment as a masquer; the Queen fills the gap left by the King ensuring that royalty remains the literal and philosophical fulcrum of the court. The absolutist implications of masque remain intact, although the shift in focus from King to Queen may indicate a wider anxiety about her undue influence and unprecedented role.

The conceit behind the masque is the King's 'heroic love' for his 'unmatchable lady', and this encompasses two dominant features of the masque: the cult of neo-platonic love and the Queen's exceptional status apart from other women.[11] Her importance is symbolised by the fact that, as I noted earlier, she provides a second, alternative focus for the perspective set. A divine messenger finds the Queen enthroned, presumably within the audience rather than on the masque stage, although the text is not precise on this point, and informs her that the city of Callipolis (the City of Beauty) has been infiltrated by depraved lovers. King Charles, however, formed another symbolic focus in other ways. The King appears on the masque 'stage' in a group of fifteen lovers who symbolise the positive and platonic aspects of love as opposed to the earlier aberrant, humorous lovers of the antimasque. The virtuous lovers are arranged on the page of the text and in the masque itself in two columns of seven with King Charles making up the fifteenth in the middle. There is possible some number symbolism at work here as well as the more obvious symbol that the two columns with Charles stood midcentre form an H for Henrietta Maria, the object of the King's heroic love.[12]

The depraved lovers reported to the Queen clearly represent all the values rejected by neo-platonism, but there is also good reason to think that Jonson is specifically attacking Puritan dissent. This is a favourite target for Jonson who had attacked Puritan influence in masques such as *Love Freed From Ignorance And Folly* (1611) and *Love Restored* (1612), and in the plays *The Alchemist* (1610) and *Bartholomew Fair* (1614). Moreover, the depraved lovers are also described as 'sectaries', a term explicitly linking with Puritans rather than with any other group, and reflecting their tendency to fragment into many autonomous sects adding to the theological confusion and power struggle in the years prior to and during the Civil War and Commonwealth.[13] These sectaries are seen as oppositional to the courtly cult of neo-platonic love, they 'neither knew the name or nature of love rightly, yet boasted themselves his followers' (ll.21-2). Similarly, in championing the authority of a Calvinist God, Puritans rejected the court fashion of a neo-platonist form of Christianity. These 'bad' lovers make up the antimasque and 'leap forth below, a mistress leading them,... with antic gesticulation' (ll.26-9). It is worth noting that the leader of the depraved lovers is specifically female, as the connection between excess of all kinds and women was of long standing.[14] The depraved lovers represent excessive emotion which is deformed by its lack of grounding in reasoned neo-platonism (as exhibited by King Charles himself who represents platonic 'heroic love' in this masque). Such 'female' incontinence is accompanied by superfluous, exaggerated or hysterical words and action; thus there is 'A glorious boasting lover / A whining ballading lover / An adventurous romance lover' etc. The fact that the lovers are led by a mistress, representing what was popularly interpreted as a specifically female lack of control reinforces the traditional sense of antimasque chaos versus the harmony of masque; but in this instance the first is pointedly female, the latter male and represented by King Charles himself. This emphasis on excess as a threat to the traditional structures of order and reason connects with much that I have said about the grotesque in the previous chapter, and it may be that the incontinent 'mistress' is deliberately intended as a carnivalesque inversion of, or anti-type to Henrietta Maria, a figure on to which anxiety about the Queen's excessive influence and rejection of the traditional subordinate role could be displayed or projected.

What is intriguing about these lovers is that they are separated into four groups 'in the scenicall persons and habits of the four prime European nations'. Orgel and Strong assert that 'Jones' designs do not bear this out', on the grounds that many of the costumes in the masque sketches are derived from the Italian *commedia dell'arte* and a few are in Northern European style (pp.409-15). This is doubtless true, but does not prevent these designs from being allocated to specific national groups. Jones's sketch of the scornful lover, for example, features a costume described by Orgel and Strong as 'North European, ... old-fashioned, with the ruff and trunk hose of the late Elizabethan and Jacobean period'. What they omit is the fact that although the costume became fashionable in England, it originated in Spain and was associated with that country. Appropriately, the courtier wearing a ruff is described on the sketch as the 'scornful lover', fitting with popular notions about Spanish pride. So, although the masque text is silent on the point of which European nations are specifically referred to, it is possible to speculate in this area (perhaps the text's silence on the nationality of the lovers is an instance of Jonson's diplomacy, as to satirise French lovers, among others, in a masque celebrating Henrietta Maria's virtues would be politically inflammatory). It is likely that France, Italy and Spain would be included here, and certainly three of the groups fit in with popular caricatures of the Mediterranean nations as 'boasting', 'corrupt' and 'scornful' lovers. The French were traditional targets for British jingoism, the Italians had produced Machiavelli and were renown for deceit and intrigue, just as the Spaniards were known for their pride. The fourth group is characterised by 'A melencholic despairing lover' who possibly represents the Protestant Northern states; in Northern Europe melancholy had become a fashionable mode of behaviour, probably partly because of its roots in Calvinist theology – in this respect it is significant that the most famous melancholic dramatic protagonist, Hamlet, is a Dane. The Calvinist emphasis on predestination impelled believers to seek out signs in their lives indicating if they were to be saved or damned. The potential impossibility of this task, coupled with a deep fear of preordained damnation which the individual was powerless to alter must have often produced acute despair or melancholy. It is unlikely that British or English lovers make up one of these groups, as

Britain did not then regard itself as part of Europe, as many British people still do not. In fact, what is going on in this masque is a very typical form of British jingoism, or a celebration of 'little England'. Serious political powers are ridiculed and denigrated, belittled into nothing more than ridiculous lovers, whereas the British lovers (i.e. Charles and his gentlemen) appear in all pomp and ceremony. This national stereotyping aggrandises a financially and militarily weak Britain by ridiculing those countries which posed the greatest threat to domestic security.[15]

The antimasque is banished with the descent of Euphemus whose name means 'Well-omened', he heralds harmony and platonic love. Interestingly, he is Euphemus rather than Euphema, that is, he is specifically male and represents the opposite of the 'mistress' who lead the 'depraved lovers' – thus the antimasque and masque draw on gendered stereotypes to reinforce the contrast between chaos and harmony that is traditionally embodied in the antimasque/masque structure. Euphemus uses specifically neo-platonic language and imagery in his paean to love, he speaks of 'chaste desires' and 'a harmony of parts'. This platonic love also has a separate time scheme and is immune to decay. With reference to the Queen, Euphemus describes Callipolis as 'by the splendour of your rays made bright' and this language is particularly notable here as sun imagery of this sort usually describes the King's symbolic powers. In this masque, however, the sun imagery is devoted to the Queen, constituting another instance of the Queen's role as an alternative focus in the masque and indicating a greater concern with gender in the form. In the traditional discourse of the Stuart masque the King is always the apotheosis of mortal man because of his semi-divine nature. *Love's Triumph* extends this status to the Queen and focuses on her exalted nature, while less rigorously emphasising this aspect of the King. One pragmatic reason for this is that *Love's Triumph* is only the first part of a pair of masques, which focuses on the Queen, and designed around the King's performance. Although the second masque of this pair, *Chloridia*, was performed by the Queen and her ladies, there is not, however, a complete reversal of the pattern seen in *Love's Triumph*, i.e. a masque concentrating on the nature of King Charles. *Chloridia*, rather, draws on a completely different conceit, that of 'some rites done to the goddess Chloris'. What this suggests is that *Love's Triumph* exhibits a unique concern to explore the nature and role of the Queen, which is not mirrored in the companion masque by a consideration of the King's role. The shift in focus away from Charles (a stark contrast from the earlier Jacobean masque) may indicate that Caroline masques are interesting largely for what they do not say or show, as the idealised fictions of the stage increasingly diverged from political realities. So, although Charles performs in *Love's Triumph*, any direct reference to him as King is occluded, perhaps suggesting the King's desire to deflect any speculation about his own political function, while the focus on Henrietta Maria and her cult of neo-platonic love allows the political ideology of the Caroline court to be represented in its most aesthetic and abstract form. The shift in focus from King to Queen may be additionally explained by the fact that the King's role in the political hierarchy was already understood by the court, whereas the Queen's role caused some anxiety; she was the first significant consort of a Tudor or Stuart monarch and further disadvantaged by being a French Catholic. The qualities attributed to the archetypal female have already been exhibited by the 'mistress' in the antimasque, and this necessarily problematises Henrietta Maria's position. How can a state be influenced and the King advised by such a flawed sex? There is a risk that his own claim to semi-divine status could be undermined by this anomaly. The masque of *Love's Triumph* circumvents such anxieties by displacing then on to another, and openly vilified female figure (the 'mistress') and by insisting that although the Queen is female, she is exceptional and not representative of her sex.[16] Euphemus initiates the process of distancing Henrietta Maria from ordinary women:

> To you that are by excellence a queen,
>   The top of beauty! but of such an air
> As only by the mind's eye may be seen
>   Your interwoven lines of good and fair.

(ll.61–4)

These lines distinguish the Queen as the height of her sex's beauty and then go further to remove her from this set of terms altogether: her real beauty is metaphysical and can only be perceived by the mind. This may well be a stock conceit deployed by Jonson when praising his aristocratic patronesses and acts as a diplomatic assurance that moral virtue and intellectual qualities do not necessarily preclude physical charms; his well known poem 'Epistle. To Katherine, Lady Aubigny' also rests largely on this governing conceit. In *Love's Triumph* this abstracting conceit is taken to its extreme and Henrietta Maria becomes a neo-platonic principle, or a geometrical symbol whose lines are 'good and fair'. In fact, this ethereal, extraordinary nature is extended to all the court ladies as a justification of their exalted positions in society. Their breasts are transformed into altars and they become marmoreal and symbolic versions of themselves:

> Here, perfect lovers, you must pay
> First fruits, and on these altars lay
> (The ladies' breasts) your ample vows
> Such as Love brings, and beauty best allows.

(ll.109–12)

Femaleness is reformulated into an aesthetic of passive beauty waiting to be distinguished by active male love, in contrast to the more disconcerting representation in the antimasque of the female 'mistress' whose centrifugal influence heralds a disruption similar to the destructive effect of Puritan dissent on the authority of the Crown. This reformulation of femaleness could be seen as another strategy for containing Henrietta Maria's influence and diffusing the potential threat to the political order which she represents. Such a strategy resembles the convention of courtly love, which at once elevates the woman to the status of a goddess and places her more firmly under male control. In this masque, the Queen herself is literally translated to pure geometry:

> *Euphemus*: The queen of what is wonder in the place!
> *Amphitrite*: Pure object of heroic love alone!
> *Euphemus*: The centre of proportion –
> *Amphitrite*:   Sweetness –
> *Euphemus*:   Grace!
> *Amphitrite*: Deign to receive all lines of love in one.
> *Euphemus*: And by reflecting them fill this space.
> *Chorus*: Till it a circle of those glories prove
>   Fit to be sought in beauty, found by Love.
>
> (ll.116–22)

The Queen becomes a passive symbol sought out by the geometrician 'Love' or in this case the King. The masque then goes on specifically to associate this geometrical, classically based neo-platonism with traditional Christian language and symbolism, and draws on the creation myth in Genesis:

> So Love, emergent out of chaos, brought
>   The world to light!
> And gently moving on the waters, wrought
>   All form to sight!
>
> (ll.135–8)

The Christian creation myth is aligned with classical mythology and philosophy, 'And Neptune too / Shows what his waves can do'. Orgel and Strong find a platonic basis for the sea imagery, 'if we consult the mythographers we will learn that Henrietta Maria's official persona, the Queen of Love, was born from the sea, and that Neptune was the creator and tamer of horses, the Platonic emblem of the passions' (p.54). This imagery also fits in with Charles's foreign and domestic ambitions. Kevin Sharpe writes that 'Charles I regarded a strong navy as essential to the maintenance of English security and the preservation of England's and his own authority'.[17] The King pursued a policy of building up a navy for trade and military defence, and his claims to the sea are reflected in John Selden's legal treatise *Mare Clausum* (Selden was, of course, a close acquaintance of Jonson's). Charles's personal commitment to the navy is illustrated further by his pursuit of the unpopular Ship Money tax.

Venus sings the closing hymn of the masque after the throne has disappeared and is replaced by a palm tree with an imperial crown at the top, entwined with lilies and roses, emblems of France and Britain. The palm tree is said to be emblematic of 'Beauty and Love, whose story is mysterial'. This mystical discourse attempts to obscure the real anxieties about gender that have informed this court entertainment; we are presented with an image that suggests harmony and equality between Queen and King, Beauty and Love, Lily and Rose, thereby erasing any suggestions of undue power and influence on the part of Henrietta Maria. The agents of dissent are expelled (i.e. the 'mistress' and depraved lovers) or reformulated and absorbed by the masque itself, as in the Queen's case. Henrietta Maria becomes a geometrical and philosophical principle and, while she is made symbolically central, is shown to lack any real power as she is dependent on the active male principle of love for her definition and identity. The final absorption of her difference is achieved through the manipulation of her name in the last lines of the masque; she is no longer disconcertingly French Henrietta Maria, but an anglicised Mary.

The collapse of the dialogic masque

The two Caroline masques written by Jonson differ in that they lack significant structures of dissent running through them. The antimasque is silenced and reduced to pantomime; significantly, the 'bad' lovers in *Love's Triumph* are described in terms of *Pantomimi* or Roman mimes, thereby relating them to the antimasque of *Queens* rather than to any of the later antimasques. In *The Masque of Queens* the antimasque is made up of witches who perform bizarre dances to cacophonous music and then are banished suddenly by the appearance of the masque and its 'mystical' powers. The antimasque lovers in *Love's Triumph* perform actions similar to those of the witches and are also banished suddenly. Most importantly, this antimasque lacks dialogue, thus depriving it of the capacity to articulate verbally values contradicting those of the masque; thus the antimasque is silenced and its powers of dissent enfeebled. This disempowerment of the antimasque is not complete, however, because, as I discussed in Chapter 3, in order for the masque to deal with dissent it must first represent it, thereby, paradoxically, empowering it to some extent. In their silent representation of chaos, the antimasque characters still present a different order of values to those of the masque. Notably, the antimasque's weakened powers of contradiction are matched by the expansion of the masque itself – a direct reversal of the earlier pattern of development where the expanded antimasque threatened to consume the masque, as I describe in Chapter 4. However, Jonson comes full circle, as it were, with the late entertainments, because the masque of *Love's Triumph* still evinces the internal contradictions distinguishing the early *Masque of Blackness*, which, together with the presence of the antimasque, ensure a qualification of dominant state ideology.

Caroline masque as absolutist ritual

Discussion of the court masque often assumes the absolutism of the Stuart monarchy to be the fundamental explanation for the symbolic form and content of the court entertainment, foregrounding the masque as an emphatic confirmation of political hegemony. I have already disputed this view at some length and suggested that Jonson's masques involve criticism as well as confirmation. At the end of Chapter 4 I questioned the nature of this royal absolutism on the grounds that any degree of contradiction represented by the court masque undermines pure absolutism. Alan Sinfield has used the work of historians, (some Marxist, but not all) to explore the claims of absolutism surrounding the Stuart court and revealed them to be questionable. This weakening of absolutism, in practice, accelerated in Charles's reign and resulted in masques that, by way of compensation, even more stridently assert the principle of a divinely sanctioned monarchy and occlude any reference to the political world outside the court's pastoral fantasies. Nicos Poulantzas makes a significant point when he remarks that in early modern England political power and economic wealth were not commensurate: 'The dominance of the feudal type in the state continues even after the bourgeoisie have obtained political power, providing a characteristic example of the dislocation between the state's structures and its political powers'. So, the monarchy and its aristocratic network controlled ideology even after Parliament had begun to take control of the purse strings, and while the monarchy was seen to be invested with total power, it suffered from economic and even political weakness. Poulantzas views the 'absolutist' state more as a period of transition between feudalism and capitalism, a view corroborated by Perry Anderson who describes England's absolutism as 'the weakest and shortest' in western Europe. W.T. MacCaffrey recognises a consolidation of monarchical power under Henry VIII and a leaking away of royal power thereafter: 'In short, the effort of the monarchy to deploy its authority more widely and more variously was being checked even before 1603 by the marked revival of aristocratic initiative'.[18] If loss of royal power can be seen as an increasing trend culminating under Charles I, the nature of Jonson's Caroline masques becomes clearer. The King's traditional manipulation of state ideology is all that is left him as Parliament whittles away at the royal prerogative, and assertion of that ideology becomes all the more imperative, the more it is attacked or eroded. In such an economically weakened position the control of ideology becomes increasingly important. The King must be represented as omnipotent and self-sufficient even if this is not strictly true. This seems to be a characteristic move of political hegemonies; to retain their authority they must be represented as all-powerful, even if this an illusion which is not economically backed up. As Charles suffered from growing disempowerment, ideological pressure increased in the masque, and there could be little room for contradiction of royal claims, although, even in these circumstances, Jonson's masques manifest mute anomalies qualifying the dominant hegemony that shaped them. By contrast, more overt contradiction was still allowable in the Jacobean masque since the monarchy's role was relatively unquestioned; this position of relatively assured power allowed greater scope for discussion of how royal policy should be directed. Hence, Jonson's Jacobean antimasques enact dialectical strategies, whereas the Caroline masques appear to be largely monologic, apparently conforming rigorously with the requirements of a royal ideology under siege. Perhaps it should also be recalled that at the end of his career Jonson was both sick and impoverished, and suffering a reversal in fortune similar of that of the Stuart monarchy. He had been one of the chief arbiters of literary debate and the forefront of moulding a distinctive tradition in English writing. He moved easily among court circles and the intellegensia, and his cultural impact should not be underestimated. However, by 1631, the date of *Love's Triumph Through Callipolis*, Jonson's fortune and status were waning, although in composing the court masques that year he presented himself to the world as still an important and influential court poet. It could be said that Jonson was engaged in the same kind of damage limitation exercise as the King; Jonson's fortunes had been tied largely to the court, and he could not afford to alienate his court sponsors, just as the King could not afford any ideological contradiction.

Notes

1. The historical material in this introduction is largely taken from Parry (1989), 28–41.

184 Ben Jonson's Antimasques

2. For more detail on the significance of the term 'inventor' see Gordon (1949), 152-78.
3. Orgel and Strong (1973), vol.1, 16. Further references to this book are given after quotations in the text.
4. Jonson prepared a quarto edition of *Love's Triumph Through Callipolis* for press around the time of the masque's performance. There is also a version of the masque in the 1640 folio prepared for press from Jonson's papers by Sir Kenelm Digby. The masque text that I refer to in this chapter is found in *Ben Jonson: The Complete Masques*, ed. Stephen Orgel (1975). Orgel's version of the *Love's Triumph* text draws on both the earlier quarto and the 1640 folio edition.
5. On 'rhetorical bravery' see Rhodes (1992), 34-41.
6. Strong (1984), 48.
7. Jonson's attitude to the visual arts is complicated. He often associates excessive visual display with a lack of internal substance, see, for example, the poems 'Expostulation with Inigo Jones', 'On Something that Walks Somewhere', 'On Court Worm', 'To Sir Annual Tilter'. However, in *Discoveries* Jonson writes less dismissively of the visual arts, and links them with poetry, albeit in a secondary position: 'Poetry and picture, are arts of a like nature; and both are busy about imitation. It was excellently said of Plutarch, poetry was a speaking picture, and picture a mute poesy. For they both invent, feign and devise many things, and accommodate all they invent to the use and service of nature. Yet of the two, the pen [poetry] is more noble than the pencil [visual art]. For that can speak to the understanding; the other but to the sense'; *Discoveries*, ll.1867-75, Parfitt (1988), 419.
8. For an authoritative version of the view that the masque idealises its participants without any qualification see Orgel, *The Illusion of Power* (1975a), ch.2.
9. It should be noted that by the seventeenth century convex mirrors had largely been replaced by flat mirrors, which were certainly more, if not wholly accurate.
10. The perspective set had been used for the earliest masques, up to the late Caroline masques. However, in early masques such as *Blackness* the set was not wholly integrated with the text; such an integrated setting did not occur until *The Masque of Queens* (1609). Perhaps Jones's most important development in the masque after the death of James I, is the localisation of the set, in that it represented actual places familiar to the audience. Localisation, added to the use of perspective in set design, emphasised that the harmony imaged in the masque was a reflection of current reality, an emphasis in keeping with Charles's intensified absolutist discourse. Jones's perpectival set drew on the philosophy of neo-platonism, where the universe is perfectly ordered into a harmony of parts. In the set, this harmony is imaged in carefully measured lines of perspective which have the King as their vanishing point; the monarch is the culmination of this harmony of parts. For more detail on the implications of the perspective set see Orgel and Strong (1975), vol. 1, 'The mechanics of platonism'.
11. Neo-platonic ideas were made fashionable at court by the Queen's interest in them. For a good general introduction to the basic tenets of neo-platonism see Willey (1934: 1986), ch.8; Orgel and Strong, vol.1, ch.4. As Queen, Henrietta Maria not only possessed a status above other women, but also above that of other earlier Queen consorts. She is said to have greatly influenced Charles in domestic and foreign policy. This influence was initially resented by Buckingham, the King's favourite, who reputedly taunted the Queen with the fact that, 'there

had been queens in England who had lost their heads'. After Buckingham's assassination, Parliament was the chief opponent of the Queen's influence over the King, and viewed Henrietta Maria as a dangerous focus and promoter of Roman Catholicism in Britain; Ashley (1963), ch.9 & 10; Gregg (1981), 172-3, 538, 839-42.

12. Although I have found no firm evidence for number symbolism in this masque, it is probably at work here. Such symbolism would be in keeping with renaissance literary practice and with the platonic emphasis of this masque, There may also be a connection between the 'H' formed by King Charles's masquers and the image or emblem of the pillars of Hercules, representing the extremes of knowledge. It is not my purpose here to explore in depth the significance of this iconography in *Love's Triumph*, but I mention it as an aspect of the masque that deserves further research. For an example of number symbolism at work see, Alistair Fowler (1964; 1970).

13. *The Concise Oxford English Dictionary*, 7th edition (1984), defines sectary as 'a member of a sect esp. (Hist) of the Independents, Presbyterians, etc. at the time of the English Civil War'.

14. Gail Kern Paster has written on incontinent women in city comedy, and although her essay is anchored on instances of bladder incontinence she shows how in early modern semantic structures this was linked with verbal and moral incontinence; Paster (1987), 43-65. On the links between various types of female excess see Parker (1987) and Sinfield (1992), 131.

15. Sharpe (1992), describes the foreign policy of Charles's financially weak monarchy in 1631 as a diplomatic playing of nations against each other. Although England remained neutral at this time, France, Spain and the Netherlands were consistently keen to maintain that neutrality, and prevent hostile action from the English navy. Sharpe quotes Secretary Sir John Coke: 'as we are friends to all sides and enemies to none, so we will not tie ourselves to any neutrality which may hinder us from treating with any party that shall offer best conditions' (p.87). This policy ensured that the prime European nations were always a consideration in Caroline foreign and domestic policy. A number of recent clashes may also have helped to reinforce popular stereotypes of these nations. The treatment of Charles on his trip to Spain to woo the Infanta (1624/5) confirmed the notion of Spanish pride and formality. French treatment of the Protestant Huguenots led to war in 1626, and reinforced English vilification of (particularly French) Catholics. The Venetian diplomats in London noted and reported home all this activity, perhaps reinforcing the view of the wily and intriguing Italian. The victories of Swedish Gustavus Adolphus and competition over trade with the Netherlands put Scandinavia and Northern Europe at the forefront of popular imagination, and Adolphus was hailed as a Protestant hero.

16 Much has been written on similar mythologies surrounding Elizabeth I. See Yates (1975); Strong (1987); Berry (1989); King (1990), 30-74; King (1985), 41-84; Erler (1987), 359-71.

17. Sharpe (1992), 97.

18. Sinfield (1992); Poulantzas (1973), 171; Anderson (1974), 113; MacCaffrey (1965), 52-64 (61).

Postscript
Jonson's heirs: Shirley and Milton

This postscript is intended as a substitute for the traditional conclusion that completes or closes down debate in academic works, and the reasoning behind this more tentative approach to closure is that my own thoughts on the development of the antimasque and masque are continually evolving as critical debate on this topic moves forward; in many ways masque criticism has benefited from the general resurgence of interest in Jonson himself. However, at the final stage of this book it may be useful to summarise my position. The Jonsonian antimasque developed out of incoherencies and anomalies in the early masques, and became a significant structure of dissent, offsetting and questioning the assertions of royal hegemony in the masque proper. Yet, as I have been at pains to emphasise throughout, this destabilising impetus of the antimasque does not completely negate or undermine the assertions of masque, but complements it in a dialectical investigation of contemporary government and how it may be improved. In this way, the antimasque was involved in an essentially didactic project that sought to reform the court and the Crown from within. Nevertheless, the expanded satirical antimasque became a dominant part of the court entertainment, so that, in its full-blown form, it threatened to consume the eulogistic masque. However, a key aspect to this critical perspective is the belief that such a consumption is never complete as the structure of the court entertainment demands that masque is always reinstated after the antimasque, no matter how perfunctory this reinstatement may seem. After reaching a peak, the antimasque declines dramatically, and this collapse can be explicitly linked with Charles I's accession to the throne in 1625, and concomitant aesthetic and political developments.

In the previous chapter I discussed in some depth the apparent collapse of the dialogic Jonsonian court entertainment into royal monologism, and the enfeebling of the once dominant antimasque. However, I also suggested that discrepancies exist within the Caroline masques themselves that put pressure on their expression of royal hegemony. A critical impulse is so integral to the Jonsonian masque that no matter how marginalised it becomes, it is never completely extinguished. It may be argued that the capacity to articulate dissent was the distinguishing feature of the Jonsonian masque, a feature recognised and adapted by later masque poets. I suggest that Jonson's shaping of the masque was definitive to the extent that later writers used the Jonsonian model as a basis for their own versions of the form and in support of this assertion I will briefly consider two masques written shortly after Jonson's last masques of 1631, and only a few years before his death in 1637.

The Triumph Of Peace

There is an unusual amount of detail available regarding the circumstances and planning of *The Triumph Of Peace* (1633), written by James Shirley, on account of Bulstrode Whitelock's meticulous notes and diaries; Whitelock was an important member of the committee that commissioned the masque and largely determined its style and content.[1] The other outstanding feature of this masque was its unparalleled scale and splendour. The masque was given to the King and Queen by the Inns of Court in compensation for the apparent insults of one of their members, William Prynne. As is well known, Prynne had written *Histriomastix*, an attack on the stage which he intended to publish. The most infamous entry in this work was a side-heading, 'women actors, notorious whores', which, with the encouragement of Archbishop Laud, was taken by King Charles to be a slanderous reference to Henrietta Maria's participation in court theatricals. Charles actively discouraged any reflection on his personal behaviour or policies, and his anger in this instance was fanned by the fact that he interpreted Prynne's comments as an outrageous insult to the Queen. However, it should be noted that in attacking Prynne, Laud quoted him out of context and seized on the opportunity to ruin a man whom he despised for his religious views. Prynne was duly prosecuted, and severely punished. The Inns of Court were keen to distance themselves from Prynne's controversial views, and thus commissioned a masque to be performed by some of their members in honour of Charles and Henrietta Maria. Yet, we should not regard this masque as merely an act of unqualified obeisance to the monarch, as Whitelock clearly records that the committee in charge of commissioning the masque had its own agenda, and used the occasion to air certain grievances, in particular, concerning the granting of monopolies.[2] It is significant, that a court masque was recognised as a suitable vehicle for articulating views that implicitly criticised the current government, and I would argue that this aspect of the *Triumph Of Peace* places it firmly in the tradition of the Jonsonian masque.

The Triumph Of Peace also draws on Jonsonian masque in its antimasques. The first of these opens with the appearance of Fancy, Opinion and Confidence, who express 'humours' or personality traits taken to the extreme, and, as such, resemble characters in Jonson's antimasques as well as in his early satiric drama.[3] They indulge in the kind of nonsensical banter that is familiar from earlier antimasques, and Fancy, in apparent ignorance that he is part of the antimasque, enquires,

> How many antimasques have they? of what nature
> For these are fancies that take most; your dull
> And phlegmatic inventions are exploded
> Give me a nimble antimasque.

These comments are probably intended as a jibe at the Jacobean type of bawdy antimasque developed by Jonson, that was once fashionable. The ironic point being that this elite court audience was probably well aware that this type of antimasque was now viewed as comically outmoded. Although *The Triumph Of Peace* features several antimasques as a prelude to the masque, the first antimasque invites us to laugh at the form itself as anachronistic, a strategy linking with Jonson's practice of making oblique criticisms of the state through a protective veil of antic humour.

Fancy introduces the following antimasques, the most unusual of which is an antimasque of cripples and beggars. Their presence causes some confusion between Fancy and Opinion:

> *Opin.* I am glad they are off:
> Are these the effects of peace?
> Corruption, rather.
>
> *Fan.* Oh, the beggars show
> The benefit of peace.

Fancy's view is based on the fact that in this antimasque the beggars receive charity from a gentleman; however, it seems quite clear that the very presence of beggars powerfully qualifies the idea of the nation's harmony and plenty which the discourse of the Crown promoted. This implicit destabilising of the monarch's assertions is similar to the strategies of covert irony that I have traced in Jonson's masques. The first antimasque is followed by Rabelaisian grotesques, who are specifically pointed to as such when opinion declares of one of them, 'what thing's this? / A chimera out of Rabelais?'. In Chapter 4 I noted the connection between such Rabelaisian grotesques and figures in the Jonsonian antimasque, and Shirley's grotesques may be directly indebted to those found in Jonson's *The Vision Of Delight* (1617) and *Pleasure Reconciled To Virtue* (1618). In their absurd costumes the figures in Shirley's entertainment represent projectors or monopolists. One of these, for example, is dressed 'in a case of black leather, vast to the middle, and round on the top, with glass eyes, and bellows under each arm; a capon perched upon his fist'. Fancy glosses this character as,

> A new project,
> A case to walk you all day under water;
> So vast for the necessity of air,
> Which, with an artificial bellows cooled,
> Under each arm is kept still from corruption;
> With those glass eyes he sees, and can fetch up
> Gold or whatever jewels have been lost,
> In any river o' the world.

As ludicrous as this figure appears, this antimasque is concerned to make an important point about those who have gained from the King monopolies over certain goods and their methods of production, and are thereby able to inflate artificially the prices of these goods because they have no economic competition. The direct result of this practice was increased suffering for the poor, who often could not afford to buy basic necessities such as soap. Whitelock records that this antimasque was a deliberate attack on the practice of granting monopolies, which many believed were illegal:

> By it an information was covertly given to the King, of the unfitness, and ridiculousness of these Projects against the Law; and the Attorney Noy, who had most knowledge of them, had a great hand in this antimasque of the Projectors.[4]

Criticism of the Crown is not confined to the antimasque, and the Inns of Court make a significant point in the masque, when Irene (Peace) is shown to be dependent on Eunomia (Law) and Diche (Justice). This may be viewed as a reminder to the increasingly autocratic King that effective government had to be conducted within the law; there had been some suggestion that Laud had peremptorily attacked Prynne and may have had him illegally punished and imprisoned. Charles, however, continued to consider his prerogative to be superior to the law, an attitude demonstrated by his behaviour over John Hampden's trial in 1637, when the King directly intervened in the legal process to secure Hampden's conviction.[5]

The form, socio-political content and dissenting implications of this entertainment mark it out as a successor to the Jonsonian masque and in briefly analysing *The Triumph Of Peace* I have tried to describe those features that make it analogous with Jonson's masques. Milton's *Comus*, written a year after Shirley's masque, is not so obviously indebted to Jonson, but there are grounds for suggesting that Milton used a Jonsonian model in the creation of his masque, as I will outline below.

Comus

Milton wrote this masque in 1634 for the Earl of Bridgewater and his family; this alone, constitutes a major departure from the Jonsonian masque, as these entertainments were usually staged at court.[6] While Milton's masque was not performed at court, it did have an aristocratic audience and the lack of the monarch's presence on this occasion informs the masque text to the extent that it represents the difficulty of pursuing virtue without divine aid (traditionally figured in the masque by the King). The chaos initiated by Comus and his crew is all the more dangerous as Milton does draw upon the orthodox mechanism of masque, which traditionally presented the King's influence as a divine power effortlessly dissolving chaos and instituting order. In this sense, Milton adapts his masque to express the concerns of its audience and the role morality plays in their lives, rather than the exploration of royal hegemony that is apparent in the Jonsonian masque. Although *Comus* demonstrates the values traditionally exhibited in the masque as a whole, it departs further from the Jonsonian court entertainment in that it lacks a clear delineation between antimasque and masque. On the one hand Milton's masque is more of an integrated drama, where the antimasque merges seamlessly with the masque; on the other hand, it may be argued that, while departing from the Jonsonian court entertainment in many ways, Milton takes the dramatic impulse manifested in Jonson's antimasques to its logical conclusion, making his entertainment into a more integrated dramatic whole.

The character of Comus had also appeared in Jonson's 1618 masque, *Pleasure Reconciled To Virtue* (as well as in the poem 'To Sir Robert Wroth') where he is described as 'the god of the bouncing belly'. Although it is probable that Milton used this source in his creation of Comus, he chose to place a more sinister significance on Comus's traditional love of wine and carousal. Recently, the symbolism of Comus has been discussed in relation to Milton's views on witchcraft and the female sex, and associated with the resurgence of the debate over country sports.[7] As I showed in Chapter 3, Jonson's *Love Restored* (1612) also imaged this controversy, but in this earlier masque, country sports are shown to have a rural integrity in comparison with the often excessive and superficial court masque. Milton's views were clearly in greater sympathy with Puritan criticism of country sports on the Sabbath, than with Jonson's exoneration of them. The revelry of Comus and his crew is linked in this masque with the seduction of virtue, and its spiritual consequences. The debate over Sunday sports had become topical again because in 1633 Charles had reissued James I's *Book Of Sports* in defence of these pastimes. Milton clearly wrote his masque in such a way as to question the royal view on this matter. Milton's masque offsets the degeneracy of the revellers in the wild wood with the chastity and temperance of the Lady, and it is on account of these qualities that she is unharmed by Comus's sorcery. Despite the fact that this masque departs from the Jonsonian masque in many ways, I would argue that the way in which Milton shapes its topical socio-political content, and exploits it to articulate views that obliquely criticise the Crown, demonstrate its indebtedness to the Jonsonian masque. It was Jonson who had developed the court masque from an uncomplicated yet magnificent eulogy of the monarch, into a dialectical investigation of the nature of monarchical government, while creating a space for the poet's own voice to be heard. The importance Jonson attached to the poet's critical integrity can be deduced from the implicit criticism running through his court entertainments in varying degrees; thus, it is likely that Milton drew on the Jonsonian masque as a model for his incorporation of socio-political dissent in *Comus*.

The careers of Whitelock and Milton emphasise the mixed nature of the masque. Both became known as prominent Puritans, and yet despite their religious and political sympathies both were responsible for masques. This underlines the fact that masques had become more complex than aristocratic eulogies of the monarchy, despised by Puritans for their excess and superficiality. Despite what I have termed the later enfeeblement and collapse of the antimasque, Jonson's artistic legacy to Whitelock and Milton was a genre that could articulate the need for reform in government, while upholding the infrastructure of state. Whitelock and Milton responded to the masque's capacity to speak to the social and intellectual elite, pointing out the need for internal reform, without alienating this cultural group as other more radical expressions of dissent appeared to do. Unfortunately, the pressure of events culminating in the Civil War, meant that this subtle approach to the need for reform degenerated into polarised positions either for or against the Crown. During this time, society and culture became radically oppositional, and there was no longer any room for the delicate negotiation of extremes that characterised the Jonsonian masque.

Notes

1. Spalding (1853: 1990), vol.1, 53-62.
2. For the circumstances, music and text of *The Triumph of Peace*, and Whitelock's description of its deliberate attack on the abuse of monopolies, see Lefkowitz (1970), 27-109 (32-3).
3. Examples of these 'humorous' characters include Morose in the comical satire *Epicoene* (1609) and Fant'sy in the court masque, *The Vision of Delight* (1617). These characters are dominated by a particular folly to such an extent that they behave in bizarre and ludicrous ways. There is an implicit didacticism in this comedy of humours that warns against excess and advocates the pursuit of self-knowledge and moderation.
4. Lefkowitz (1970), 32-3.
5. For detail on the prosecution of John Hampden for his refusal to pay the Ship Money tax see, Hill (1989), 46.
6. The text of *Comus* referred to here is found in Bush (1988), 112-39.
7. Among the many articles covering these topics see Disalvo (1990), 204-27; Norbrook (1984b), 94-110. Norbrook's article also discusses Shirley's *The Triumph of Peace*.

Bibliography

Primary texts

Herford, C. H., Simpson, E. and P. (eds) (1925-52), *Ben Jonson*, Clarendon Press, Oxford.
Orgel, S. (ed.) (1975), *Ben Jonson: The Complete Masques*, Yale University Press, New Haven.
Parfitt, G. (ed.) (1988), *Ben Jonson. The Complete Poems*, Penguin Books, Harmondsworth.
Wilkes, G. (1988), *Ben Jonson. Five Plays*, Oxford University Press, Oxford.

The last three are the editions generally used in this book, except where Herford and Simpson are referred to; this is indicated in the end notes or in the text itself with the abbreviation HS, followed by the volume number, page and line reference.

Secondary texts

Aasand, H. (1992), '"To Blanch An Ethiop White, And Revive A Corse": Queen Anne And *The Masque Of Blackness*', *Studies In English Literature 1500-1900*, vol.32.
Akrigg, G. P. V. (1962), *The Jacobean Pageant*, Hamish Hamilton, London.
Anderson, P. (1974), *Lineages Of The Absolute State*, New Left Books, London.
Ascham, R. (1570: 1974), *The Schoolmaster*, ed. L. V. Ryan, University of Virginia Press, Charlottesville.
Ashley, M. (1963), *The Stuarts In Love, With Some Reflections On Love And Marriage In The Sixteeenth And Seventeenth Centuries*, Hodder & Stoughton, London.
Ashton, R. (1969), *James I By His Contemporaries*, Hutchinson, London.
Ayres, P. J. (1987), 'The Nature Of Jonson's Roman Historicism', in

Kinney, A. and Collins, D. S. (eds) (1987).
Bacon, Francis (1625: 1986), *Essays*, introd. M. J. Hawkins, J. M. Dent & Sons, London & Melbourne.
―――― (1605: 1988), *The Advancement of Learning*, (ed.) Johnston, A., Clarenden Press, Oxford.
Bakhtin, Mikhail (1981), *The Dialogic Imagination: Four Essays*, ed. M. Holquist, trans. C. Emerson, Texas University Press, Austin.
―――― (1986), *Rabelais And His World*, trans. H. Iswolsky, The MIT Press, Cambridge, MA.
Barish, J. A. (1963), *Ben Jonson. A Collection Of Critical Essays*, Prentice Hall, Englewood Cliffs, NJ.
―――― (1981), *The Anti-Theatrical Prejudice*, University of California Press, Berkeley.
Barker, F. and Hume, P. (1985), 'Nymphs and reapers heavily vanish: the discursive con-texts of *The Tempest*', in Drakakis (1985).
Barthelemy, A. (1987), *Black Face, Maligned Race. The Representation Of Blacks In English Drama From Shakespeare To Southerne*, Louisiana State University Press, Baton Rouge and London.
Barthes, R. (1977), 'The Death of the Author', in *Image Music Text*, Heath, S. (ed.), Fontana Press, London.
―――― (1987), *Criticism and Truth*, The Athlone Press, London.
Barton, Anne (1983), 'Shakespeare and Jonson', in Muir, K., *et al* (eds), *Proceedings of the second annual congress of The International Shakespeare Association, 1981*, University of Delaware Press, Newark.
―――― (1986), *Ben Jonson, Dramatist*, Cambridge University Press, Cambridge.
Beaurline, L. A. (1978), *Jonson and Elizabethan Comedy. Essays In Dramatic Rhetoric*, The Huntingdon Library, San Marino.
Belsey, C. (1985a), 'Disrupting Sexual Difference: Meaning And Gender In The Comedies', in Drakakis (1985).
―――― (1985b), *The Subject of Tragedy. Identity and Difference In Renaissance Drama*, Methuen, London.
Bergeron, D. (1985), *Shakespeare's Romances And The Royal Family*, University Press of Kansas, Lawrence.
Berry, P. (1989), *Of Chastity and Power: Elizabethan Literature And The Unmarried Queen*, Routledge, London.
Bingham, C. (1981), *James I Of England*, Wiedenfield and Nicolson, London.
Blisset, W. *et al* (eds) (1973), *A Celebration Of Jonson. Papers Presented at the University of Toronto in October 1972*, University of Toronto Press, Toronto.

Boehrer, B. T. (1997), *The Fury Of Men's Gullets: Ben Jonson And The Digestive Canal*, University of Pennsylvania Press, Philadelphia.
Brady, J. and Herendeen, W. H. (eds) (1991), *Ben Jonson's 1616 Folio*, Associated University Presses, London, Newark, Cranbury NJ.
Briggs, Julia (1983), *This Stage-Play World. English Literature And Its Background, 1580–1625*, Oxford University Press, Oxford.
Brinkley, R. (1932), *Arthurian Legend In The Seventeenth Century*, Johns Hopkins University Press, Baltimore.
Bryant, J. (1954), '*Catiline* And The Nature Of Jonson's Tragic Fable', *Papers of the Modern Language Association*.
Burt, R. (1987), '"Licensed By Authority": Ben Jonson And The Politics Of Early Stuart Theatre', *English Literary History*.
Bush, D. (1988), *Milton. Poetical Works*, Oxford University Press, Oxford.
Butler, M. (1991), '"We are one mans all": Jonson's *The Gypsies Metamorphosed*', *The Year Book Of English Studies*, vol. 21.
Butler, M. and Lindley, D. (1994), 'Restoring Astrea: Jonson's Masque for the Fall of Somerset', *English Literary History*, vol. 61, no. 4, Winter.
Cartelli, T. (1983), '*Bartholomew Fair* As Urban Arcadia: Jonson Responds To Shakespeare', *Renaissance Drama*, vol. XIV.
Cave, T. (1979), *The Cornucopian Text*, Oxford University Press, Oxford.
Chalfant, F. (1978), *Ben Jonson's London, A Jacobean Place Name Dictionary*, University of Georgia Press, Athens, Georgia.
Chan, M. (1980), *Music In The Theatre Of Ben Jonson*, Clarendon Press, Oxford.
Chedgzoy, K. (1995), *Shakespeare's Queer Children*, Manchester University Press, Manchester.
Creaser, J. (1984), '"The present aid of this occasion": The setting of *Comus*', in Lindley, D. (ed.), *The Court Masque*, Manchester University Press, Manchester.
Daniel, S. (1604: 1967), 'The Vision of the Twelve Goddesses', in Spencer, S. and Wells, T. (eds), *A Book of Masques in Honour of Allardyce Nicol*, Cambridge University Press, Cambridge.
De Luna, B. (1967), *Jonson's Romish Plot, A Study of 'Catiline' And Its Historical Context*, Clarendon Press, Oxford.
Deloney, T. (1597: 1987), *Jack of Newbury*, in Salzman (1987).
Derrida, J. (1980), *Of Grammatology*, introd. & ed. G. Spivak, The Johns Hopkins University Press, Baltimore.
Dick, O. (ed.) (?1693: 1949), *Aubrey's Brief Lives*, Secker & Warburg, London.
Disalvo, J. (1990), 'Fear of Flying: Milton On The Boundaries Between Witchcraft And Inspiration', in Farrell, K. *et al*, *Renaissance Women*, University of Massachussets Press, Amherst.

Dollimore, J. (1989), *Radical Tragedy. Religion, Ideology and Power in the Drama of Shakespeare and his Contemporaries*, Harvester Wheatsheaf, Hemel Hempstead.
Dollimore, J. and Sinfield, A. (1985), 'History and Ideology: the instance of *Henry V*', in Drakakis (1985).
Drakakis, J. (ed.) (1985), *Alternative Shakespeares*, Methuen, London.
Dutton, R. (1983), *Ben Jonson: To The First Folio*, Cambridge University Press, Cambridge.
────── (ed.) (1987), *Sir Philip Sidney, Selected Works*, Carcanet, Manchester.
Eagleton, Terry (1981), *Walter Benjamin: Towards A Revolutionary Criticism*, Verso, London.
────── (1987), *Marxism and Literary Criticism*, Methuen, London.
────── (1990), *The Ideology of the Aesthetic*, Blackwell, Oxford.
Eco, U. (1984), 'The Frames of Comic Freedom', in Eco, U. *et al* (eds), *Carnival!*, Mouton Publishers, Berlin.
Edwards, P. (1979), *Threshold Of A Nation. A Study Of English And Irish Drama*, Cambridge University Press, Cambridge.
Elias, N. (1969: 1983), *The Court Society*, trans. E. Jephcott, Blackwell, Oxford.
Elyot, T. (1531: 1883), *The Boke Named The Gouerner*, ed. H. H. Croft, Kegan, Paul, Trench, London.
Erasmus (1515/16: 1936), *The Education of a Christian Prince*, trans. L. K. Born, Columbia University Press, New York.
Erler, M. C. (1987), 'Sir John Davies and the Rainbow Portrait of Queen Elizabeth I', *Modern Philology*, vol. 84 (4).
Evans, R. C. (1992), 'Jonson, Weston And The Digbys: Patronage Relations In Some Later Poems', *Renaissance and Reformation*, vol.XVI, no.1, Winter.
Evett, D. (1990), *Literature and the Visual Arts in Tudor England*, University of Georgia Press, Athens, Georgia.
Fanon, F. (1994), 'On National Culture', in Williams, P. and Chrisman, L. (eds), *Colonial Discourse And Postcolonial Theory*, Harvester Wheatsheaf, Hemel Hempstead.
Ferguson, Arthur B. (1960), *The Indian Summer Of English Chivalry*, Duke University Press, Durham.
────── (1986), *The Chivalric Tradition In Renaissance England*, Associated University Presses, Washington, Cranbury NJ and London.
Ferguson, M. W. *et al* (eds) (1986), *Rewriting The Renaissance. The Discourses of Sexual Difference In Early Modern Europe*, University of Chicago Press, Chicago and London.

Finkelstein, R. (1987), 'Ben Jonson On Spectacle', *Comparative Drama*, vol.21, no.2, Summer.

Fish, Stanley (1980), *Is There A Text In This Class?*, Harvard University Press, Cambridge MA. and London.

——— (1987), 'Authors-Readers: Jonson's Community Of The Same', in Kinney and Collins (eds) (1987).

Fisher, A. (1997), 'Jonson's Funnybone', *Studies In Philology*, vol.XCIV, no.1, Winter.

Fowler, Alistair (1964), *Spenser and the Numbers of his Time*, Routledge and Kegan Paul, London.

——— (1970), *Silent Poetry: Essays in numerological analysis*, Routledge and Kegan Paul, London.

Gascoigne, G. (1574: 1987), 'The Adventures Of Master F.J.', in Salzman, P. (ed.), *An Anthology of Elizabethan Prose Fiction*, Oxford University Press, Oxford.

Gent, L. and Llewellyn, N. (eds) (1990), *Renaissance Bodies, The Human Figure In English Culture c. 1540-1660*, Reaktion Books, London.

Girouard, M. (1978), *Life In The English Country House. A Social And Architectural History*, Yale University Press, New Haven.

Goldberg, J. (1983), *James I And The Politics Of Literature - Jonson, Shakespeare, Donne And Their Contemporaries*, Johns Hopkins University Press, Baltimore.

Gordon, D. J. (1949), 'Poet and Architect', *Journal Of The Warburg and Courtauld Institutes*, vol.XII.

——— (1975), 'Hymenaie: Ben Jonson's masque of union', in Orgel, S. (ed.), *The Renaissance Imagination*, University of California Press, Berkeley and London.

Gossett, S. (1988), '"Man-Maid, begone!": Women In Masques', *English Literary Renaissance*, vol.18.

Gotch, J. A. (1901), *Early Renaissance Architecture In England*, B.T. Batsford, London.

Greenblatt, Stephen (1980), *Renaissance Self-Fashioning. From More To Shakespeare*, University of Chicago Press, Chicago and London.

——— (ed.) (1988), *Representing The Renaissance*, University of California Press, Berkeley.

——— (1992a), 'The Cultivation Of Anxiety: King Lear And His Heirs', in Newton, K. M. (ed.), *Theory Into Practice*, Macmillan, Houndmills.

——— (1992b), *Learning To Curse. Essays In Early Modern Culture*, Routledge, London.

——— (1992c), *Marvellous Possessions. The Wonder Of The New World*, Oxford University Press, Oxford.

―――― (1992d), 'Murdering Peasants: Status, Genre and the representation of Rebellion', in *Learning To Curse. Essays In Early Modern Culture*, Routledge, London.
Greene, T. M. (1970), 'Ben Jonson and The Centred Self', *Studies In English Literature 1500-1900*, vol.10.
―――― (1982), *The Light In Troy. Imitation And Discovery In Renaissance Poetry*, Yale University Press, New Haven.
―――― (1987), 'Magic and Festivity at the Renaissance Court', *Renaissance Quarterly*, vol.XL.
Gregg, P. (1981), *King Charles I*, J.M. Dent & Sons, London.
Hall, K. (1991), 'Sexual Politics And Cultural Identity In *The Masque Of Blackness*', in Case, S. E. and Reinelt, J. (eds), *The Performance Of Power. Theatrical Discourse And Politics*, University Of Iowa Press, Iowa City.
Haynes, J. (1984), 'Festivity And The Dramatic Economy Of Jonson's *Bartholomew Fair*', *English Literary History*, vol.51.
Heich, A. (1975), 'Queen Elizabeth I: Parliamentary Rhetoric And The Exercise Of Power', *Signs*, vol.1.
Heineman, M. (1980), *Puritanism and Theatre. Thomas Middleton And Opposition Drama Under The Early Stuarts*, Cambridge University Press, Cambridge.
Helgerson, R. (1992), *Forms Of Nationhood. The Elizabethan Writing Of England*, University of Chicago Press, Chicago and London.
Hendricks, M. and Parker, P. (eds) (1994), *Women, Race And Writing*, Routledge, London.
Hill, C. (1986), *Society and Puritanism In Pre-Revolutionary England*, Penguin Books, Harmondsworth.
―――― (1989), *The Century Of Revolution 1603-1714*, Van Nostrand Reinhold (International), London.
Howard, J. E. (1987), 'The New Historicism In Renaissance Studies', in Kinney and Collins (1987).
Hutchinson, L. (1806: 1973), *Memoirs Of The Life Of Colonel Hutchinson*, ed. J. Sutherland, Oxford University Press, Oxford.
James I, King (1599: 1969), *Basilikon Doron*, Scolar Press, Menston (facsimile edition).
Johnstone, A. F. (1991), 'English Puritanism And Festive Custom', *Renaissance and Reformation*, vol.XXVII, no.4.
Jones, Eldred (1965), *Othello's Countrymen. The African In English Renaissance Drama*, Oxford University Press, Oxford.
Jones, Emrys (1961), 'Stuart *Cymbeline*', *Essays In Criticism*, vol.II.
Kenyon, J. P. (1966), *The Stuarts*, Fontana, London.

Kiernan, V. G. (1965), 'State and Nation in Western Europe', *Past and Present*, no.31.

King, John N. (1985), 'The Goodly Woman in Elizabethan Iconography', *Renaissance Quarterly*, vol.38(1), Spring.

—— (1990), 'Queen Elizabeth I: representations of the Virgin Queen', *Renaissance Quarterly*, vol.43(1), Spring.

Kinney, A. (1986) *Humanist Poetics*, University of Massachussets Press, Amherst.

Kinney, A. and Collins, D. S. (eds) (1987), *Renaissance Historicism*, University of Massachussets Press, Amherst.

Kinser, S. (1990), *Rabelais's Carnival Text, Context and Metatext*, University of California Press, Berkeley.

Lee, J. (1989), *Ben Jonson's Poesis, A Literary Dialectic Of Ideal And History*, University Press of Virginia, Charlottesville.

Lefkowitz, M. (ed.) (1970), *Trois Masques A La Cour De Charles Ier D'Angleterre*, Editions Du Centre National De La Recherche Scientifique, Paris.

Leinwand, T. (1990), 'Negotiation And New Historicism', *Papers of the Modern Language Association*, vol.105.

Lever, J. W. (1971), *The Tragedy Of State*, Methuen, London.

Levin, C. (1989), 'Power, Politics, Sexuality: Images of Elizabeth I', in Brink, J. R., et al (eds), *The Politics Of Gender In Early Modern Europe*, Sixteenth Century Journal Publishers, Kirksville, MO.

Lewalski, B. (1973), *Donne's Anniversaries And The Poetry Of Praise. The Creation Of A Symbolic Mode*, Princeton University Press, Princeton.

Limon, J. (1990), *The Masque Of Stuart Culture*, Associated University Press, Newark and London.

—— (1991), 'The Masque Of Stuart Culture', in Peck, L. L. (ed.), *The Mental World Of The Jacobean Court*, Cambridge University Press, Cambridge.

Lindley, David (ed.) (1984), *The Court Masque*, Manchester University Press, Manchester.

—— (1987), 'Embarrassing Ben: The Masques For Frances Howard', in Kinney and Collins (1987).

—— (1994), *The Trials Of Frances Howard*, Manchester University Press, Manchester.

Loewenstein, J. (1988), 'The Script in the Marketplace', in Greenblatt (1988).

—— (1991), 'Printing And The "Multitudinous Press": The Contentious Texts Of Ben Jonson's Masques', in Brady and Herendeen (1991).

MacCaffrey, W. T. (1965), 'England: The Crown And The New Aristocracy', *Past and Present*, no.30.
Macherey, P. (1966: 1978), *A Theory of Literary Production*, Trans. Wall, G., Routledge, London.
────── (1981), 'On Literature As An Ideological Form', in Young, R. (ed.), *Untying The Text, A Post-Structuralist Reader*, Routledge and Kegan Paul, London.
McGee, C. E. and Meagher, J. C. (1988), 'Preliminary Check List Of Tudor And Stuart Entertainments 1614-1625', *Research Opportunities In Renaissance Drama*, vol.XXX.
Marcus, L. S. (1981), 'Masquing Occasions And Masque Structure', *Research Opportunities In Renaissance Drama*, vol.XXIV.
────── (1986), *The Politics of Mirth: Herrick, Milton, Marrell and the Defence of Old Holiday Pastimes*, University of Chicago Press, Chicago and London.
Mathew, D. (1938), *The Jacobean Age*, Longman, London.
Meagher, J. C. (1966), *Method and Meaning In Jonson's Masques*, University of Notre Dame Press, Notre Dame and London.
Miles, R. (1986), *Ben Jonson. His Life And Work*, Routledge and Kegan Paul, London.
Mill, A. J. (1924: 1969), *Medieval Plays In Scotland*, Benjamin Blom, New York and London.
Milton, J. (1637: 1988), *Comus*, in Bush, D. (ed.), *Milton. Poetical Works*, Oxford University Press, Oxford.
Moryson, F. (1605?: 1890), 'Description of Ireland 1600-1603', in Morley, H. (ed.), *Ireland Under Elizabeth and James I*, Routledge, London.
Murray, T. (1983), 'From Foul Sheets To Legitimate Model: Antitheater, Text, Ben Jonson', *New Literary History*, vol.14.
Neale, J. E. (1934: 1979), *Queen Elizabeth I*, Triad/Panther Books, St Albans, U.K.
Newton, K. M. (ed.) (1988), *Twentieth Century Literary Criticism. A Reader*, Macmillan, London.
Norbrook, D. (1984a), *Poetry and Politics in the English Renaissance*, Routledge, London.
────── (1984b), 'The Reformation Of The Masque', in Lindley (1984).
Orgel, Stephen and Strong, R. (1973), *Inigo Jones. The Theatre Of The Stuart Court*, Vols 1 and 2, University of California Press, Berkeley.
Orgel, S. (1965), *The Jonsonian Masque*, Yale University Press, New Haven.
────── (1975a), *The Illusion Of Power*, University of California Press, Berkeley.
────── (ed.) (1975b), *The Renaissance Imagination. Essays And Lectures*

By D. J. Gordon, University of California Press, Berkeley.
—— (1991), 'What Is A Text?', in Kastan, D. S. and Stallybrass, P., *Staging The Renaissance. Reinterpretations of Elizabethan and Jacobean Drama*, Routledge, London.
Palmer, D. W. (1992), 'Ben Jonson As Other: Recent Trends In The Criticism Of Jonson's Drama', *Research Opportunities In Renaissance Drama*, vol.XXXI.
Parker, P. (1987), *Literary Fat Ladies: Rhetoric, Gender, Property*, Methuen, London.
Parry, Graham (1981), *The Golden Age Restor'd*, Manchester University Press, Manchester.
—— (1985), *Seventeenth Century Poetry, The Social Context*, Hutchinson, London.
—— (1989), *The Intellectual And Cultural Context Of English Literature 1603-1700*, Longman, London.
Paster, G. K. (1987), 'Leaky Vessels: The Incontinent Women Of City Comedy', *Renaissance Drama*, vol.XIV.
Patterson, A. (1984), *Censorship And Interpretation. The Conditions Of Writing And Reading In Early Modern England*, University of Wisconsin Press, Madison, WI.
Peacock, J. (1995), *The Stage Designs Of Inigo Jones. The European Context*, Cambridge University Press, Cambridge.
Peterson, Richard S. (1975), 'The Iconography Of Jonson's *Pleasure Reconciled To Virtue*', *The Journal Of Medieval And Renaissance Studies*, vol.5, no.1, Spring.
—— (1981), *Imitation And Praise In The Poems Of Ben Jonson*, Yale University Press, New Haven.
Poulantzas, N. (1973), *Political Power And Social Classes*, New Left Books, London.
Prescott, Anne L. (1984), 'The Stuart Masque And Pantagruel's Dreams', *English Literary History*, vol.51.
Rabelais (1534: 1955), *Gargantua*, trans. and introd., J. M. Cohen, Penguin Books, Harmondsworth.
Rackin, P. (1990), *Stages Of History. Shakespeare's English Chronicles*, Routledge, London.
Randall, D. B. J. (1975), *Jonson's Gypsies Unmasked*, Duke University Press, Durham.
Rhodes, N. (1980), *Elizabethan Grotesque*, Routledge and Kegan Paul, London.
—— (1992), *The Power Of Eloquence And English Renaissance Literature*, Harvester Wheatsheaf, Hemel Hempstead.

Ricks, C. (1961), 'Sejanus and Dismemberment', *Modern Language Notes*.
Riggs, D. (1989), *Ben Jonson. A Life*, Harvard University Press, Cambridge, MA.
Sallust (1963), *Jugurthine War, Conspiracy Of Catiline*, ed. and trans. S. A. Handford, Penguin Books, Harmondsworth.
Salzman, P. (ed.) (1987), *An Anthology Of Elizabethan Prose Fiction*, Oxford University Press, Oxford.
Sharpe, K. (1992), *The Personal Rule of Charles I*, Yale University Press, New Haven and London.
Shepherd, R. (1985), 'Royal Favourites In The Political Discourse Of Tudor And Stuart England', unpublished PhD thesis, Claremont Graduate School.
Shepherd, S. (1986), *Marlowe And The Politics Of Elizabethan Theatre*, The Harvester Press, Brighton.
Shirley, J. (1633: 1974), *The Triumph of Peace*, in Lefkowitz (1970).
Siddiqui, Y. (1992), 'Dark Incontinents: The Discourses Of Race And Gender In Three Renaissance Masques', *Renaissance Drama*, vol.XXIII.
Sidney, P. (1595: 1987), *The Defence Of Poesy*, in Dutton, R. (ed.), *Sir Philip Sidney, Selected Writings*, Carcanet Press, Manchester.
Sinfield, A. (1992), *Faultlines. Cultural Materialism And the Politics Of Dissident Reading*, Oxford University Press, Oxford.
Smuts, M. R. (1987), *Court Culture And The Origins Of A Royalist Tradition In Early Stuart England*, University of Pennsylvania Press, Philadelphia.
Spalding, R (ed.) (1853: 1990), *The Diary Of Bulstrode Whitelock 1605-1675*, Oxford University Press, Oxford.
Spencer, T. J. B. and Wells, S. (eds) (1967), *A Book Of Masques In Honour Of Allardyce Nicol*, Cambridge University Press, Cambridge.
Stallybrass, P. and White, A. (1986), *The Politics And Poetics Of Transgression*, Methuen, London.
Stone, Lawrence (1967), *The Crisis Of The Aristocracy 1558-1641*, Oxford University Press, Oxford.
Stone, L. and Stone, J. C. F. (1984), *An Open Elite? England 1540-1880*, Clarendon Press, Oxford.
Strong, R. (1967), 'Inigo Jones And The Revival Of Chivalry', *Apollo*, August.
—— (1984), *Art And Power. Renaissance Festivals 1450-1650*, The Boydell Press, London.
—— (1986), *Henry Prince Of Wales And England's Lost Renaissance*, Thames and Hudson, London.
—— (1987), *Gloriana: The Portraits Of Elizabeth I*, Thames and Hudson, London.

Sweeney, J. G. (1985), *Jonson And The Psychology Of Public Theater: To Coin The Spirit, Spend The Soul*, Princeton University Press, Princeton.
Swinburne, A. C. (1889), *A Study Of Ben Jonson*, Chatto and Windus, London.
Tait, R. S. (ed.) (1901), *Lusus Regius. Being Poems And Other Pieces By James Ye First*, Westminster.
Teague, F. (1985), *The Curious History Of Bartholomew Fair*, Associated University Presses, Lewisburg and London.
Tennenhouse, L. (1986), *Power On Display. The Politics Of Shakespeare's Genres*, Methuen, London.
Trimpi, W. (1962), *Ben Jonson's Poems. A Study Of The Plain Style*, Stanford University Press, Stanford.
Virgil (1978), *The Aeneid*, trans. and ed. W. F. J. Knight, Penguin Books, Harmondsworth.
Waller, G. (1993), *The Sidney Family Romance: Mary Wroth, William Herbert And The Early Modern Construction Of Gender*, University of Delaware Press, Detroit.
Walls, P. (1996), *Music In The English Courtly Masque 1604-1640*, Clarendon Press, New York, Oxford.
Warner, M. (1976), *Alone Of All Her Sex. The Myth And Cult Of The Virgin Mary*, Weidenfeld and Nicolson, London.
Watson, R. N. (1987), *Ben Jonson's Parodic Strategy. Literary Imperialism In The Comedies*, Harvard University Press, Harvard, Massachussets.
Weiman, R. (1985), 'Mimesis in *Hamlet*', in Parker, P. and Hartman, G. (eds), *Shakespeare And The Question Of Theory*, Methuen, London.
Weiman, R. and Shwartz., R. (1978), *Shakespeare And The Popular Tradition In The Theater*, Johns Hopkins University Press, Baltimore.
Wells, R. H. (1986), *Shakespeare, Politics And The State*, Macmillan, Houndmills.
Welsford, E. (1927), *The Court Masque*, Cambridge University Press, Cambridge.
Wheeler, C. (1938), *Classical Mythology In The Plays, Masques And Poems Of Ben Jonson*, Princeton University Press, Princeton and London.
Whigham, F. (1984), *Ambition And Privilege: The Social Tropes Of Elizabethan Courtesy Theory*, University of California Press, Berkeley.
Willey, B. (1934: 1986), *The Seventeenth Century Background*, Routledge and Kegan Paul, London.
Williams, R. (1985), *The Country And The City*, Hogarth Press, London.
Wooton, D. (1988), *Divine Right And Democracy. An Anthology Of Political Writing In Stuart England*, Penguin Books, Harmondsworth.
Yates, Frances, (1957), 'Elizabethan Chivalry: The Source Of The Accession

Day Tilts', *The Journal Of The Warburg And Courtauld Institutes*, vol.XX.
—— (1975), *Astrea: The Imperial Theme In The Sixteenth Century*, Routledge and Kegan Paul, London.
Yoch, J. L. (1988), 'A Very Wild Regularity: The Character Of Landscape In The Work Of Inigo Jones', *Research Opportunities In Renaissance Drama*, vol.XXX.
Young, A. R. (1992), 'The Emblematic Art Of Ben Jonson', *Emblematica*, vol.6, no.1, Summer.

Index

Aasand, Hardin 20, 47, 52-4, 57
absolutism 2, 165-6, 172, 182-3
Akrigg, G.P.V. 115
alchemy 122
Anderson, Perry 182
Anne of Denmark 44, 49, 52, 53-4, 57, 111, 128
Aristophanes 87
Arthurian myth 8, 51, 63-95

Bacchus 39
Bacon, Francis 42, 64-5, 106
Bakhtin, Mikhail 9, 133-40, 142, 144, 159-60
Barthelemy, Anthony 20, 52
Barthes, Roland 11, 13, 123
Barton, Anne 29
Belsey, Catherine 13, 35
Boehrer, Bruce Thomas 101
Breton, Richard 148
Bryant, Joseph 90
Buckingham, Duke of 114-15, 117, 172
Bulstrode, Cecilia 29-30
Burt, Richard A. 45
Butler, Martin 19-20

Caesar 22, 134, 135
Campion, Thomas 120, 163
Carr, Robert 155, 164
Comus 38-9
Carew, Thomas
    'To Saxham' 34
Carleton, Dudley 52-3, 122, 127-8, 129
Cartelli, Thomas 143
Cave, Terence 167
Cecil, Robert 110
Charles I 4, 67-8, 121, 165-6, 171-3, 175-81, 183, 186-7, 189
Chaucer, Geoffrey 30-1

chivalric myth *see* Arthurian myth
Cicero 128
Circe 38
classical 138, 139, 141, 144, 146, 160
Comus 40, 205
Cultural Materialism 10, 15-17, 102, 104, 164

Daniel, Samuel 42-3, 120, 163
    Tethys' Festival 71
Deloney, Thomas 23
Dollimore, Jonathan 104, 117
Donaldson, Ian 19
Drayton, Michael 73
Drummond, William 78, 109

Eagleton, Terry 159
Elizabeth I 48, 66-7, 69, 73, 153, 155
Elyot, Thomas 64
Erasmus, Desiderius 32, 35
Essex, Earl of 58, 113, 114, 121
Euripides 40

Fish, Stanley 122, 125
Fisher, Alan 135
Foucault, Michel 16

Gascoigne, George 23
Girouard, Mark 79
golden age 39
Gordon, D.J. 18, 43, 49, 106
Gosset, Suzanne 20
Gotch, J. Alfred 79
Greenblatt, Stephen 103-4, 118
Greene, Thomas M. 33-4
grotesque 138, 141, 143-4, 147, 152, 160, 166

Hall, Kim 20, 47, 52, 53, 57

Hampden, John 203
Helgerson, Richard 77
Henrietta-Maria, Queen 4, 121, 171, 173, 175-81, 187
Henry V 73-4, 76, 84
Henry, Prince 68, 70-5, 78-81, 83-4, 88, 108, 111
Herford, Charles 19, 52
Horace 37, 82, 91, 126
Howard-Essex divorce 22, 114
Howard, Jean E. 103

iconography 3
imitatio 26, 37
irony 6, 26, 32-8, 46

James I 5, 7, 21, 28, 44, 47, 48-51, 56, 67-72, 75, 80-1, 84-5, 88, 106, 116, 119, 153, 155
 Basilikon Doron 50, 68, 72, 113, 161
 Book of Sports 46, 110, 191
Jones, Inigo 7, 67, 79, 148, 171, 173-4, 177
Jonson, Ben
 A Challenge At Tilt 86, 157
 'An Epigram on the Court Pucell' 29
 'An Epistle to a Friend to Persuade Him to the Wars' 40
 'An Epistle to Master John Selden' 29, 33, 39
 'An Execration Upon Vulcan' 77, 83
 Bartholomew Fair 5, 6, 9, 77, 86, 122, 134-50, 152, 156-7, 160-2, 166, 176
 Catiline 8, 64, 88-91, 93, 95
 Chloridia 172-3, 178
 Conversations 28-9, 125
 Discoveries 26, 44, 82, 84, 91, 94-5
 'Epistle to Katherine, Lady Aubigny' 33, 179
 Eastward Ho 122, 125-7
 'Expostulation With Inigo Jones' 187
 For The Honour Of Wales 136
 Hymenaei 9, 19, 42-3, 55, 104-12, 116, 119, 124
 Love Freed From Ignorance And Folly 4, 8, 51, 79, 120, 134, 145, 148-57, 176

Love Restored 4, 9, 110-14, 151, 157, 176, 190
Love's Triumph Through Callipolis 10, 124, 172-83
Masque of Beauty 7, 19, 26-8, 34, 41-2, 44-7, 52, 55-8, 63
Masque of Blackness 7, 19, 21, 27-8, 34, 41-2, 44-56, 58, 63, 86, 101, 104, 111, 120, 122, 127, 163, 167, 182
Masque of Queens 3-4, 51, 62, 127, 149, 181
Mercury Vindicated From The Alchemists At Court 4, 9, 21, 114-17, 119-20, 134, 157, 166
Oberon The Fairy Prince 4, 7, 21, 63-4, 68, 71-2, 76-9, 85-8, 93-4, 104, 111
'Of Life and Death' 40
'On Giles and Joan' 14, 110
'On Groin' 139
'On Gut' 139
'On My First Daughter' 40
'On Sir Cod The Perfumed' 96
'On Something That Walks Somewhere' 89
Pleasure Reconciled To Virtue 38, 46, 51, 122, 128, 188, 190
Poetaster 8, 21, 88, 91, 95, 126
Prince Henry's Barriers 4, 7, 21, 62, 66, 68, 70-80, 83-8
Sejanus 8, 75, 80-1, 88, 89, 91-3, 95, 122, 127
The Alchemist 119-20, 123, 176
The Irish Masque At Court 4, 9-10, 21, 86, 134, 145, 148, 157-64
The Isle of Dogs 122, 127
The Masque of Owls 105
'The Praises Of A Country Life' 37
The Vision Of Delight 188
'To Alphonso Ferrabosco, On His Book' 14
'To Court Worm' 29, 89
'To Master John Selden' 28, 31, 33
'To My Book' 36
'To My Muse' 32
'To Lord Ignorant' 29
'To Penshurst' 34, 38, 40
'To Sir Cod The Perfumed' 28, 89
'To Sir Henry Cary' 39
'To Sir Robert Wroth' 7, 14, 27, 34-40, 43-4, 51

'To The Immortal Memory And Friendship Of That Noble Pair, Sir Lucius Cary and Sir H. Morison' 31
'To The Reader' 14
'To William, Earl of Pembroke' 124
Volpone 80, 87, 119, 120
Works 3, 12, 114

Lee, Jongsook 29, 40-1
Leinwand, Theodore B. 16, 118
Lever, J.W. 89
Limon, Jerzy 3
Lindley, David 20, 158, 164
Loewenstein, Joseph 3, 126, 129

MacCaffrey, W.T. 182
Macherey, Pierre 16, 118, 159
Mantegna 174
Marcus, Leah 15, 20, 46, 51, 107, 117
Martial 173
Marvell, Andrew
  'Upon Appleton House' 34
Mary, Queen of Scots 153
Meagher, John 19
Marlowe, Christopher
  Tamburlaine 80, 81
Milton, John 10, 205
  Comus 10, 12, 38, 189-91

New Historicism 12, 15-17, 102-4, 118, 165
Neo-platonism 23, 121, 176, 178, 180
Norbrook, David 35, 40

Orgel, Stephen 15, 19, 46-7, 53, 62, 85, 102-3, 117, 166, 173, 177
Overbury, Thomas 121

panegyric 2, 6, 8, 26, 28-9, 32, 34-8, 41, 46, 119
paradiastole 70
Parmigianino 175
Parry, Graham 20, 94
pastoral 37
Patterson, Annabel 127
Peacock, John 67, 72
Peele 66
Pembroke, Earl of 31, 34

perspective 175-6
Peterson, Richard 26
Poulantzas, Nicos 182
Prescott, Anne Lake 20, 148, 151
Prynne, William
  Histriomastix 187, 189
Puritanism 49, 151-2, 156, 176, 190-1

Rabelais 20, 148, 188
Raleigh, Walter 78
Rhodes, Neil 136, 174
Roman Catholicism 49, 52, 69, 158, 161-2
Rubens 171

satire 8, 26, 33, 39, 45, 119, 159, 163
Sallust 89-90
Selden, John 181
Shakespeare, William
  The Tempest 77, 143
Sharpe, Kevin 180
Shirley, James
  The Triumph of Peace 10, 121-2, 157, 187-90
Siddiqui, Yumna 47-8
Sidney, Philip 64
  The Defence of Poetry 31-2, 64
Simpson, Evelyn and Percy 19, 55
Sinfield, Alan 182
Smuts, R. Malcolm 68, 70
Stallybrass, Peter 133, 139, 153, 159
Stone, Lawrence 38
Strong, Roy 20, 65-6, 68, 78, 165, 173-4, 177

Tacitus 89
Trimpi, Wesley 26

Virgil 82, 92

Waller, Gary 34
Walls, Peter 3
Welsford, Enid 18, 119
Wheeler, Charles 38
Whigham, Frank 65
White, Allon 133, 139, 153, 159
Whitelock, Bulstrode 187, 189, 191
Williams, Raymond 38,
Wroth, Lady Mary 34, 36